Robert Kee was born in 1919 and educated at Stowe School, Buckingham and Magdalen College, Oxford where he read History. He was a pupil and friend of A.J.P. Taylor. He began his career as a writer, journalist and broadcaster immediately after the end of World War Two in which he had been a RAF bomber pilot. He worked for the weekly magazine *Picture Post*, the *Observer*, *The Sunday Times* and other papers before moving in 1958 to television on which he has appeared over many years on both BBC and ITV as reporter, interviewer and presenter, and made many documentaries including the thirteen-part BBC *Ireland: A Television History* on which this book, *Ireland: A History*, is closely based. He has written twelve other books including *A Crowd Is Not Company* (an account of his experience as a prisoner of war), *The Green Flag* (a history of Irish nationalism), *1945: The World We Fought For*, *Trial and Error* (about the Maguires and the Guildford Four) and *The Laurel and The Ivy* (about Charles Stewart Parnell and Irish nationalism).

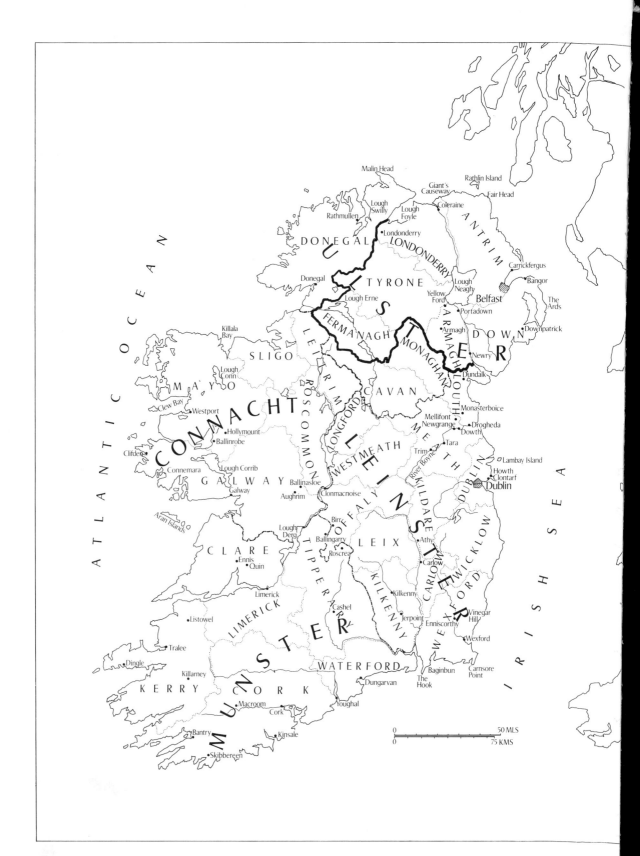

Malin Head

Giant's
Causeway

Rathlin Island

Fair Head

Coleraine

Lough
Swilly

Lough
Foyle

ANTRIM

Rathmullen

DONEGAL

Londonderry

LONDONDERRY

Carrickfergus

Bangor

TYRONE

Lough
Neagh

The
Ards

Donegal

Lough Erne

Yellow
Ford

Belfast

U L S T E R

Killala
Bay

FERMANAGH

Armagh

Portadown

DOWN

Downpatrick

SLIGO

LEITRIM

MONAGHAN

Newry

Lough
Conn

Dundalk

MAYO

ROSCOMMON

CAVAN

Clew Bay

Westport

CONNACHT

Monasterboice

Hollymount

Mellifont
Newgrange

Drogheda

Ballinrobe

LONGFORD

MEATH

Dowth

Clifden

Lough Corrib

WESTMEATH

Trim

Tara

Lambay Island

Connemara

River Boyne

Howth

GALWAY

Ballinasloe

Clontarf

Galway

Aughrim

Clonmacnoise

KILDARE

DUBLIN

Dublin

Aran Islands

LEINSTER

Birr

OFFALY

Lough
Derg

Ballingarry

LEIX

Athy

CLARE

Roscrea

CARLOW

Ennis

Quin

TIPPERARY

Carlow

WICKLOW

Limerick

KILKENNY

Kilkenny

WEXFORD

LIMERICK

Cashel

Jerpoint

Vinegar
Hill

Listowel

Enniscorthy

Wexford

Tralee

MUNSTER

WATERFORD

Baginbun

Carnsore
Point

Dingle

Dungarvan

The
Hook

Killarney

KERRY

CORK

Macroom

Youghal

Bantry

Cork

Kinsale

Skibbereen

ATLANTIC OCEAN

IRISH SEA

0   50 MLS

0   75 KMS

Robert Kee

Ireland

A HISTORY

An *Abacus* Book

First published in Great Britain by Weidenfeld & Nicolson Ltd 1980
Abacus edition published in 1982
Reprinted 1991, 1992, 1993, 1994
This revised edition published in 1995
Reprinted 1996, 1997, 1998

A CIP catalogue record for this book is
available from the British Library.

ISBN 0 349 10678 9

Typeset by M Rules
Printed and bound in Great Britain by
Butler & Tanner Ltd, Frome and London

Abacus
A Division of
Little, Brown and Company (UK)
Brettenham House
Lancaster Place
London WC2E 7EN

Contents

Preface to the revised edition

The BBC television series on which most of this book is based was first shown when the IRA campaign in Northern Ireland of the second half of the twentieth century had already been going on for nearly ten years. Writing the book then, it seemed almost incredible that these 'troubles' could have gone on so long and resolved nothing, leaving more than two thousand people dead, thousands more injured and senseless material damage inflicted on the economic life of Northern Ireland.

But the killing and the destruction were to go on for more than twice that amount of time, making twenty-five years altogether, still without resolving anything other than an end to the lives of a thousand more people, with the same consequent trauma.

The IRA were by then further than ever from achieving their self-proclaimed ideological goal of driving British sovereignty out of Northern Ireland; the British security forces were as far as ever from being able wholly to contain the IRA.

Then, on 15 December 1993, came the Downing Street Declaration. This signed agreement between a British Conservative Government and a coalition Government of the Republic of Ireland, led by the political party with the strongest Irish republican tradition, outlined firm broad principles upon which republicans from both parts of Ireland and Unionists in the North – those who had believed in the use of political violence and those who had not – could come together through the democratic process to seek a new departure from their ancient troubles.

In the light of this Declaration, some three quarters of a year later, both the IRA and the so-called Loyalist paramilitaries who had been opposing them, solemnly declared that they had decided to end their violence. Whatever was to happen in future, that particular twenty-five years at last had a finite identity; it was over. It seemed time to bring this book up to date.

In the Preface to the previous edition it was stressed that 'a' history such as this, based on 'a television history' – which was how the Ireland series was subtitled – is largely determined in both form and content by its television origins. Not only does the story get rather arbitrarily broken up into the number of programme sections proscribed (thirteen in the BBC case), but the television need to prevent the viewer from switching off, or at least going off to make a cup of tea and losing the narrative thread, often drives narrative on at a pace that would not be natural in a normal book. Bold things get done. Swathes are cut through history; qualifications and reservations that should be made get left out; many fascinating details get left out too, while some achieve a dimension to which they are hardly entitled. Then there are the weekly gaps between programmes down which may be dropped much superfluous chronology too difficult to be dealt with otherwise. In other words, a professional discipline other than that of history itself is at work. Which does not mean, of course, that in both film and book standard historical discipline is not at work too as far as possible, but 'as far as possible' is not the sort of qualification an academic historian much likes.

Up to a point, however, for readers who begin with almost no knowledge of the subject, all this can prove something of an advantage. The television discipline is here to make things easier for them too. And they actually have an advantage over viewers of the series. They get the best of both worlds. If you want a continuous message, you have it here in the printed word in a way you might have missed through temporary distraction on the box. But should you be distracted here, the message waits for you to go back to it. At the same time 'skipping' is built into the text.

Here is an example of this sort of in-built skipping. Chapter 4 here deals with the appearance of two nations in Ireland, one of which was virtually to take over Irish nationalism. This chapter contains four major themes, any one of which in a conventional popular short history would require a chapter to itself. These are: the separate growth of the Catholic nation; the establishment of the Protestant nation; the failed attempt to bring the two together in the disastrous rebellion of 1798; and the final achievement of the Catholic nation's political status under Daniel O'Connell. All four roll through here as one statement.

There are fine disadvantages in all this. The short-lived rebellion of Robert Emmet receives a mention because of its importance as myth, but details of the far more interesting intervention of the French at Killala Bay in 1798 and the actual events of the rebellion of that time in Ulster had to be ignored.

In Chapter 5, much essential detail for a proper appreciation of the social and economic origins of the Great Famine has been omitted, together with material that can make more humanly comprehensible the otherwise apparently often unfeeling attitude of the British Government. The important thing to get across in television terms was the full horrific impact of what had happened under British Government in Ireland and the consequences in folk-memory of that impact even today, not least in the United States of America. No academic could regard the treatment here of the British Treasury official, Charles Trevelyan, as sufficiently fair, but from the point of view of the television programme there were more important considerations than being fair to Trevelyan.

Such are the liberties that have had to be taken in each of the chapters based on the series as it was transmitted.

In this revised edition I have made a number of very minor amendments, principally of style, to the text which previously covered the thirteen original programmes. For a later repeat transmission of the series, the thirteenth programme had to be brought up to date and that new content is here covered in the text for the first time. The new material as a whole here runs from the second part of Chapter 13 to the end of the book. The original Chapter 13 ended with a cursory account in only a few lines of the Sunningdale Agreement of 1973 and its destruction by the Ulster Workers' strike of 1974. It seemed at the time of writing – some fourteen years ago – to have been no more than a sad dead end, an oasis that had turned out to be a mirage in the desert of continuing violence and political sterility through which Northern Ireland was for ever passing. Now, as we again appear to be entering new territory, that early ambitious failure to 'solve the problem' acquires a certain resonant significance on which it can be useful to reflect.

In general, given the entirely new circumstances which the Downing Street Declaration of 1993 and the subsequent IRA and Loyalist paramilitary ceasefires of 1994 have inaugurated, my purpose here, as in the rest of the book, has been not so much to give a fully detailed narrative of the course of all events but to relate events to the Irish history out of which they grew, in the hope that the great problems that remain may at least seem more understandable, if not necessarily easier to resolve. I wrote in the introduction to my long history of Irish nationalism, *The Green Flag*, on which the research for much of the BBC TV series was based: 'knowledge and understanding do not in themselves provide solutions but there can be no solutions without them'.

For those who may want to fill in some of the gaps in the story, I have added a short list of further reading at the end of the book.

Since this text is for the greater part so closely related to the television programmes, I owe an immense debt to all who helped to make these, primarily to the BBC itself and to the brilliant and indefatigable executive producer of the series, Jeremy Isaacs, then simultaneously preparing to set up Channel 4.

Particularly among those who also helped to shape or otherwise expedite the programmes, I should like to thank across many years Jenny Barraclough, John Bird, Jenny Cropper, Deirdre Devane, Simon Hammond, Maureen Hardman, Peter Harris, June Leech, Keith Long, Louise Maclean, John Ranelagh, Paul Rapley, Roy Sharman, Michael Waldman, the late Gordon Watkins, Vicky Wegg-Prosser, Brian Wenham and Will Wyatt. It is people like them who have helped to make the BBC what it continues to be: the finest broadcasting organization in the world.

The enterprising publishers of the very first edition of *Ireland: A History* were Weidenfeld & Nicolson and I am much indebted to George Weidenfeld for acquiring it and to Colin Webb and Rose Bean who then worked there for helping by day and by night to get it ready for publication in time for the showing of the programmes.

Robert Kee 1995

Robert Kee

9

Chronology of Events

December British General Election
Sinn Fein victory over
Parliamentary Party in Ireland

1919 *January* Dail Eireann meets in
Dublin – not banned
Catholic constables of Royal Irish
Constabulary killed by Dan Breen
at Soloheadbeg
Killing of police organized by
Collins

1920 *March* First Black and Tan members
of RIC arrive from England
July First RIC Auxiliaries arrive
November Kevin Barry hanged (first
of 24 British executions to June
1921) 'Bloody Sunday'
Kilmichael Ambush
December Burning of Cork by
Auxiliaries

1921 *May* IRA setback at burning of
Dublin Custom House
July King opens Northern Ireland
Parliament in Belfast; Sir James
Craig, Prime Minister of Northern
Ireland
Truce
December Anglo-Irish Treaty

CHAPTER 11

1922 *April* Four Courts occupied by anti-
Treaty IRA
June General Election in Ireland
gives pro-Treaty majority
Four Courts attacked by Free State
troops
Civil War starts
August Deaths of Arthur Griffith
and Michael Collins
William Cosgrave, President of
Executive Council
November First executions of anti-
Treaty IRA by Free State in Dublin,
followed by executions of Erskine
Childers, O'Connor, Mellowes
etc. – total executions by Free State
to May 1923: 77

CHAPTER 12

1923 End of Civil War
IRA 'dump arms'

1926 De Valera founds Fianna Fail
1927 General Election in Ireland
Killing of Kevin O'Higgins
De Valera and Fianna Fail take oath
without taking oath and enter Dail
1932 General Election in Ireland: Fianna
Fail victory
IRA prisoners released
'Economic War' with Britain over
land Annuities
1937 Constitution of 'Eire'
1938 Agreement with Britain: economic
war ended; Britain gives up military
and naval rights in 'Treaty' ports
1939 IRA bombing campaign in Britain
September Outbreak of Second
World War
Eire neutral
December IRA raid on Magazine
Fort, Phoenix Park, Dublin
1945 *May* End of Second World War
Churchill's and de Valera's radio
speeches
July Labour Government in power
in Britain until 1951
1948 General Election in Ireland: defeat
of Fianna Fail: de Valera out of
office for first time in 16 years
1949 Republic of Ireland declared
Accepted by Britain with guarantee
of support to Northern Ireland

CHAPTERS 13–16

1956–62 IRA campaign in North
1965 O'Neill-Lemass Talks
1967 Northern Ireland Civil Rights
Association founded
1968 *August* First Civil Rights March
October Derry Civil Rights March
banned by William Craig, Minister
of Home Affairs, but held and
broken up with brutality by police
November O'Neill reforms
announced
1969 *January* People's Democracy Belfast
to Derry Civil Rights March
4 January Marchers attacked at
Burntollet bridge
April O'Neill resigns: Chichester
Clark Prime Minister

	August B Specials out of hand in Derry and Belfast
	14 August British troops sent to Derry
	October Protestant riot in Belfast protesting against Hunt Commission's report on RUC
1970	Dublin Arms Trial
1971	*February* First British soldier killed by IRA in Belfast
	Chichester Clark resigns: Faulkner Prime Minister
	August Faulkner gets British government's agreement to internment: 342 arrested
1971	*December* 1,576 arrested
1972	*30 January* Bloody Sunday in Derry
	March Direct Rule; Stormont suspended
1973	*December* Sunningdale Agreement; Assembly established with Power-sharing
1974	*May* Ulster Workers' Strike brings down Faulkner and Assembly
	Direct rule re-imposed
1975	Northern Ireland Convention elections
1976	Convention dissolved
	Roy Mason Northern Ireland Secretary
1979	Atkins Northern Ireland Secretary
1980	Haughey/Thatcher meeting
1981	Prior Northern Ireland Secretary
	IRA Hunger Strikes
1982	Assembly elections Provisional Sinn Fein stands for first time wins 5 of the 78 seats
1985	Tom King Northern Ireland Secretary
	Anglo-Irish Agreement
1986	Assembly dissolved
1989	Brooke Northern Ireland Secretary
1992	Mayhew Northern Ireland Secretary
1993	Downing Street Declaration
1994	*August* IRA Ceasefire
	October Loyalist Ceasefire
	First official British government contact with Sinn Fein

Chapter 1

Dangerous Altercations

When trouble started in Northern Ireland in the late 1960s it took most people in the world by surprise. It has bewildered them ever since. This is largely because, for most people who don't live there, the late 1960s seemed to be the beginning. But the years of violence and suffering which Northern Ireland then experienced for the next twenty-five years are simply the latest events in an old story which began long ago.

Some people think it is dangerous to go into Irish history, because by looking into old troubles you may aggravate new ones. But as a historian of Ireland, Dr A.G. Richey, replied over a hundred years ago to people who made this same charge then:

. . . a knowledge of the truth is never dangerous, though ignorance may be so; and still more so is that half knowledge of history which enables political intriguers to influence the passions of their dupes, misleading them with garbled accounts of the past.

Northern Ireland has had its fair share of political intriguers and their dupes, and more than its fair share of garbled accounts of the past. Ungarbling the past is what this book is about.

But in trying to ungarble a past which has made such a hideous present, where do you start? In one way you could do worse than start away from Ireland altogether, in London, the seat of British government; this is because, for more than 800 years, government in London has made a claim to concern itself with Ireland. You could quite reasonably oversimplify matters and say that this is the cause of the Irish problem. It is certainly the cause of Britain's Irish problem. The attempt to assert that claim has given government in London the most consistent problem of her long domestic history.

Nearly four centuries ago, on 1 December 1598, Queen Elizabeth I was complaining that although she was spending an excessive amount of money on 'these late dangerous altercations in Ireland . . . yet we receive naught else but news of fresh losses and calamities. . . .' She continued: 'We will not suffer our subjects any longer to be oppressed by those vile rebels. . . .'

Two centuries later, on 23 January 1799, the Prime Minister of the day, William Pitt, was still struggling with the problem, saying in the House of Commons:

Ireland is subject to great and deplorable evils which have a deep root, for they lie in the situation of the country itself – in the present character, manners and habits of the inhabitants – in their want of intelligence, or in other words their ignorance . . . in its religious distinctions, in the rancour which bigotry engenders and which superstition rears and cherishes.

On 12 June 1846, Sir Robert Peel, the Prime Minister of that day, was using words in the House of Commons which have an extraordinarily familiar ring today:

Her Majesty's Government have found that in four or five counties in Ireland . . . there have been for several successive years outrages so grievous and dangerous to life and property, so alarming, that those who lived in those counties prepared to give their allegiance to their sovereign, have not received that which they have a right to expect in return – protection from the law and institutions of their country. Her Majesty's Government have found not only that life is in danger, not only that the free liberty of action is controlled by a grievous tyranny, but they found that the law has been paralysed, that evidence cannot be procured, that repeated murders are committed, and that no trace can be discovered of the murderers. . . .

And William Ewart Gladstone, the Prime Minister who, more than any other, tirelessly gave his considerable mind to the problems of Ireland, exclaimed in the House of Commons on 4 April 1893, near the end of his life: 'We say that the Irish question is the curse of this House. It is the great and standing impediment to the effective performance of its duties. . . . You have not got in Ireland a state of contentment.'

Eighty-six years later, the Irish problem physically hit the Palace of Westminster itself when, on 30 March 1979, the Conservative Opposition spokesman on Northern Ireland, Airey Neave, was killed by a bomb placed under his car by Irish republicans. But even this was only new inasmuch as a prominent politician was killed. The House of Commons chamber itself had been severely damaged by an Irish Republican bomb in Gladstone's time. And this was only one of a number of bombs that went off in London over a hundred years ago in the name of the Irish Republican cause.

Perhaps the most momentous of all such bomb explosions occurred at the site of what is now an Adult Education College in the London Borough of Clerkenwell in 1867. The present building is an old Victorian school, but it was built on the site of an old Victorian prison. In one of the prison's cells late in 1867 there sat Richard O'Sullivan Burke, a leader of the Fenians, the Irish Republican movement of that day which already boasted an Irish Republican Army.

An attempt by some of Burke's comrades to rescue him by blowing up part of the outer wall of the prison failed because the authorities had got wind of the plot. But the explosion took place and not only blew an enormous hole in the prison wall but also destroyed a number of houses. This resulted in a number of casualties comparable with those in the Birmingham IRA bombing of 1974. (Twenty-one people were killed in Birmingham; twelve were killed as a result of the Clerkenwell explosion and many others mutilated.)

An Irishman named Michael Barrett was eventually hanged for the

TOP LEFT: Elizabeth I:
'. . . those vile rebels.'

TOP RIGHT: William Pitt:
'. . . deplorable evils.'

CENTRE LEFT: Robert Peel:
'. . . repeated murders.'

CENTRE RIGHT: William
Gladstone: '. . . the curse of
this House.'

BOTTOM LEFT: Lloyd George:
'. . . murder by the throat.'

BOTTOM RIGHT: Margaret
Thatcher . . . flak jacket,
South Armagh.

THE ILLUSTRATED

POLICE NEWS.

LAW COURTS AND WEEKLY RECORD.

THE EXECUTION OF BARRETT.

LAW-COURTS AND WEEKLY RECORD.

LONDON, SATURDAY, DECEMBER 21, 1867.

Clerkenwell explosion. The execution of far too many Irishmen will be recorded in the course of this book – more than one hundred in the lifetime of its author – but Michael Barrett is in a way special because, it was partly the Clerkenwell explosion and other Irish Republican activities of the time which, by the candid admission of the Prime Minister, Gladstone, 'first induced the British people to embrace, in a manner foreign to their habits in other times, the vast importance of the Irish controversy.'

Certainly it helped induce Gladstone himself to start reforming the land system of Ireland, around which centred the main grievances of the Irish people of the day. Eventually he even committed his own party, the Liberals, to the principle that Ireland should have its own domestic government under the Crown, known as Home Rule. And, although he personally was unable to carry Home Rule through Parliament, the continuing promise of it in the programme of one of the two major British political parties, together with the reality of continuing land reforms, was enough to ensure that by the turn of the century Ireland was quieter than at any other time in her history.

When Queen Victoria visited Dublin in 1900, vast crowds turned out to welcome her to the capital and hardly a Republican voice was to be heard. Similar scenes of loyalty to the Crown were witnessed when her son Edward VII visited Dublin in 1903, and it seemed as if the bad times in the relations between the two countries had gone for ever. When, in 1914, Britain was drawn into the greatest war in her history, the vast majority of Irishmen were with her. North and South, Catholic and Protestant volunteered for the British army in tens of thousands.

Suddenly, less than two years later, at Easter 1916, the country was taken aback by an obscure and tiny minority of Irish men and women who came out in arms in open Republican rebellion against the British government. Within a week much of the centre of Dublin lay in ruins.

Four years later all Ireland was seething with unrest again on a scale unknown for over a hundred years. 'Coercion' – as the Irish had long called the British government's periodic suspension of the normal forms of law-ruled supreme. On both sides murder walked the streets: murder by special British forces known as the Black and Tans; murder by the IRA.

The British Prime Minister, David Lloyd George, like so many British prime ministers before him was determined to come to grips with the Irish problem. In November 1920, he declared exuberantly: 'We have murder by the throat!' A year later he concluded a treaty with the leader of the so-called murderers, an Irish Republican from County Cork called Michael Collins, on whose head he had put a price of £10,000 (nearer £100,000 in today's money) only a few months before.

So it becomes clear why some people could think it dangerous to look too closely into Irish history. The Clerkenwell explosion helped change British government policy: the violence of 1920 changed British government policy; the IRA of today have hoped by violence to change British government policy. Examination of the past might well be said to be encouragement to them. But the past is already encouragement to them. This book explains how it came to be so.

LEFT: A century of Irish Republican explosions in London: Airey Neave dies at Westminster.

A 'special relationship' between Irish identity and the Christian
Church. Sixth-century monastery at Inishmurray, County Sligo.

Chapter 2

A Nation Once Again?

The history of modern Ireland begins on 6 December 1921 when, under the 'treaty' concluded between the British government and the leader of the IRA of that day Michael Collins and his colleagues, the foundations were laid for Ireland to be divided into two separate areas of sovereignty: that of the new Irish 'Free State', which covered twenty-six of Ireland's thirty-two counties; and that of the remaining six counties, to be known as 'Northern Ireland', with a devolved Parliament of its own but under the overall sovereignty of the British government at Westminster.

That this was far from being a neat or indeed logical solution of the Irish problem is made clear by one simple geographical fact. The most northerly point in Ireland, Malin Head in County Donegal, was, and still is, as a result of that treaty, not in Northern Ireland at all but in what has popularly come to be known as the South. Perhaps the geography, rather than the history, of Ireland is a more reliable starting point.

If you go to Malin Head and take, as it were, a bird's flight out to sea from there, going past the Giant's Causeway (which *is* officially in Northern Ireland) and Rathlin Island to Fair Head, on a clear day you can see, only thirteen miles away, the coast of Britain. And the very first inhabitants of Ireland arrived across that channel perhaps some 8,000 years ago. A look at the map shows at once what geography does to history: the physical closeness of Britain made its attentions inevitable.

Whichever way you turn the map, the larger of these two islands off the north-east coast of Europe can hardly help appearing to want to grasp the smaller in its arms. You can't get rid of that brooding matronly (or motherly, if you like) figure in the background – the Grand Old Dame Britannia, as an Irish anti-recruiting song of the First World War described her, a grand old dame preoccupied with her own interests to the detriment of an Ireland seeking an identity of her own.

If, however, you move away from the coast towards the centre of Ireland it becomes easier to forget that grasping motherly figure. There have been 800 years of attention from London, but there were some *8,000* years of human life in Ireland before that.

The first substantial traces of independent Irish life are to be found in the valley of the river Boyne, and they are substantial indeed: the great passage-graves of Dowth, Knowth and Newgrange with their numerous satellite tombs. They were built about 3,000 BC by the new Stone Age successors of those first inhabitants to come across the straits from Britain, and they are the burial chambers of their tribal kings – kings of a simple agricultural society which already carried the unmistakable imprints of civilization. The decorated carvings of the interior are executed without the help of any iron tools. You could call them the earliest personal signatures of an Irish identity. Outside too, on the stones that surround the vast burial mound at ground level, are further sophisticated examples of this early Irish art.

These people had come as invaders and they were to be followed by successive waves of invaders, moving across from Britain and Europe or arriving direct from France and Spain, and developing still more sophisticated ornaments of civilization: Bronze Age and Celtic Iron Age jewellery, collars, necklaces and ear-rings; Iron Age decorated weaponry – ornaments of civilization made in Ireland.

It was the last of these successive waves of invaders, the Gaels, arriving in Ireland probably just before the birth of Christ, who were to set the most conspicuous and enduring imprint on what 'Irishness' was to be like. Their language was to remain the language of the majority of people of Ireland until only 150 years ago.

When, in the fifth century AD, the Romans finally left Britain, this Gaelic-Irish imprint in its pagan form had been for a long time the only Irish identity. Though the Romans had been in Britain for 400 years, no Roman administrator had ever set foot in Ireland. No Roman pattern of organization or of centralized administration had imposed itself on Gaelic Irish society. This remained what it had always been: a society made up of lesser or greater independent tribal kingdoms living by agriculture, raiding and fighting each other for cattle and land, and forming shifting alliances among themselves in order to do so.

Today, great deep ring-forts, or raths, on the hill of Tara in central Ireland still mark the home of the early pagan Gaels' High Kings. Such High Kings, while claiming eventually to be 'rulers of all Ireland', were not so in any modern centralized sense and they had no law-making powers. In fact they spent much of their time defending the semi-sacred symbolic title they claimed against the many other kings and over-kings of their society's constantly-warring tribal groups.

And yet, despite their tribal groupings and their wars these people shared a common language, a common code of law (the Brehon Law), a common tradition of oral poetry and music and a common history adapted from ancient legend. And when they came to write down their language they wrote of themselves as 'men of Ireland'. At a time when no country was a nation in a modern centralized sense, but when British society had been at least to some extent shaped by the Romans, Ireland had its own individual cultural unity which you could certainly call a sort of nationhood. Many great shocks were in store for it.

The first shock came when the traditional pagan rites of the Gaelic world were finally driven from the hill of Tara and eventually out of Ireland altogether by Christianity with the assistance of a self-appointed Romano-British missionary, later to be canonized as St Patrick. A rather crude nineteenth-century statue of St Patrick now stands on the hill of Tara. It marks not just the triumph of Christianity over paganism, but something

ABOVE: '. . . the earliest personal signatures of an Irish identity . . . ' Passage-grave at Newgrange, County Meath.

BELOW: Tara – home of pagan Gaelic High Kings.

The first shock for Gaelic Ireland: St Patrick. But in the end 'triumphant fusion'.

For this Irish world a new great shock. Round towers to watch for Vikings. Monasterboice, County Louth.

more subtle and specifically Irish: the triumphant fusion of Christianity with the Gaelic world.

One of the remarkable features of Gaelic society was to be its resilience. Within the framework of Christianity, Gaelic culture flourished as never before. In turn, Christianity shone from Gaelic Ireland through the dark ages after the fall of Rome like a beacon in Europe. There has ever since remained an especially close relationship between Irish identity and the Christian Church.

Irish monasteries such as those at Clonmacnoise and Monasterboice provided the setting for a Gaelic golden age. It was there that the details of an already ancient Irish society were first written down. It was there that magnificent works of art were fashioned: the *Book of Durrow* (a seventh-century transcription of the Gospels); the Ardagh chalice of the early eighth century; the *Book of Kells* (the Gospels again), a masterpiece of that century's end. From such monasteries Irishmen set out to found and strengthen other monasteries all over Europe.

Then, suddenly, one day in AD 795, this Irish world experienced a new great shock. The first of thousands of long, beautifully-curving high-prowed open boats filled with fierce and terrible strange warriors from beyond the sea beached on Lambay Island off the Dublin coast. It was the beginning of the Norsemen's invasion of Ireland. Known as 'Danes' in Irish popular history, they came mainly from Norway. They came slaughtering, burning and ransacking their way into Irish history, terrorizing and looting Gaelic homestead and monastery alike. More than a century later an Irish chronicler was still writing of 'immense floods and countless sea-vomiting of ships and fleets so that there was not a harbour or landport in the whole of Munster without floods of Danes and pirates. . . .'

There was no organized national resistance to the invasions. It is true that in 1014 a king from County Clare named Brian Boru, who had managed to fight his way against other Irishmen up to the High Kingship, defeated, at Clontarf, a great army consisting partly of the Norsemen of Dublin. But the other part of the army that he defeated consisted of the Irishmen of Leinster, and other great kings of Ireland stood aloof on the sidelines to see what pickings there might be when the battle was over.

Round towers, which can still be seen in many parts of Ireland, were built as combined belfries and refuges for the monasteries which the Norsemen continually sacked. The entrance to them was set high above the ground and, at the sound of the alarm from the belfry above, those seeking safety would mount rapidly, pulling their ladder up after them. Appalling scenes of brutality and terror must have been enacted below – not once but many times in what are now such peaceful places.

The Norsemen, the Vikings, became in time part of Ireland, building on the coasts the first Irish towns such as Arklow and Wexford, settling into the Gaelic pattern of warring kings, above all inter-marrying with the Gaelic Irish and becoming Irish themselves. As new Irish, they were to experience Ireland's next great shock to come:

> At the creek of Baginbun
> Ireland was lost and won

It was at Baginbun on the south-western tip of County Wexford that a small party of Normans, who had sailed across the sea from Wales, landed on 1 May 1170, and built across the promontory there a vast rampart which, overgrown as it is with gorse and bramble, is still impressive today after eight centuries of Irish wind and weather. The rampart sealed off the neck of the promontory which the Normans were then able to use as a bridgehead. What a bridgehead into Irish history it was to prove. Eight centuries of conflict were to flow from it – a conflict that is still not over.

These Norman invaders were soldiers not of the king of England but of one of his barons, the earl of Pembroke, known as Strongbow, and they had been invited over by the Irish king of Leinster, Dermot Macmurrough, to help him in a fight he was having with his own High King. Strongbow obviously hoped for something in return. Macmurrough, said to have a voice hoarse from shouting in the din of battle, for his part wanted the amazingly superior Norman military technology – equipment unknown in Ireland: knights in armour, and archers (the Irish were only using slings and stones at the time).

Strongbow himself, whose advance party this had been, arrived from across the sea soon afterwards to claim the reward for his help. He came with more knights and archers, and within a year had not only captured Dublin for Macmurrough but married his daughter and, when Macmurrough died, became king of Leinster himself.

It was then that the king of England, Henry II, intervened. He came not principally to subdue the Irish but to subdue Strongbow who was clearly having ideas above his station as one of the king's feudal subjects. And that was the beginning of London's claim to concern itself with Ireland. The problem of eventually subduing the Irish as well was taken on almost without realizing it.

The immediate impact on the Gaelic world of the Norman adventurers who stormed into Ireland in the wake of Strongbow was devastating. Entering into alliances with some Irish chieftains they seized land and cattle from others, building great castles as bastions to protect their gains as they penetrated, with their superior military technology, into all parts of Ireland except western and central Ulster.

Although these Normans owed nominal allegiance to their overlord, the English king, on the other side of the Irish Sea, they were only in pursuit of their own interests; and they spread their castles across the country in that pursuit. They were after land and wealth, which, to the strong – and they *were* strong – was there for the taking. Irish literature of the time is full of lamentation at the strangers' ruthless ways. And yet, now remote from their nominal allegiance to the English king, they in turn became an element in the traditional Gaelic political pattern of warring tribal anarchy; literally, with their castles, a part of the landscape. Intermarrying with the Irish and exchanging their own Norman French for Irish, adopting Irish ways and Irish laws, very many of the Normans became, as the saying went, 'more Irish than the Irish'.

Numerous attempts were made by kings of England to stop this process of assimilation. One of the early Irish parliaments, held at Kilkenny in 1366, tried to legislate against the wearing of Irish clothes and Irish hair-styles, and the use of the Irish language and Irish laws, by what were referred to as

LEFT ABOVE: '. . . long, beautifully curving, high-prowed open boats filled with fierce and terrible strange warriors from beyond the sea . . .' Viking ship carved by one who saw them.

LEFT: '. . . .in pursuit of their own interests . . . they spread their castles across the country . . .' Norman castle at Dunamase, County Leix.

'the English born in Ireland'. All to no permanent avail. They became known as the 'degenerate English'. Even those great Norman-Irish barons who were entrusted by the English king, their nominal overlord, with the role of deputy for his interests in Ireland tended to become an independent power. Royal government shrank increasingly to a beleaguered, ineffectual thing, enclosed within a self-isolating defensive frontier of a few hundred square miles round Dublin known as 'the Pale'.

Part of the Pale as it was at the end of the fifteenth century can still be seen at Clongowes, some twenty miles west of Dublin. It makes a pleasant woodland walk along a raised rampart standing now about four feet high between and above the double ditch that marked the boundary. The term 'beyond the Pale' is still used to describe people whose behaviour cannot be coped with or controlled. The Gaelic Irish and the Gaelicized English were the original models. The Crown of England's writ simply did not apply west of the Irish Pale. Less than fifty years later the boundary had shrunk still closer to Dublin, and the former Pale at Clongowes was itself 'west of the law'. But by that time there was a new line of monarchs on the English throne, the Tudors, and, with their ideas of modern, centrally-controlled government they were determined that the anarchy that thrived in Ireland should end.

We know exactly what the state of Ireland was like when Henry VIII came to the throne almost four and a half centuries after the Norman invasion because we have an account of it in the state papers for 1515:

More than sixty counties called regions inhabited with the King's Irish enemies . . . where reigneth more than sixty chief captains wherein some call themselves Kings, some Princes, some Dukes, some Archdukes that liveth only by the sword and obeyeth unto no other temporal person . . . and every of the said captains maketh war and peace for himself. . . . Also there be thirty great captains of the English folk that follow the same Irish order . . . and every of them maketh war and peace for himself without any licence of the King . . .

It was in 1534 that Henry VIII decided to put an end to such a state of affairs. Ireland was in a particularly advanced state of anarchy that year because the great House of Fitzgerald, earls of Kildare – the very House that was meant to represent the royal authority in Ireland – was itself in open rebellion against the Crown. Henry laid down an all-important change on paper: all lands in Ireland, whether owned by Gaelic Irish or Gaelicized English, were to be surrendered to the Crown and then re-granted, thus asserting unquestionably the Crown's claim to ultimate control over them. His daughter, Elizabeth I, was to make this control a reality and apply it with a ruthless severity.

To the Old English the change in land tenure meant, theoretically, nothing new – simply a re-affirmation of the relationship with their overlord, the king, which was supposed to have existed all along. What *was* new was that the relationship would now be enforced. For the Gaelic chieftains the change was enormous, both in theory and in practice. They now no longer held their lands according to ancient Gaelic law and tradition but by the English king's law and by the English king's goodwill, which required in return their good behaviour.

Contemporary woodcuts by John Derricke:

TOP: 'A barbarous country must first be broken by war before it will be capable of good government.'

ABOVE: Submission of Gaelic chieftains to Elizabeth I's English Deputy. The end of one sort of Gaelic Ireland.

At first they did not seem to recognize the danger. Perhaps they just assumed that the new English government was going to be as ineffective as the old. Of this notion they were soon to be sadly disabused. Their very habits and customs were to be held up as excuses for the Government's new rigour: 'The Irish live like beasts,' wrote one contemporary English observer, '. . . are more uncivil, more uncleanly, more barbarous in their customs and demeanours than in any part of the world that is known.' The contemporary woodcut artist John Derricke, revealing the extent to which Irish chieftains had adopted some Elizabethan domestic principles along with Elizabethan dress, also took pains to stress how in other respects they fell crudely below Elizabethan standards.

Resolution in imposing new obedience to English law was greatly strengthened by a sense of missionary licence to civilize:

Martial law [wrote an official] is very necessary and ought to be granted to all governors of remote and savage places where Your Majesty's laws are not received . . . until such time as the people all become civil.

Queen Elizabeth I herself approved the ground rules:

We perceive that when occasion doth present you do rather allure and bring in that rude and barbarous nation to civility by discreet handling rather than by force and shedding of blood; yet when necessity requireth you are ready also to oppose yourself and your forces to those whom reason cannot bridle . . .

Her deputies in Ireland were Englishmen newly appointed from England, and no longer those old Norman-English Irish lords who had so often proved to be simply their own masters in the past. The Crown's army was now mainly composed of English soldiers from England – not just the Irish retainers of those lords. Force 'when necessity requireth' was applied equally against the Old English and the Gaelic Irish, with unprecedented savagery.

There were no less than six separate rebellions of the Old English themselves, with or without Gaelic Irish allies, against Elizabeth's new order. And, although as part of the traditional pattern of warring alliances, Gaelic chieftains also fought on the side of Elizabeth's armies, other Gaelic chieftains resisted that new order with equal determination. In all this it was the ordinary Gaelic Irish population who took the brunt of the punishment. These new English of Elizabeth's saw Ireland and its natives as a territory and a population to be conquered and civilized much as the Spanish conquistadors of the same century viewed South America. And they acted in much the same way.

Sir Henry Sidney, one of Elizabeth's deputies in Ireland, wrote to the Privy Council in 1576:

I write not to your honours the name of each particular varlet that hath died since I arrived, as well by the ordinary course of the law, and martial law as flat fighting with them. . . . But I do assure you, the number of them is great, and some of the best, and the rest tremble for the most part. . . . Down they go in every corner and down they shall go . . .

LEFT: St Patrick on the hill of Tara. First shock for pagan Gaelic Ireland.

BELOW: Cross at Clonmacnoise monastery. For Ireland: a 'special relationship' with the Christian church.

RIGHT: The Book of Kells (end of eighth century) – Gaelic culture flourishing as never before.

OPPOSITE

ABOVE LEFT: Strongbow, earl of Pembroke. Military technology on offer to Macmurrough for something in return.

BELOW LEFT: Dermot Macmurrough, King of Leinster. 'A voice hoarse from shouting in the din of battle . . .'

ABOVE RIGHT AND BELOW RIGHT: The 'degenerate English'. Gaelicized Norman knights out of control.

Of another deputy, Sir Humphrey Gilbert, a contemporary wrote:

His manner was that the heads of all those which were killed in the day should be cut off from their bodies and brought to the place where he encamped at night, and should there be laid on the ground by each side of the way leading into his own tent, so that none should come into his tent for any cause but commonly he must pass through a lane of heads, which he used *ad terrorem* [to terrorize] – the dead feeling nothing the more pains thereby. And yet it did bring great terror to the people when they saw the heads of their dead fathers, brothers, children, kinsfolk and friends lie on the ground before their faces . . .

For some of Elizabeth's officials the methods used went too far. A former Tudor deputy, Sir James Croft, denounced 'these unexpert captains and soldiers that hath slain and destroyed as well the unarmed as the armed, even to the plowman that never bare weapon, extending cruelty upon all ages, from the babe in the cradle to the decrepit age . . .'

And the poet Spenser who witnessed campaigns in Munster wrote of the Irish there:

They were brought to such wretchedness as that any stony heart would have rued the same. Out of every corner of the woods and glens they came creeping forth upon their hands, for their legs would not bear them. They looked anatomies of death, they spake like ghosts crying out of their graves . . .

But the voice of Elizabethan officialdom felt few such scruples. The earl of Leicester in the 1570s declared: '. . . temporizing [or moderately conducted] wars are to be used with civil and expert men, but savages and those rural rascals are only by force and fear to be vanquished.' And Sir John Davies stated: 'A barbarous country must first be broken by a war before it will be capable of good government.'

This was the consensus, and in practical terms it worked. By the end of Elizabeth's reign Ireland was for the first time ever under something like the effective control of the English government. But there was another consensus: an Irish one. In this time of Elizabeth there was laid that foundation of traditional Irish hatred for governing Englishmen, which was to remain so deep in Irish consciousness.

Other foundations for the future – and indeed our own present – were also laid at this time. In the first place, the early faint traces of a modern Irish nation can, with hindsight, be discerned in a new closer association of the Old English and the Gaelic Irish. They already shared much Gaelic blood and culture, but now the common adversity in experiencing a new, ruthlessly interfering English government brought them closer to each other. A further century of adversity would complete their amalgamation.

Secondly, something had already happened that encouraged that amalgamation – the failure of the Reformation in Ireland. The Reformation of the Church – which had made England Protestant and the English monarch supreme head of the Church instead of the Pope – had not taken effect in Ireland. The simplest reason for this was a straight-forward physical one: the same as that which aggravated all England's problems in Ireland. Communication was extremely difficult with a population of about

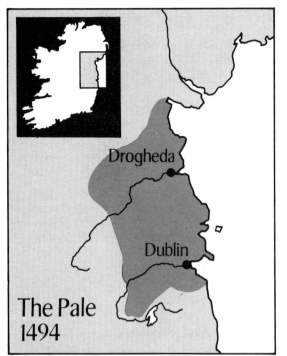

The Pale
1494

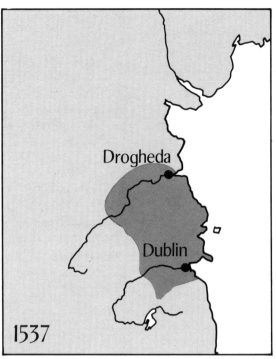

1537

Hugh O'Neill, earl of Tyrone.
'His Gaelic self got the better of
his Elizabethan self.'

a million people scattered across an Ireland half covered with bog and scrub, and with almost no roads at all. Even if the English government had not had its work cut out trying to impose civil law, let alone religious doctrine, the Irish Church – which had itself shown no interest in the new Lutheran ideas – was to a great extent still more inaccessible behind the major barrier of the Irish language.

As a result, although Ireland was by sovereign and government technically committed to the reformed Protestant religion, Protestantism remained virtually a dead letter except in and around the seat of government, Dublin. There was a political reason too why Elizabeth was in no hurry to press the Protestant point. A real danger existed that her difficult subjects in Ireland would make an ideological religious appeal for help in their troubles to Catholic powers in Europe like Spain, who might wish to use Ireland as a back door into England. Elizabeth did not want to strain unnecessarily the loyalty of those who *were* prepared to be loyal by over-antagonizing them on points of religious doctrine.

The Gaelic Irish and the Old English thus acquired a further distinctive badge of difference from the new English officials and settlers by remaining Catholic while the new men were Protestant.

The last of the great Gaelic Irish chieftains to make a stand against the intrusions of government on the civil front was a fascinating if complex figure from the wilds of Ulster, Hugh O'Neill, whom Queen Elizabeth had made earl of Tyrone. Anxious to secure support for English rule in Ulster, which was then the least penetrated of all the four provinces of Ireland, she had helped him since childhood in his disputes with other branches of the O'Neills of Ulster. He had even been brought up for eight years in England as a boy and man – a young protégé of leading Englishmen with access to Elizabeth's court. Loyalty to the queen, in one sense, was in his blood. Yet also in his blood was a feeling of descent from those Ui Nialls who had been High Kings of Ireland for centuries before. His Ulster was still little different from the territories they had ruled, and he wanted to keep it that way. Indeed, he wanted to have it both ways. He wanted the queen's favour; but he wanted to be free of her rule when he felt like it. This was not a formula for success with someone like Queen Elizabeth.

Finally Tyrone's Gaelic self got the better of his Elizabethan self. In alliance with his powerful Ulster neighbour Hugh O'Donnell, he resolved to make a last stand for the independence of the Gaelic way of life. And though he had earlier fought *for* Elizabeth in her armies, confronting the rebellious Old English of Munster, now, in his native Ulster, he rose in arms against her.

It was on the southern borders of his Ulster kingdom, a few miles north of Armagh, that in 1598 at a place known as the Yellow Ford he came closest to success. Here Tyrone dramatically defeated an English army which had set out from Armagh to try and relieve an isolated English fort on the river Blackwater. This victory of his at the Yellow Ford (over an English commander, incidentally, who was his own brother-in-law) was a major disaster for the new English government in Ireland – 'shaking it', as a contemporary put it, 'till it tottered'.

But Tyrone was fighting in his own interest for an Irish way of life. It is

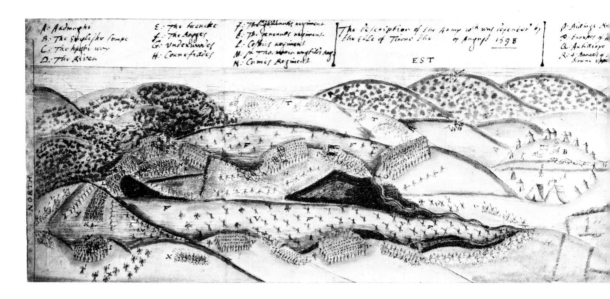

The Battle of the Yellow Ford –
momentarily '. . . shaking English
government in Ireland till it
tottered.'

anachronistic to regard him as fighting for 'Ireland' in a modern national-istic sense. Irish political nationalism was something that had to be synthesized later.

When, in September 1601, a great Spanish fleet set sail for Ireland to help Tyrone and his ally O'Donnell, and anchored in the harbour of Kinsale, Tyrone and O'Donnell were at the very other end of Ireland in their native Ulster. To meet the threat, the latest British deputy, the Protestant Mountjoy, marched south at once to besiege the Spaniards in Kinsale. And it was then that Tyrone and O'Donnell marched south too, brilliantly evading English forces sent to intercept them. They in turn besieged Mountjoy as he sat before Kinsale.

What can now be seen as the final battle for Gaelic Ireland took place there, outside Kinsale, on Christmas Eve 1601. But when Tyrone's forces attacked Mountjoy his men were fighting out in the open in conditions far less favourable to their special skills than the bogs and woods around the Yellow Ford. Mountjoy routed them and they scattered north in disorder. And that, at last, was the end of the old Gaelic Ireland.

Tyrone finally made his formal submission to the Crown and, to the fury of many Englishmen who had been fighting him, obtained pardon, after kneeling humbly for a long time before Mountjoy and then being taken to Dublin Castle. Over three centuries later Dublin Castle was to be taken over by Irish troops in Irish uniforms and a new Irish flag raised above it to replace the Union Jack. What is the real connection between these two events separated by over 300 years? What thread, if any, is there between Tyrone and those Irish Fenians who blew up Clerkenwell prison in the 1860s; between Tyrone and the present IRA?

When modern Irish nationalism first began to try and express itself in the nineteenth century a number of unofficial national anthems arose in Ireland (the official one being 'God Save The Queen'). One of these, reg-ularly sung at the end of political meetings and other Irish gatherings, went as follows:

A Nation once again
A Nation once again,
That Ireland long a province be
A Nation once again.

But how far was it realistic to say that the sort of 'nation' Ireland had been in the past was relevant to the present? What if a large minority of the Irish population in the counties of North-East Ulster did not want to be 'a Nation once again' at all?

The Flight of the Earls from Rathmullen, County Donegal. Begin here for the history of modern Northern Ireland. (*Painting by Thomas Ryan.*)

Chapter 3

No Surrender!

When the Protestant citizens of Belfast parade on 12 July every year, with their fine bands and banners and fancy dress, to celebrate the victory of William of Orange at the Battle of the Boyne in 1690, there is a solemn revelry about them, almost as if they had just won that victory themselves. And in a way they have. They have been winning it ever since.

Why, a complete stranger might ask, do quite a lot of the men wear bowler hats? Bowler hats are no more normal headgear today than they were at the Battle of the Boyne. The answer is that with those bowler hats they specifically celebrate two victories in one. The first was at the Boyne in 1690; the second was won just before the First World War in 1914, when their grandfathers and great-grandfathers – who did wear bowler hats – marched like this to stop the British government of the day from carrying out its intention to give a united Ireland the limited form of national independence known as Home Rule.

But this answer in turn raises another question: how is it that these men, whose ancestors came to Ireland 300 years ago and more, want nothing to do with the idea of Irish national independence? Why do they insist so vehemently that Ireland 'a Nation' should not include them? To answer that one needs to go back further than the Battle of the Boyne.

On the western side of the beautiful long sea inlet in the north of Ireland known as Lough Swilly, sits the amiable little seaside town of Rathmullen. It is a good deal further north in Ireland than Belfast but it is not in official 'Northern Ireland'. It is in fact in today's Irish Republic and a corvette of that Republic's navy can sometimes be seen tied up at the little harbour there flying the Republican flag. Yet it is here that the history of official modern Northern Ireland really begins.

It was at Rathmullen on 4 September 1607 that a ship which had been tied up here for a few days, flying French colours, pulled up anchor and sailed away, carrying with it into voluntary exile in Europe the two last great Gaelic Catholic chieftains to try to stop English rule from becoming effective in Ireland: Hugh O'Neill, the earl of Tyrone and his ally, the earl of Tyrconnell, Rory, Hugh O'Donnell's heir.

This 'flight of the earls' took English officials completely by surprise. After his submission to the Crown in 1603, and subsequent pardon, Tyrone had been allowed to retain possession of his lands in Ulster, a fact that had caused much resentment among English soldiers and officials who had been locked in a grim struggle with him as an arch-traitor for many years. Why then did he suddenly go off like this?

Essentially: because he was weighed down with the sad realization that he could no longer be master in his own house in Ulster in anything but name. He was suffering continual harassment from English officials, who were not only asserting the rights of English law in his territories in accordance with the terms of his submission, but also penalizing his Catholic religion and exacting fines for its practice according to that law. In addition, some who had been thwarted of the chance to get their hands on his territories for their personal profit after his pardon, had been suggesting, falsely as it turned out, that he was implicated in a treasonable plot with Spain and he feared for his life. So he could stand it no longer and was off. The implication of treason seemed momentarily substantiated; his and Tyrconnell's lands were forfeit to the Crown.

The four counties of Donegal, Tyrone, Derry and Armagh (the territories of the earls) together with the two counties of Cavan and Fermanagh became subject to the most systematic attempt yet to plant or settle in Ireland strangers from England and Scotland. This was the so-called Plantation of Ulster, worked out on a government drawing-board between 1608 and 1610.

The idea of planting colonies of settlers in Ireland with the specific aim of stabilizing English government rule, was by no means new. It had been tried first in the reign of the Catholic sovereigns Philip and Mary in the 1550s – Leix and Offaly were then re-named King's and Queen's Counties. It had been tried in Munster in the south-west in the 1560s and again in the 1580s. It had even been tried twice on a small scale in Ulster in the 1570s. But all such previous plantations had in the end been failures, collapsing for lack of human support or capital, or else being physically wiped out by the rebellion of those who had been dispossessed to make room for them.

What was different about this 1610 plantation in Ulster was both its scale and its systematized attempt to avoid former failures, not least, for example, by its part provision of capital through the City of London companies.

In a calm and quiet little street close to the cathedral in the centre of the City of Derry there is a door painted purple bearing a brass plate on which are engraved the words: 'The Honourable the Irish Society', as if some rather distinguished person lived there.

The building still houses that 'Irish Society' which in 1610, composed of functionaries of the City of London and its companies, was made responsible for colonizing – 'civilizing' was then very much the thought – those parts of the forfeited lands of the flown earls which lay thereabouts. It was the Irish Society which changed the name of the city from Derry to Londonderry.

The City of London, with its great capital resources, had undertaken the task of colonizing not only Derry itself but also the whole county. The Irish Society's role was similar to that of the Virginia Society for colonizing – and civilizing – America. The land was divided among wealthy City companies – drapers, salters, fishmongers, haberdashers and the rest. (There are still a Draperstown and a Salterstown in County Londonderry.) The plan, at least on the drawing-board, was that almost all the land of the County of Derry should go through these City companies to Scottish and English settlers who would not be allowed to take Irish tenants. A small proportion of the county – about five per cent – was to go to former soldiers who *were* allowed to take Irish tenants: the rest – about ten per cent – was allotted to the native Irish, former occupants of the whole of it, who now had to pay the Crown double the rent the settlers paid. And it was largely to the less fertile lands on the hills that the native Irish were to be officially confined.

In the other confiscated counties, other 'undertakers' of the settlement were found. But the principles of land allocation were similar. Here too the Irish were supposed to be allotted only the less fertile lands, though rather larger proportions were given both to them and to those former soldiers who were allowed to take Irish tenants.

However, drawing-board schemes involving human beings seldom work out as planned. The City companies and others who undertook to implement the settlement often allowed the native Irish to stay on the land despite the new regulations, either as much-needed labourers for the settlers, or as rent-paying tenants who could be charged high rents without incurring the capital investment needed to bring in cross-Channel settlers.

Settlers certainly came in. By 1622 there were about 13,000 of them – half-English and half-Scots – but the Irish still lived all around them. Thus from the start the main political purpose of the plantation was weakened. The chance of totally colonizing the forfeited counties was lost and the native population were not brought neatly into the 'civilizing' conformity of the English Protestant cultural pattern.

As a result the Catholic Gaelic Irish, while actually occupying a good deal more land than had originally been allotted to them, lost none of their resentment because they regarded it all as theirs in the first place. And the Protestants, less numerous, less dominant than had been intended, felt insecure and more like a beleaguered garrison surrounded by enemies than masters in their own new homes. Living daily among the Irish whose rights to land they had usurped, they fortified their farms and made security their watchword; security against whatever trouble might be brewing for them in the woods and bogs outside their windows.

The really effective plantation of Ulster took place from a different source altogether – through an originally small privately-organized Protestant settlement of Scots that had begun on the Ards peninsula of Ulster's east coast a few years earlier. There, Scotland lies only just across the water. For centuries, before the Reformation, Scots had been coming across this North Channel and settling in this part of Ireland, usually becoming indistinguishable from the Gaelic Irish people among whom they settled. But just before the 1610 plantation – in 1606 – a private settlement had been undertaken by two Scottish Protestant adventurers named Montgomery and Hamilton after a deal with the local Gaelic chieftain. This eastern Protestant plantation of Ulster prospered rapidly and became the bridgehead by which, for the rest of the century and beyond, individual Scottish settlers flocked to Northern Ireland. They spread outward from there through the town of Belfast, over the whole area of Antrim and Down. They even spread right across Ulster to fill out the gaps left in the official plantation of the west. The geographical distributions of Protestant and Catholic in Northern Ireland today still reveal clearly the two separate settlements of Ulster of over 300 years ago.

The success of the eastern Ulster settlement meant that the overwhelming number of settlers in Ulster were Scots rather than English. More significant still, they were Presbyterian rather than Anglican, and when they first arrived, were being penalized by the English Church as dissenters. It is on record that one Sunday afternoon over 500 people from County Down crossed the sea to Stranraer in Scotland to receive the sacrament in a manner forbidden to them by the English law at the time in Ireland – and such journeys were a regular occurrence. Though Presbyterians are of course no longer penalized as dissenters, the psychological tradition of that sort of independence of spirit vigorously survives today as a political force. The Presbyterian determination to pursue what they see as *their* interest, both material and spiritual, figures continuously through the Irish history of the next 300 years and more, and is one of the principal factors in the contemporary situation.

Thus, gradually and overwhelmingly, the English and Scottish Protestant settlement of Ulster was established. Ulster, once the most Gaelic Irish and Catholic province of all, now had a mixed population of opposed interests and beliefs, often so closely entangled with each other that streets even in the same town would be named 'Scotch quarter' and 'Irish quarter'.

From the very start fear was in the minds of the new settlers. Quite apart from the feelings of those original inhabitants who, as labourers or tenants, were all about them, it was well known that there were some 5,000 former swordsmen of the two Gaelic earls still lurking resentfully in the bogs and mists. And on 23 September 1641, what Protestants had long been dreading happened: there was a great rebellion of the Gaelic Irish Catholics who, though loudly proclaiming their loyalty to the Crown, struck swiftly and fiercely for the return of their lands.

The rebellion was directed against all new settlements everywhere in Ireland but, because the Ulster settlement was the largest, it was there that the effect was most shattering. What made the effect so shattering were the atrocities, or more particularly the reports of the atrocities, with which the rebellion's outbreak was accompanied. For instance, one of the many colourful banners carried by Orange Lodges in 12 July processions through Belfast to this day vividly depicts what happened on the bridge at Portadown on a cold November day in 1641.

On that day – and there is contemporary evidence to substantiate the incident – a party of some 100 Protestant men, women and children who had been seized from their homes, robbed, and stripped of most of their clothes, were herded together onto the bridge. They were then thrown or driven over the parapet into the water below where they were drowned or if they could swim were shot or knocked on the head as they came to shore. Some of the Irish even took to boats and bashed them with oars as they floundered in the waters. There was said to be a ghostly figure which arose from the waters for months afterwards – a woman, naked to the waist, very white, her hair dishevelled, 'her eyes', it was said, 'seeming to twinkle in her head as she cried, "Revenge! Revenge!"'

That last detail in particular and the exact number of people murdered at Portadown may well not be strictly accurate but there is too much verbatim contemporary evidence for this atrocity and for others that took place against Protestants at the outbreak of the 1641 rebellion to doubt that some such things did happen.

That evidence, now lying in some thirty-two volumes in Trinity College, Dublin, was collected from Protestant men and women who had often experienced such things at first hand and was sworn to and taken down before Royal Commissioners often quite shortly afterwards. It comes uncannily alive in the case of one Elizabeth Prize of Armagh whose five children were taken from her to be pushed from that bridge at Portadown:

And as for this deponent and many others that were stayed behind, diverse tortures were used upon them . . . and this deponent for her part was thrice hanged up to confess to money, and afterwards let down, and had the soles of her feet fried and burnt at the fire and was often scourged and whipt . . .

And a great number of other Protestants, principally women and children, whom the rebels would take, they pricked and stabbed with their pitchforks, skeans and swords and would slash, mangle and cut them in their heads and breasts, faces, arms, and hands and other parts of their bodies, but not kill them outright but leave them wallowing in their blood to languish and starve them to death.

The Revd Robert Maxwell, Protestant Rector of Finnane, County Armagh, deposed 'that the rebels buried many of the British Protestants alive, and took great pleasure to hear them speak unto them as they digged down old ditches upon them.' The Rector further deposed that the rebels dragged his brother, Lt. James Maxwell

. . . out of his bed in the rage and height of a burning fever and . . . cruelly butchered him. . . . And . . . his wife Grizell Maxwell being in childbirth, the child half-born and half-unborn, they stripped stark naked and drove her to the Blackwater and drowned her. The like they did to another Englishwoman in the same parish which was little inferior if not more unnatural and barbarous than the roasting of Mr Watson alive, after they had cut a collop out of either buttock . . .

And there is much more of the same sort of thing.

However, much of this 'evidence' of sworn personal statements is hearsay and must thus contain at least exaggeration as well as some straight untruths. Some is sworn many years after the alleged event and therefore is very suspect, though some is sworn within a few weeks of the day described by the witness. Some shows the Irish rebel commanders, particularly Owen Roe O'Neill – nephew of the great Hugh – who came from Spain in 1642 to command the rebel forces, to have been humane and considerate with their prisoners, and it seems that atrocities were committed on the whole as a result of wild indiscipline rather than policy. Much of the evidence in these famous thirty-two volumes does not concern Ulster at all but other counties of Ireland where the rebels rose against further recent plantations which had taken place on the Ulster model – in Longford, Leitrim, Clare, Mayo, Wexford, Kilkenny, Wicklow and other counties. Some of it is even evidence of atrocities committed by government forces against the Irish.

But the central conclusion must be that a not inconsiderable number of atrocities were committed in the early stages of the 1641 rebellion against the English and Scottish settlers in Ulster. And though the numbers were often fantastically exaggerated (one Protestant historian put the Protestant dead at over 150,000 – more than the entire Protestant population of Ireland at the time), on balance historians seem to think that about 12,000 Protestant men, women and children were either murdered or died of their privations in the early days of the 1641 rebellion.

The real point is that exaggerated versions of the atrocities have been as important as the reality in conditioning later attitudes in Northern Ireland. There is in the Northern Protestant historical subconscious no limit at all to the horrors that might have been or might still be inflicted on them. It must be remembered that the 1641 rebellion took place when Protestants were far outnumbered by the Irish Catholics they lived among. Northern Ireland Protestant attitudes today are still conditioned by the fact that they are a minority in the whole of Ireland rather than by the fact that they are now a majority in the North.

Quite apart from the atrocities and their effect on Ulster, the rebellion of 1641 had a further all-important effect on the way things were to go in Ireland. The Gaelic Irish had risen in the Catholic cause as well as the cause of their own lands lost to the new settlers. But the Old English settlers in Ireland were Catholics too, like the Gaelic Irish. As the English parliament became more and more Puritan – moving as it was towards a civil war with the king – and more and more zealously anti-Catholic, *all* Catholics in Ireland, both Gaelic Catholic and Old English, became more and more anxious that their religion would prejudice their rights to land. In other words the two Catholic groups in Ireland became increasingly identified in interest and now joined in rebellion to begin what was at first a slightly uneasy, but for the future all-important, self-protective alliance.

An early phase of this new social grouping is illustrated by an incident that took place in 1641 at Clongowes Castle, County Kildare, the former bulwark on the Pale of the Dublin-based English government. The later building that stands there today houses a Catholic boys' public school – and the harmony of English culture with Irish Catholic zeal is appropriate. For it was here in 1641 that the owner, one James Eustace, an English Catholic whose family had already intermarried with Gaelic stock, drew his sword for the Catholic religion and Ireland against the English government in Ireland. And here there were Protestant atrocities to record. Women and children on the estate were slaughtered and the garrison was hanged when it surrendered. Eustace's ninety-year-old mother, who had been hiding the key to a secret room of the castle in her mouth, died when her jaws were smashed.

Awful events were slowly hammering the people of Ireland into two nations regardless of race: one Catholic and the other Protestant. And the man who was to do so much to further that process was to arrive in Ireland at the end of the decade. His name: Oliver Cromwell.

Cromwell had by then won the Civil War against King Charles I in England, but in Ireland there were still strong Royalist armies in alliance with Irish Catholic rebels. In August 1649 Cromwell came over.

'Cromwell came over,' wrote someone who experienced it, 'and like a lightning passed through the land.' He struck first at Drogheda, branding

RIGHT: Rebellion of Gaelic Irish Catholics: the bridge at Portadown. Horrors for the Northern Protestant subconscious.

BELOW: Drogheda. A brand name for English 'frightfulness' in Ireland. But Cromwell was attacking an English commander.

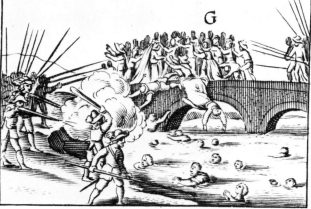

Driuinge Men Women & children by hund: reds vpon Briges & casting them into Riuers, who drowned not were killed with poles & shot with muskets.

G

Fol: 159

the name of the town into Irish history, as a traditionally classical example of English 'frightfulness' in Ireland.

But Cromwell's ruthless action at Drogheda cannot be seen simply as the crude anti-Irish racialism of Irish nationalist legend. The garrison at Drogheda was commanded by an English Catholic, Sir Arthur Aston, and was largely under English officers – all Royalists fighting Cromwell in this the last stage of the great Civil War.

Cromwell had brought over with him siege artillery superior to anything then in Ireland and after some 300 cannon shot succeeded in breaching the walls. But on his first attempt to storm the breach his men were driven back with considerable loss. This set-back so inflamed him that when his men did succeed in breaking through he behaved as he did.

'Being in the heat of the action', he wrote soon afterwards, 'I forbade them to spare any that were in arms in the town.' And although the order was thus theoretically confined to the garrison itself, it seems more than probable that women and children were caught up in the process. On his own later admission no priest was left alive.

Attacking with sword in hand, he and his men drove the defenders back to a high tower known as Millmount. Trapped there, the commander and his officers surrendered, but were immediately put to the sword, though that is a euphemism where Sir Arthur Aston is concerned, for he was beaten to death with his own wooden leg. Those of the garrison who had temporarily managed to escape across the river to the other part of the town took refuge in various places, one of which was the tower of St Peter's Church. Cromwell had it burned down and those who fled from it massacred. Of the surrender of a party of some 120 defenders caught in another tower, he wrote: 'The officers were knocked on the head, every tenth man of the soldiers killed and the rest shipped to the Barbadoes . . . I think that we put to the sword altogether about 2,000 men.' And to assuage any feelings of remorse or guilt he might have felt he added that all this was done by the Spirit of God: 'And therefore it is right that God alone should have all the glory.'

In a confused way Cromwell seems to have seen himself at Drogheda as accomplishing God's work by avenging the atrocities of the rebellion of 1641. But the inhabitants of Drogheda had played no part in the rebellion of 1641; the town had always been within the confines of the English Pale. And although it is possible that some Irish soldiers of the garrison might have taken part in such atrocities, this cannot have been true of the English officers.

Nevertheless the effect of this, Cromwell's final ruthless campaign of the Civil War, on the future history of Ireland was devastating. In the name of English government, all Irish Catholics, as suitors of the whore of Babylon, were to be trodden under and Irish Protestants were to triumph.

From Drogheda Cromwell's Puritan Parliamentary armies marched victoriously south through Ireland. Some surrendering garrisons were treated with mercy, even with honour. But one town, Wexford, suffered even worse than Drogheda, being stormed while still negotiating surrender. Cromwell's men ran amok in the town, killing at least 2,000, of whom 200 were said to be women and children slaughtered in the market-place.

After Wexford the rest of the Parliamentary army's campaign was soon

OPPOSITE

ABOVE: Siege of Derry, 1689. For James II's armies only mortars. For the besieged a diet of dogs, mice and candles.

BELOW: Relief of Derry, 1689. '. . . Those English ships in the Foyle which had so long appeared to lack the courage to burst the boom . . .'

over, and when it was over Cromwell enacted a draconian measure against those of the defeated Irish Catholics who owned land. Catholic land in Ireland east of the Shannon was to be distributed among his soldiers and the adventurers who had financed his campaigns; those thus dispossessed were transplanted beyond the Shannon to the more barren province of Connaught. And with this final humiliation of the Irish Catholic landowners – their banishment to a remote corner of their own country in the beautiful sad lands of the west – what came to be known as 'the curse of Cromwell' was complete.

Only the *landowners*, their families and retainers were transplanted. The rest of the population, former tenants and landless labourers of those who now had to make their homes in Connaught, stayed behind in the same capacity to serve the new Protestant settlers. But the transplantation to Connaught was a symbol of humiliated status to all Irish Catholics everywhere. The curse of Cromwell marked them all.

The percentage of the land of Ireland owned by Catholics which had shrunk by the time of the great rebellion to fifty-nine per cent, was reduced by the Cromwellian land settlement to a mere twenty-two per cent. After further Catholic humiliation in great events to come it was to shrink by 1695 to fourteen per cent and by 1714 still further to seven per cent.

When the restored monarch Charles II replaced the Cromwellian regime in 1660, Irish Catholics hoped that he would restore them to their former status too. But he was too wily to upset Protestants who had given him back his crown. It was only when his Catholic brother James II succeeded to the throne that Irish Catholics felt their moment had come. James appointed Catholics to high offices of State in Ireland and a Catholic-dominated Irish parliament passed an Act revoking the Cromwellian land settlement. But before it could be implemented the kingdoms of England and Ireland were split temporarily in two.

If you look at a map of Ireland and follow, from right to left, the border which partitions it, you will arrive in the end at the City of Londonderry. For nearly 300 years it has been the definitive symbol of Irish Protestant determination to stand firm against all apparent threats to their way of life. So long as life in Ireland continues to be dominated by symbols from the distant past, Londonderry will continue to be required as one.

For it was here, in 1688, as the citizens of that day heard how England was replacing the Catholic King James II with the Protestant William of Orange that, on the walls of Londonderry, the crisis which this inevitably meant for Ireland began to be played out. And the first stage of that crisis is still re-enacted here every year on the anniversary of these great events. Protestants of Londonderry, with their sashes of the Orange Order and other ceremonial equipment, assemble every 7 December to celebrate the action of thirteen apprentice boys of the City who on that day in 1688, helped save Ireland for William of Orange.

The sequence of events was as follows. In the late autumn of that year, tension in the city had been mounting as a story began to spread that Catholics in Ireland loyal to James II against William of Orange were turning on Protestants and massacring them again, as in 1641. On top of this, news suddenly arrived in Londonderry that a new garrison was to be sent to the city in King James's name to relieve the previous one – the new garrison being a *Catholic* regiment of Lord Antrim's Redshanks.

Though the citizens could not but acknowledge that James was still their legitimate king, voices began to be heard among them saying that with such rumours of massacre around it would be madness at such a moment to let Catholic troops in to garrison the place. Other voices, shocked, declared that it would be unthinkable to try and keep royal troops out of a royal garrison. The Protestant Bishop of Londonderry and other Protestant establishment figures were among the latter, although the Presbyterians with their naturally independent attitude to authority were less troubled by such scruples.

The official decision, however, had been taken to admit the troops in the normal way, when suddenly thirteen apprentice boys of the city took matters into their own hands, seized the keys of the gates of Londonderry and on 7 December 1688 slammed them firmly in the face of Lord Antrim's Redshanks – King James's troops.

The siege of the town by James's forces did not start until some months later in April 1689 and was not really pressed in earnest until two months after that, lasting in full intensity only about six weeks. When James presented himself before the walls in person, the Protestant soldier in command of the unchanged garrison, a Lieutenant-Colonel Robert Lundy, was actually in favour of surrendering the city to him but his authority was overthrown by the citizens and Lundy had to flee the city disguised as a common soldier with a load of matchwood on his back. Today the name of Lundy is still used as a term of abuse in Northern Ireland for any Protestant who weakens in his radical fervour for the Protestant cause.

Just as the siege itself was starting in April, ships bringing troops from William of Orange in England to relieve the city arrived in the River Foyle, but judging that it had no chance of holding out they rather timidly withdrew again. When, in May, more ships with supplies from England arrived in the Foyle, a wooden boom had been drawn across the river by the besieging army. The officer in charge of the expedition decided that it presented too intimidating a barrier for him to be able to proceed.

Meanwhile some 30,000 Protestants, including many from the countryside round about, had collected behind the walls and seemed to present a sitting-target to be starved out. They should have been a sitting-target for siege artillery too but the besieging army had only one gun, a 24-pounder, capable of breaching the walls. The army did, however, have mortars which did much damage to houses, and this in an overcrowded city, short of food, caused considerable hardship and, in what turned out a wet summer, much sickness.

Dogs, cats, mice, candles and leather were soon being eaten; and there is a famous story of one fat citizen of Derry who felt he had to stay indoors because he thought he noticed his neighbours eyeing him greedily. Not that it can have been any sort of joke at all to have been in the city at the time: thousands of people died of starvation and disease. But it was a strange sort of siege; there were one or two skirmishes outside the walls, but only one serious attempt to breach them, which was driven off. The besieging army was in fact ill-trained, outnumbered and ill-equipped. Many of James's soldiers had only primitive pikes, pointed sticks without even iron tips, as weapons. Twice parties of non-combatants were allowed to leave – 10,000 of them in May accepting a pardon from James and going.

Once the commander of the besieging army tried to take the town by rounding up thousands of Protestants from the neighbouring countryside and driving them to a place out in the open in front of the walls where he said he was going to leave them without food or water until the town surrendered. The citizens retaliated by erecting a gallows up on the wall in full view of the besieging army from which they said they would hang Catholic prisoners unless these wretched people below the walls were released. James II's commander – James himself disapproved of such a ruthless initiative – then thought better of it and released the Protestants, though he had hoped at least that they would have to be taken inside the walls to swell the numbers already so short of food.

Still preserved on a stand in the entrance to the cathedral in Londonderry is one of the round iron 'bomb-shells' fired into the town in June 1689. It has a small hole in the top and contained in fact not explosive at all but a letter giving terms on which the inhabitants were invited to surrender. But it has proved explosive enough in subsequent history, because 'No Surrender!' was the final answer which the besieged sent out and it has been the watchword of the northern Protestants ever since.

On 28 July 1689 the British ships in the Foyle finally summoned up the courage to try and break the boom. Under fire from James II's artillery on the shore they replied with vigour and eventually succeeded in bursting through and sailing into the quay below the walls with the desperately needed supplies. The siege of Londonderry was over.

In addition to the slogan 'No Surrender' there is one other all-important memory that survives from the famous siege, at least in the Protestant subconscious. And that is the memory of the attitude of those British ships down in the Foyle who either gave up Derry for lost, or for so long appeared to lack the courage to burst the boom. In reality, but for the arrival of British help, Derry would have surrendered; some within it were already negotiating for surrender when help arrived; but the only reality which later history has allowed to count is that it did *not* surrender, together with the awareness that however much the northern Protestant may need British help he is also on his own. In that sense, the siege of Derry still goes on today though it was raised three centuries ago.

The raising of the siege *then* led to the eventual total defeat of James II in Ireland. William of Orange landed at Carrickfergus Castle the next year, 1690, and won great victories in battles at the Boyne and at Aughrim. In 1691 all the Catholic armies in Ireland totally surrendered at Limerick, under their Old English-Gaelic Catholic commander Patrick Sarsfield. He and thousands of his troops were allowed to go into exile to serve in the armies of Louis XIV and became known as 'Wild Geese'. This was the foundation of that triumph of Protestant over Catholic, Orange over Green, still perpetuated in memory by Protestants in Northern Ireland today because it is a memory they think they need.

If you ask a Protestant working-man in Belfast painting a fine popular portrait of William III on a street wall in his spare time why he is doing it and what William III means to him, he will answer to the effect that William III saved people like him from being taken over by the Papists. And if you ask him who Papists are he will answer that they are the people from whom he needs to be saved from being taken over, people who committed the atrocities of the 1641 rebellion and on whom the gates of Londonderry had to be slammed – most of the people of Ireland in fact against whom, as further momentous events unrolled over three centuries, he has felt it necessary to remain continually on guard. It is as simple, and as complicated, as that.

The first Irish nationalists – Protestant Volunteers in arms.

Chapter 4

Two Nations?

'From the very beginning of its faith', said Pope John Paul II, speaking in Phoenix Park, Dublin, on 29 September 1979, 'Ireland has been linked with the Apostolic See of Rome.' And, in the same place, later: 'On Sunday mornings in Ireland, no-one seeing the great crowds making their way to and from Mass could have any doubt about Ireland's devotion to the Mass.'

Roman Catholicism, for better or worse, is so much part of the atmosphere of Ireland that Irish national identity can seem inseparable from it. The Pope himself apparently assumed that it was inseparable. The Constitution which republicans wrote for Ireland in 1937 actually went out of its way to suggest that this was so, formally recognizing the Catholic Church to be the Church of the majority of the people. Yet here is a strange paradox: the very nationalists who wrote that Constitution also insisted that the people of the whole island were members of one 'nation'. The fact that about a quarter of the Irish people do not want to be part of the Irish nation just because they do not like Roman Catholicism has somehow always been blandly ignored by such nationalists as if it were an irrelevant fact.

The theory of Wolfe Tone, one of the first modern Irish nationalists – who talked of achieving Irish independence by substituting the common name of Irishman for Catholic and Protestant – has always been recited by nationalist Irishmen as if it had the sanctity of the Creed. As sometimes with the Creed, a different set of beliefs has been practised in everyday life. Irish nationalism, though it has had many prominent Protestant supporters, has in modern times been a nationalism which expresses the aspirations of the Catholic people of Ireland. Perhaps it should not have been so. Perhaps it need not have been so. But events determined that it would be so.

The eventual establishment of the Reformation in Ireland had given all church buildings to a triumphant Protestant State. By the mid-nineteenth century, churches specifically for Catholics had already been built again, though there were still some localities which were not to have one until the twentieth century. At the beginning of the eighteenth century however, Irish Catholics had to celebrate Mass on primitive altar tables in ruined churches and other desperate places simply because there was nowhere else where they could do so.

A rough stone table on the outside wall of a church in County Wexford bears the following inscription:

During the penal times this structure served as an altar in the ruins of the Church of St James in the parish of Wexford. Erected in the ground of the Church of the Assumption 1887.

In a religious age, the great majority of the Irish population had to follow their religion where they could – in primitive structures on the outskirts of towns if they were lucky enough to find one available, more often in the open air. A fine photograph of an open-air Mass in the middle of the nineteenth century depicts what the normal scene of worship must have been like for very many Catholics for much of the eighteenth.

But shortage of religious accommodation was by no means their only handicap. At the beginning of the eighteenth century, after the triumph of William III, a series of harsh laws had penalized the majority of the Irish population just because they were Roman Catholics. These 'penal laws' decreed that a Catholic could not hold any office of state, nor stand for Parliament, vote, join the army or navy, practise at the bar, nor, what was even more important for the social future of the country, buy land. A Catholic could not, by law, even hold land on a lease longer than thirty-one years; nor could he bequeath as he wished what he did hold. On his death his land had to be divided among all his children, unless one of them turned Protestant, in which case he inherited the lot. As a result, by the third quarter of the eighteenth century, barely five per cent of the land of Ireland remained in Catholic hands.

The penal laws did not, as is sometimes popularly supposed in Ireland, prohibit worship of the Catholic religion as such. But even in religious matters the letter of the law at least was harsh, placing severe limitations on the activity of the Catholic priesthood. Parish priests were allowed to officiate in Ireland provided they registered with the authorities – but *only* parish priests. *Not* allowed by law, banned on pain of transportation and even death, and forced into precarious secrecy, if they did remain, were friars of the regular orders of clergy (Augustinians, Dominicans etc.), and all bishops and archbishops. Theoretically this meant that all new ordinations of priests would be impossible and that the Catholic Church in Ireland would thus eventually die out.

But the Catholic Church in Ireland did not die out. This was because the religious sections of the penal laws were in fact applied much less severely in practice than in theory. Certainly, friars and unregistered priests had to perform their duties furtively. Furtively, too, bishops and archbishops had to go about their business, by no means living in the style to which bishops and archbishops are accustomed. There were occasional official drives against what everyone knew was actually happening, but alongside the official harshness went an unofficial tolerance.

The chief reason for this was a simple one: enforcement of the religious sections of the penal laws was impossible. The Catholic Church had the support of the vast majority of the people of Ireland, and to suppress the Church you would have had to suppress the people. Provided that Catholic priests and Catholic laity obeyed the civil law, and above all showed loyalty to the Protestant succession of the Crown of the two kingdoms of England and Ireland, it was easier to turn a blind eye to official breaches of the religious law.

A clear and indeed comical idea of the way in which the full rigours of the purely religious part of the penal laws neither could be, nor were, enforced, can be seen from an incident which took place in Galway in 1731. Augustine Street in Galway is so named because it contains a house of Augustinian friars – one of the most important orders of the regular clergy of the Catholic Church. In 1731 it was named Back Street but then, too, contained a house of Augustinian friars. However, under the penal laws there were not supposed to be any friars of any sort in Ireland at all. (There had even been one serious attempt to pass a law by which friars caught in Ireland should be branded on the cheek with a hot iron, so that if they did return after transportation they could be recognized and executed.) So what were these Augustinian friars doing sitting happily here in their house in the middle of Galway in 1731?

The friars knew that they had the support of the vast majority of the population thereabouts who were of course Catholic as they are today. They knew that the authorities' means of enforcement of the law were weak, even if there was the will to enforce it, and they knew too that in fact many liberal-minded Protestants disliked the aspect of purely religious persecution in the penal laws. But they also knew that the authorities had to be seen from time to time to be trying to do their duty.

Early in November 1731, the Mayor of Galway (a Protestant of course, because only Protestants could hold such an office) had just received official instructions to act firmly against the continuing strength of the Catholic Church thereabouts, and he raided the Augustinian house with his sheriffs. But, as he regrettably had to report, not a single Augustinian friar was to be found there. An entry in the Augustinian house-book, or journal, for the period does much to explain why. It does indeed report that no public Mass was held on the Sunday of that week by the friars 'because of persecution'. But it also records that on 9 November 1731 there was issued: 'A bottle of wine for ye Sheriffs . . . one shilling and one penny.'

The sheriffs were equally unsuccessful in finding any friars in their official raid on a Dominican house in another part of Galway about the same time. But they did better in other respects. The relevant entry in the Dominican journal runs '. . . for claret to treat ye Sheriffs in their search . . . two shillings and twopence'.

If the penal laws had been or could have been enforced, the Catholic Church in Ireland would have been wiped out as was the original intention. The fact that the Church was able to surmount them strengthened not only the Church itself but also its bond with the vast majority of the population of Ireland who, deprived of all political and many other rights, saw the Church as the one representative organization they had. The Church subsumed those popular energies which in other circumstances might have gone into politics.

In the absence of all political rights the only other organization which came to represent the majority of the Irish people was that network of agrarian secret societies which by the second half of the eighteenth century, under the name of 'Whiteboys', had come to exercise a powerful and often ruthless sway locally in the countryside. These agrarian secret societies offered protection to the peasantry from the worst excesses of rack-renting landlords and middlemen by threatening them with crude violence and similarly disciplining those of the peasantry themselves who offended against their code by, for instance, taking land from which another had been evicted. But although they were to continue as an all-important aspect of Irish social life until well into the following century, these secret societies seldom strayed from local agrarian affairs even into the fringes of politics. The eighteenth-century Whiteboys in particular made a point of stressing that they had no national political ambitions.

So it came about that at a time when in fact the Irish people had many grievances, being deprived by the penal laws of political and social rights and living in what every traveller described as conditions of extreme poverty, they reserved their loyalties for organizations outside politics, for their Church and the secret societies. Inasmuch as middle-class Catholics, who often made considerable fortunes in trade (from which they were not barred), looked to public life at all, it was to emphasize their loyalty to the Crown in the hope of thus ensuring the continuance of a quiet and profitable existence.

It may therefore seem a paradox to say that it was precisely during this period of the eighteenth century that the first really effective talk of the Irish nation demanding its rights began. But the paradox is easily resolved: the talk, and not only talk but action, came not from the majority of the Irish people at all, who were excluded from political rights, but from the people who were excluding them: the Protestants of Ireland.

These Protestants were mainly settlers of quite recent times, but they included a small proportion of old Catholic and even old Gaelic Catholic stock who had changed their religion for the advantages to be had by doing so. They became known as the Protestant ascendancy, and the term is apt because not only were they *above* the majority but also they had soaring aspirations on their own account, as can be seen from the magnificent country houses they built for themselves all over Ireland, from the elegant planning of their town residences which still catch the eye in Dublin, and the splendour and taste with which they adorned both. They built for themselves a whole sophisticated culture, reflected not only in their houses, but also in the literature of Swift, Sheridan, Goldsmith, Burke and others. On this culture they based a claim, as Irishmen, to be treated by Britain as an equal nation. And this, curiously as it must now seem, was the first version of modern Irish nationalism: a Protestant version. It was the nationalism of colonists expressing that sense of restless impatience with the mother country which colonists, growing away from their roots like adolescents in family life, invariably develop.

Historians are now much less certain than they used to be about the real extent to which restrictions placed on Irish trade by the English parliament seriously damaged Irish prosperity. But what is certain is that the feeling that they did so helped at the time to stir the Irish colonists' political restlessness. From the beginning of the eighteenth century they had had a proud sense of their own individual identity. It was early in that century that the Protestant Dean of St Patrick's Cathedral in Dublin, Jonathan Swift, thinking of himself and his fellow Protestants as Irishmen, had urged them to burn everything English except English coal and had helped develop a theory that the English parliament had in fact no right to legislate for Ireland at all. This, it began to be argued, was the right only of the Irish parliament.

Heady talk from Patriot
Henry Grattan in the Irish
Parliament. But what about
the other 'nation'?

This was highly questionable constitutional theory. Although an Irish parliament had been in existence since the Middle Ages (and had had to be curbed by the English parliament just because it was used by earlier colonists to assert their own interests) it had become an institution of little significance. But as, in the course of the eighteenth century, the Irish Protestants developed their culture, so they also developed the political aspirations which grew from it. Talk of 'the Protestant nation' became headier as they took their cue of spirited independence from colonists still further away from the mother country than themselves – those in America. When the Americans rebelled in the 1770s it had an important impact on Ireland. The Protestant nation took advantage of the British government's predicament to form companies of armed 'Volunteers' which, while nominally there to defend the coasts of Ireland against any invader in the absence of British regiments in America, in effect acted as a threat to the government of determined action should the 'Nation's' claim to legislative independence not be recognized.

In the splendid building in Dublin in which the Irish parliament sat (and which is today the Bank of Ireland) the 'Patriot' party was led by an eloquent lawyer, Henry Grattan. With his hand much strengthened by the existence of the Volunteers, Grattan finally won in 1782 a Declaration of Independence from the British government which on paper removed from Westminster the right to legislate for Ireland.

The new constitutional relationship between Britain and Ireland was to be that of two sovereign independent kingdoms linked by the inalienable identity of the Irish Crown with that of Britain. But it was this link which was in the end to make the Irish 'Nation's' independence little more than nominal so long as the parliamentary system of both kingdoms remained unreformed, for the control of honours and patronage, by which in the long run governmental policy was operated in each parliament, remained in the same royal ministers' hands at Westminster. There was not the same near-unanimity among the Protestant Irish for parliamentary reform as there had been for 'independence'. Nor was there unanimity for that total emancipation of Catholics to political rights which, together with reform, might have enabled Ireland to be the 'Nation' which Protestants declared her to be. The future of the 'independent Irish Nation' of 1782 was in fact deadlocked.

Then, in 1789, there occurred in Europe an event which was eventually to sharpen and redistribute Irish political thinking altogether: the French Revolution. The news of this conveyed to all deadlocked societies the remarkable message that a deadlocked society was not necessarily deadlocked at all and that 'the will of the people' in government was a practical possibility. Such news had a particularly strong emotional and intellectual impact on Ireland. An open radical organization was formed, mainly by Presbyterians from Belfast, to promote the twin objects of parliamentary reform and the unification of the Catholic and Protestant nations into one. It named itself appropriately the Society of United Irishmen, and was enthusiastically joined by that young Dublin Protestant Wolfe Tone who was to write of substituting the common name of Irishman for that of Catholic and Protestant. The United Irishmen had no success with the government and only limited success in furthering their aim with many

Protestants. By 1796 they had converted themselves into a secret society with still more radical aims, to be implemented ultimately by violent means. The year 1796 was to produce one of the most dramatic events in all Irish history and one of the most dangerous moments England ever experienced.

Bantry Bay is a magnificent stretch of water on the south-west coast of Ireland, twenty-six miles long, seven miles across, and with a draught of forty fathoms in the centre. And in this excellent deep draught of water there anchored on the evening of 21 December 1796 a great invasion fleet of thirty-five French ships, their decks crammed with thousands of French republican troops fresh from their triumphs in Europe as the greatest revolutionary army the world had ever seen. They had come to Ireland at the call of the United Irishmen to help them bring about a republican revolution there, a revolution which would unite Catholics and Protestants as one Irish nation in an Irish republic and, as Wolfe Tone himself put it: '. . . break the connection with England, the never failing source of all our political evils and to assert the independence of my country.'

This was the beginning of talk about an Irish Republic (inspired by the French and their revolution) and although Tone was then almost unknown in Ireland he was to become in retrospect, after his death, the most famous republican of them all. He had in fact done much to persuade the French to send this expedition and had come with it into the bay wearing French uniform and remarking that the shore now seemed so close that he felt he could toss a biscuit onto it.

The fleet had experienced some mishaps on the way, the most serious being that in a storm at sea it had parted company with and lost its flagship carrying the brilliant young commander of the expedition, General Hoche. After waiting in vain for him, the second-in-command decided to go ahead, but he was prevented from landing by a strong head-wind which was blowing harder every hour. There were almost no British government troops anywhere near the area and the way lay open for the French to reach Cork and beyond. But they could do nothing until the wind dropped.

Before long the wind had become a gale, and twenty of the great ships were driven down the bay and out to sea again. But the rest held on and tried to make their way up to more sheltered waters at the head of the bay. They made almost no progress at all – some fifty yards in eight hours, as the gale turned to storm with squalls of sleet and snow.

There was very little sign of human opposition, though the French were in the bay a week. About 400 men of the militia stationed at Bantry eventually drew themselves up boldly on the shore to try and make out that they were only the vanguard of some larger force. And the owner of the fine house at the head of the bay organized the local yeomanry, being afterwards created Lord Bantry for his efforts. But it was the weather that saved England. One by one the great ships found they could hold on no longer and, cutting their cables, ran back down the bay to the open sea and France again. Wolfe Tone, who went with them, remarked rightly that England had not had such an escape since the days of the Spanish Armada.

The Bantry Bay fiasco, though disappointing for the United Irishmen, was by no means wholly discouraging to them because it at least proved that the French were prepared to act on their behalf; and before very long another French expedition for Ireland was being fitted out at the Texel in Holland. However, this very fact brought home to the government the extreme seriousness of the United Irish threat and military measures were immediately taken against the secret society in its stronghold among the Presbyterians and Catholics of Ulster. The ruthless way in which the army now conducted its search for arms and information was remarkably successful and by the end of 1797 the conspiracy in that part of Ireland was virtually broken. A not inconsiderable factor in the breaking of it was a reversion on the part of many Protestants to their old sectarian ways under the auspices of the recently founded Orange Society.

A National Directory of the United Irishmen for the whole of Ireland had been formed in Dublin under the military leadership of a radical aristocrat, Lord Edward Fitzgerald, and in spite of the setbacks in Ulster, this group now tried to organize a national rebellion for the whole country, with the immediate expectation of French help. The method by which the United Irishmen hoped to bring the internal rebellion about was by incorporating within their own organization that of the peasant agrarian secret society network, particularly a mysterious but widely-spread society known as the Defenders which was already developing some vague national political thinking of its own among the Catholic peasantry.

Contact with the Defenders however had only been most imperfectly effected when the United Irish Society was devastated by the work of informers, at least three of whom were highly placed within the organization. Almost the entire National Directory was arrested in one swoop in March 1798, and although Lord Edward Fitzgerald himself escaped for a time, he too was betrayed not long afterwards and mortally wounded in the course of his arrest. Thoroughly alarmed by the scale of the conspiracy it had unearthed, and particularly by its contacts with the vast numbers of discontented peasantry in the Defenders, the government now proceeded to apply the methods of repression which had been so successful in Ulster the year before in the Midland counties of Ireland.

To extort rapidly the further detailed information it needed about the rebel organization, the army resorted to the standard military punishment of the day: flogging. Because it was the flogging which was to inspire such terror, and because it was the terror that was to set alight the one part of the rebellion that really looked dangerous, it is necessary to say something about the savage ritual and gruesome detail which such floggings involved.

It was in Athy in County Kildare, then the headquarters of the ninth Dragoons, that the wooden triangle on which the victims were spreadeagled and flogged was first set up in public in the spring of 1798. Standard army sentences of the day for their own men consisted of between 500 and 999 lashes and sometimes more – though usually only 200 to 400 were administered. So it is not difficult to imagine how they treated people they thought might be rebels, including those who, though possibly innocent themselves, might well know what the rebels were planning. In fact it is not necessary to imagine it for there are many first-hand accounts from eye-witnesses. Here is one:

There was no ceremony used in choosing victims, the first to hand done well enough. . . . They were stripped naked, tied to a triangle and their flesh cut

through without mercy. And though some stood the torture to the last gasp sooner than become informers, others did not and one single informer in the town was enough to destroy all the United Irishmen in it.

There is another account of a man who, while his flesh was being torn to shreds begged to be shot, and of another who after he had received 100 lashes cried out pitiably: 'I'm a-cutting through.' And there are many descriptions of flesh torn in lumps from the body and the baring of bones and even internal organs.

Not that the torture to extract information was confined to flogging. There was also pitch-capping, in which a brown paper cap filled with pitch was jammed on to a man's head and then, after it had begun to set a little, was set fire to; as the frantic wearer tried to tear it off, burning pitch fell into his eyes. It could usually only be got off together with much hair and scalp as well. Then there was half-hanging: pulling the rope round the victim's neck, from which it was slackened every time he lost consciousness. One particular sergeant, named Heppenstall, earned the nick-name for himself of 'The Walking Gallows' from his habit of half-hanging men over his shoulder. And, of course, there was whole hanging too.

All these tortures had an undoubtedly successful effect in extracting information. Thousands of arrests were made; thousands of stands of arms were uncovered (pikes, shotguns, swords, blunderbusses, pistols but above all pikes) and the United Irish organization in the Midlands was in such confusion by the time the signal to rise was eventually given that, though the rebels had a few local temporary successes, the whole thing went off at half-cock with great slaughter of the peasantry. But there was another effect of the military terror too, and that was to cause the government to tremble.

The County of Wexford in south-east Ireland was not one in which anyone expecting rebellion in 1798 would have expected it to be particularly menacing. Branches of the Defenders had long existed there but only the year before it had been officially noted that they were not particularly widespread; such contacts as the United Irish Society had been able to make with them had had little effect in incorporating them into a national conspiracy. For this reason it was garrisoned by relatively few government troops; and for this reason, when the government found a note from Fitzgerald naming the port of Wexford as a possible site for a French landing they at first gave the job of searching for arms and information to the local Protestant yeomanry.

Now the Protestants of Wexford were in general notoriously sectarian in outlook, so that when they immediately began to set about their business in an undisciplined and even vicious fashion appropriate to their opinion of the Roman Catholic peasantry, the fear they inspired inflamed an already strong sense of terror which had penetrated from the tales of flogging and other atrocities in the adjoining counties. When the government sent in a particularly tough regiment of the militia to assist the yeomanry – the North Cork militia – floggings started at once, though by official proclamation people were supposed to have fourteen days grace in which to surrender arms. (The rank and file of the militia was itself composed of Catholics, but they were Catholics whose chief concern seems to have been

ABOVE LEFT: The army's solution for extracting rebel information: '. . . they were stripped naked, tied to a triangle and their flesh cut without mercy.'

ABOVE: 1798. Rebel revenge.

LEFT: Driving the rebels off Vinegar Hill and into Irish nationalist mythology.

a wish to demonstrate their distinction from the Catholic rebels by the violence with which they were prepared to treat them.)

The first outbreak in Wexford seems to have resulted from a panicky determination in one locality not to submit any longer to the torture which was now spreading through the county like a sort of plague. A local priest, Father John Murphy, took charge of the peasantry in that incident and he was to become a principal figure of the rebellion in Wexford which thus assumed more the character of an indignant local peasants' revolt than that of a national rebellion.

The rebels won an important early victory over the North Cork militia in open country at Oulart Hill. Here, incidentally, the difficulty of finding any easy nationalist pattern in the rebellion is shown by the fact that the Catholic militia were refused mercy by their fellow Catholic captors though they pleaded for it in Irish, a language which Wexfordmen no longer understood. From their victory at Oulart the rebels pushed on to take the town of Enniscorthy which they partly set on fire before setting up their main camp on a nearby prominence known as Vinegar Hill.

It was not a camp in any strict military sense, being really just the place where thousands of men and women who had been terrorized by the troops in the countryside round about gathered in confusion to tell each other their sufferings and clamour for revenge. It must have been an amazing scene. Men were killing cattle which they had brought up on to the hill and boiling meat in great copper pans; people were playing musical instruments looted from Protestant houses in Enniscorthy which they had brought with them together with Wilton carpets and fine linen sheets. But there were few tents since most people had become used to lying out in the open at nights before they came there, to keep out of the way of the raiding troops.

The weather was marvellous and this was taken as a good omen. It was said that it would not rain again until the rebel cause had triumphed. How exactly that triumph was to be had without any coherent strategy or even overall leadership remained uncertain. Revenge was more easily come by and the means for that lay close at hand.

On one side of the hill was a windmill which had a green flag planted on the top and thirty-five captured Protestants from the town of Enniscorthy stuffed inside it. The overcrowding was reduced when a dozen of them were taken out, lined up in front of the door and clumsily put to death with pikes. The horribly familiar cycle of one set of atrocities breeding counter-atrocity was already at work.

An even more grisly revenge for the horrors that had long been inflicted on the population in the name of law and order followed a few days later when a barn holding Protestant men, women and children prisoners at a large farm house known as Scullabogue was set on fire and those not burned alive were shot or piked to death. The number of dead there may have been as many as 200.

Of course, such atrocities did the rebel cause no good at all, either tactically or in propaganda terms – they were in fact a particularly bad advertisement for a cause which was theoretically meant to be uniting Catholics and Protestants as fellow Irishmen. But they did make the wronged peasantry feel temporarily better, and such a mood was little

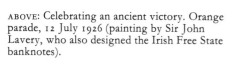
ABOVE: Celebrating an ancient victory. Orange
parade, 12 July 1926 (painting by Sir John
Lavery, who also designed the Irish Free State
banknotes).

RIGHT: Contemporary Orange Day celebrations.
But why in bowler hats?

LEST we FORGET.

1688. 1690.

WILLIAM III.

ABOVE: Battle of the Boyne 1690. The triumph of Orange over Green.

LEFT: And for Northern Irish Protestants a need to go on winning it.

RIGHT: Pope John Paul II in Ireland, 1979: '. . . no-one could have any doubt about Ireland's devotion to the mass . . .'

affected by the technical appointment of a true United Irishman as overall commander of their campaign, a civilized radical Protestant landlord named Bagenal Harvey who had been a member of the United Irish Society since its earliest days. Harvey now did his best to restrain such indulgence of revenge on the part of the rebels but was virtually as ineffectual in that respect as he was in trying to give some semblance of strategy to their cause.

The events at Scullabogue had taken place after the rebels had suffered the first of their major defeats in a hard-fought battle for the town of New Ross, and the atrocity was indeed partly a retaliation for that setback. The essential lack of strategy in their movements had been demonstrated by the fact that instead of proceeding immediately northwards from Vinegar Hill to try and join up with individual rebel groups in the Midland counties, they had first strayed southwards, capturing the town of Wexford itself but thereby giving the government forces time to concentrate against them effectively. When they eventually did try and move northwards towards Dublin after the defeat at New Ross they paid the penalty for the delay and suffered a further heavy defeat at Arklow on the Dublin road. Finally less than a month after they had first taken the field they were driven from their main encampment in a decisive battle on Vinegar Hill itself.

A vicious slaughter of scattered rebels by government troops continued for some time. (A local Protestant clergyman reckoned that more than half the estimated 50,000 dead in the rebellion had been killed in cold blood.) But the rebellion in Wexford – indeed the United Irish rebellion altogether – was over. For although there was a brave attempt at an uprising in Ulster where the United Irishmen had originated, the traditionally sectarian attitudes there had been much reinforced by news of the atrocities in the south, and the uprising ended in dismal failure with the movement quite disintegrating. And when, several months later, a small French expedition did eventually land in Ireland in County Mayo and even won an initial victory over government troops at Castlebar, there was no vestige of countrywide conspiracy left for them to co-operate with, and they soon afterwards surrendered. Finally, as if to round off the sum total of the United Irishmen's failure, Wolfe Tone himself, arriving off the northern Irish coast with a new French invasion fleet, was captured after a sea battle in which the French were defeated. He was brought for trial to Dublin where he succeeded at least in committing suicide in his cell.

The high-minded and patriotic attempt of the radical political theorists who had founded the United Irishmen to bring the two separate Irish 'nations' together had foundered on primitive confusion and prejudice. Although the great majority of the penal laws had long been repealed after falling into disuse and Catholics had actually been given the vote in 1793 (though they still could not be members of Parliament or hold offices of state), the rebellion had shown that Ireland was still composed of two very separate communities. One of these – the Protestant – after the fright it received in 1798, began to think less in terms of a Protestant 'nation' and more in terms of a simple Irish ascendancy class which sought protection for its interests in political identification with co-religionists on the English side of the Irish Sea. It is true that the Act of Union of 1800, which abolished the Irish Parliament and on 1 January 1801 united the two kingdoms

LEFT ABOVE: Protestant Irish Volunteers, College Green, Dublin, 1770s. The first Irish nationalists.

BELOW: Catholic rebels in a muddled cause defeated at the Battle of Vinegar Hill, 1798.

of England and Ireland 'for ever', was opposed at the time by many of the old Protestant patriots on Irish patriotic grounds. It is also true that the Catholics, on the whole, favoured it on the grounds that union with a more tolerant Protestant *majority*, the English, would afford better protection for their interests than they were likely to get from their own Protestant minority ascendancy. But it was self-interest on each side which determined the attitudes of both; and with the firm establishment of the Union most Protestants soon came to accept that the best hopes of preserving their ascendancy status lay in preservation of the Union, while this in turn conditioned Catholics gradually to see the repeal of that Union as the best opportunity for advancing *their* interests.

Modern Irish nationalism, which had been invented by Irish Protestants, thus came to be adopted by Irish Catholics as their own. Protestants as individuals, though not as a class, were often to support them, either as well-wishing sympathizers or, particularly in the first half of the nineteenth century, in the genuinely idealistic belief that the two nations could still achieve a common Irish patriotism. This latter concept was indeed always to remain the official policy of the new nationalist movement. But for all that, it was to degenerate into a Catholic cause with Protestant sympathizers – which is why Pope John Paul II was so effortlessly able to identify Irishness with Catholicism when he visited Ireland in 1979.

The man who was to lead Catholics to their first awareness of their modern political power had been ahead of his co-religionists in untypically opposing the Union from the start. He was a lawyer whose name was Daniel O'Connell. But before he could begin to be active on the political scene there was a short postscript to the rebellion of 1798 which must be mentioned because, for all its near-farcical character, its myth-making qualities were to be even more pervasive in Irish history than those of 1798 itself. This was the rebellion of Robert Emmet in Dublin in 1803.

In fact it turned out to be a street riot rather than a rebellion, though Emmet, an attractive figure who had been a United Irishman, was inspired by all his former colleagues' high ideals. Indeed it was his desire to assert those ideals in face of the ignominy of his failure that led him to make his most important contribution to the future: his speech from the dock before execution.

His plan had been ambitious: to seize Dublin Castle as a signal to the rest of the country to rise in arms. A proclamation of 'the Irish Republic' had been printed; contacts were arranged with a band of outlaws who had been hiding out in the Wicklow Hills ever since 1798. But the only part of the plan that really worked was the printing of the Proclamation of the Republic which was coming wet off the presses as the military arrived to seize it. (One of Emmet's arms depots in Dublin had accidentally been blown up the week before, alerting the Government to what was afoot.)

In the end, where Emmet had hoped to assemble 2,000 men to attack the Castle he mustered only eighty, and these, armed with pikes and blunderbusses, set forth into the night of Saturday, 23 July 1803, headed by Emmet himself carrying a drawn sword. Part of his following detached themselves to pike to death Lord Kilwarden, the Chief Justice, who happened to be passing through the streets in a coach at the time. Emmet, appalled by the bloodthirsty rioting into which his bid to establish an Irish

LEFT: Robert Emmet who led the 'near farcical' rebellion in Dublin in 1803. Has his epitaph been written or not?

BELOW: Emmet's execution. A later Irish nationalist was to compare his sacrifice with Christ's.

Republic immediately degenerated, abandoned the project and took himself off into hiding where he remained for a month before being caught, tried and executed. His speech from the dock which immortalized him in Irish history contained the phrase:

Let no man write my epitaph. . . . When my country takes her place among the nations of the earth, then and not till then let my epitaph be written.

Much of the patriotic theology of twentieth-century Irish nationalism has centred round discussion – often bloody – of whether it could be said to be time to write Emmet's epitaph or not. Today's IRA would answer unhesitatingly: 'No'. The fact that many other patriotic Irishmen have for more than half a century been able to answer 'Yes' to the same question is due in the first instance to one man: Daniel O'Connell.

O'Connell's house, Derrynane Abbey, lies tucked away in the remote wilds of County Kerry in the south-west of Ireland, almost like an afterthought; and he himself has sometimes been regarded as an afterthought to modern Irish nationalism. Yet O'Connell did more than any other Irishman before, or perhaps since, to give power to the Irish people – certainly more than Emmet or Wolfe Tone. A tree which he planted, when brought up as a boy in this house which the old Catholic family of the O'Connells had managed to keep even at the height of the penal laws, still stands.

The moral of the rebellion of 1798 for the Catholic people of Ireland was clear: they needed political leadership. The secret societies were too primitive to operate effectively on a national scale, even when linked to sophisticated political theorists like the United Irishmen. The Catholic Church was still the only representative organization the people had, but that clearly was going to be of marginal use for the redressing of Catholic grievances in an overwhelmingly Protestant state. It was to this political sterility of the Catholic Irish people that O'Connell put an end. He was to become known as 'the Liberator', not because he liberated Ireland from England (he did not), but because he liberated the great mass of the Irish people from their irrelevance on the political scene.

In the space of just over twenty years he inaugurated two great political campaigns in succession. The first was for Catholic Emancipation, or the removal of the remnants of legal discrimination against Catholics surviving from the penal laws. Principally this concerned the right of Roman Catholics to sit in parliament, from which they were still banned unless they took an oath abjuring certain fundamental Catholic beliefs. To campaign for Catholic Emancipation, O'Connell built up a strong mass organization with the help of able middle-class assistants and more important still of the Roman Catholic clergy. And although it could be said that the right to sit in Parliament or occupy high office of state was of little immediate interest to the ordinary Irish peasantry yet it was as a symbol of the rising status of all Catholic Irish people that it was pursued. Above all it was a rallying cry for that people's right to have a say in their own affairs, a demonstration of their ability to assert that right regardless of what a government with roots in London might say.

An essential feature of O'Connell's political organization was its broad

The country estates of the Irish Protestant Nation. 'Soaring aspirations on which they based a claim as Irishmen to be treated as a nation equal to Britain.'

democratic basis. Associate membership of his Catholic Association could be had for a penny a month and soon very large sums were flowing into it. Something not unlike the first modern political party machine, with strong clerical overtones, was created. Over the use to which this power might be put, there was always to be a query in the minds of a government all too aware of the dangers from popular fury which had threatened in Ireland a quarter of a century before.

O'Connell himself was imbued with a horror of popular violence as a result of the events of 1798 and was continually deprecating it, whether for agrarian or wider political ends. But at the same time he became adept at stressing, with disciplined crowds at great meetings and processions, the physical power that lay in the mass support behind him, and at hinting that, but for his control of it, it could unleash itself against the government with a fury that knew no bounds. Thus the dark forces of violence he was holding back became also forces at the back of him. And in drawing attention to the threat he was averting he uttered a sort of threat himself.

With the strength of this organization behind him O'Connell put up a (Protestant) pro-Emancipation candidate to contest a bye-election in Waterford, a seat in which the power of anti-Emancipation Tory landlords to have candidates of their own choice elected had previously seemed incontestable. Now for the first time the power of the Catholic Association proved itself greater still, and tenants voted in droves (against their landlords) to put in the pro-Emancipation candidate. The victory encouraged O'Connell himself to stand in one of the most famous elections in Irish history at Clare in 1828. With the same powerful organization – his supporters actually marching in step in regular columns under officers without any of the drunkenness or disorderly behaviour that normally distinguished Irish elections – O'Connell won triumphantly. The Home Secretary, Robert Peel, himself commented on the 'fearful exhibition of sobered and desperate enthusiasm' which attended the triumph. O'Connell, being a Catholic, could not of course yet take the seat he had won. But when he stood again and won the government backed down before the implications of such a menacingly disciplined display of Irish opinion. And it was this submission rather than the Emancipation Act which soon followed, which was O'Connell's real victory. He had made Irish popular opinion a force in British politics for the first time.

At the beginning of the 1840s he turned similar techniques and an even more powerful organization of a similar type – also with strong clerical backing – to an even more ambitious cause: that of Repeal of the Act of Union and a restoration of the rights of an Irish Parliament which now of course would be dominated no longer by a Protestant ascendancy minority but by the Catholic majority. In other respects he sought the same constitutional position for Ireland as Grattan had done: not separation but a close partnership between two kingdoms, each with independent legislatures, united by ancient historical blood-ties and common interests – the whole symbolized by the person of a joint monarch. It was a somewhat rose-coloured fantasy, little troubled by such realistic human considerations as what would happen to the person of the joint monarch if the partners decided to go their different ways. But the argument by which he hoped to convert English opinion was one which all constitutional nationalists were

NOTICE.

WHEREAS, there has appeared, under the Signatures of "E. B. Sugden, C., Donoughmore, Eliot, F. Blackburne, E. Blakeney, Fred. Shaw, T. B. C. Smith," a paper being, or purporting to be, a PROCLAMATION, drawn up in very loose and inaccurate terms, and manifestly misrepresenting known facts ; the objects of which appear to be, to prevent the PUBLIC MEETING, intended to be held TO-MORROW, the 8th instant, at CLONTARF, *to petition Parliament* for the REPEAL of the baleful and destructive measure of the LEGISLATIVE UNION.

AND WHEREAS, such Proclamation has not appeared until *late in the Afternoon of this Saturday, the 7th*, so that it is utterly impossible that the knowledge of its existence could be communicated in the usual Official Channels, or by the Post, in time to have its contents known to the Persons intending to meet at CLONTARF, for the purpose of Petitioning, as aforesaid, whereby ill-disposed Persons may have an opportunity, under cover of said Proclamation, to provoke Breaches of the Peace, or to commit Violence on Persons intending to proceed peaceably and legally to the said Meeting.

WE, therefore, the COMMITTEE of the LOYAL NATIONAL REPEAL ASSOCIATION, do most earnestly request and entreat, that all well-disposed persons will, IMMEDIATELY on receiving this intimation, repair to their own dwellings, and not place themselves in peril of any collision, or of receiving any ill-treatment whatsoever.

And We do further inform all such persons, that without yielding in any thing to the unfounded allegations in said alleged Proclamation, we deem it prudent and wise, and above all things humane, to DECLARE that said

Meeting is abandoned, and is not to be held.

Signed by Order,

DANIEL O'CONNELL,

Chairman of the Committee.

T. M. RAY, Secretary.

Saturday, 7th October, 1843.
3 o'Clock P. M.

RESOLVED—That the above Cautionary Notice be immediately transmitted by Express to the Very Reverend and Reverend Gentlemen who signed the Requisition for the CLONTARF MEETING, and to all adjacent Districts, SO AS TO PREVENT the influx of Persons coming to the intended Meeting.

GOD SAVE THE QUEEN.

Browne, Printer, 36, Nassau-street.

ABOVE LEFT: Derrynane, County Kerry, house of O'Connell – '. . . tucked away almost like an afterthought . . .' as was O'Connell in some versions of Irish nationalism.

LEFT: O'Connell at Monster Meeting – 'You could hear his voice a mile off, as if it were coming through honey.'

ABOVE RIGHT: *Punch* belabours O'Connell for wanting Repeal of the Union. But it was 'approaching with the strides of a giant.'

RIGHT: A setback for O'Connell. But an even more terrible one on the way.

to use in future, namely that, far from encouraging separation, such recognition of Ireland's claim to be a nation would undermine and silence all calls for it. Only failure to grant such recognition could bring separation about, ran the argument. But O'Connell did not rely chiefly on argument.

In a series of what became known as 'Monster Meetings' he once again deployed vast crowds of disciplined and good-natured supporters who by their very restraint in such numbers hinted at what they might do if unrestrained. The greatest of all such Monster Meetings took place on 15 August 1843 on the Royal Hill of Tara and its ancient Gaelic earthworks. Archaeologists who have found bones 4,000 years old at the bottom of one of the mounds there, have also found, under the grass at the top, traces of wooden platforms and bits of clay pipes and whiskey bottles from O'Connell's meeting. A writer in the *Nation* newspaper claimed 'without fear of exaggeration' that there were three quarters of a million people there that day. O'Connell himself, who never had the slightest fear of exaggeration, put it at one and a half million.

With the vast crowds mustered by O'Connell's marshals on horseback, the carriages, the banners, the bands and others in historic fancy dress, how, in the days before microphones, did they manage to hear what O'Connell was saying? Well, one small farmer said of O'Connell's voice: 'You'd hear it a mile off as if it were coming through honey.' And on this day, in his honeyed voice, the Liberator declaimed: 'We are at Tara of the Kings – the spot from which emanated the social power, the legal authority, the right to dominion over the furthest extremes of the land.' (That was largely rubbish, historically. But the rest was not rubbish.) He went on:

The strength and majority of the national movement was never exhibited so imposingly as at this great meeting. The numbers exceed any that ever before congregated in Ireland in peace or war. It is a sight not grand alone but appalling – not exciting merely pride but fear. Step by step we are approaching the great goal of Repeal of the Union, but it is at length with the strides of a giant.

To the extent that the Irish people were now, under O'Connell, manifesting something of the strength of a giant in British politics this was true. It was a strength which in the future was often to lie dormant but which when roused would finally prove more than Westminster could deal with. All subsequent Irish nationalists were to benefit from this strength which O'Connell had stored. But the goal of Repeal itself was still a long way off. When the government called the bluff of the Monster Meetings and banned one planned for Clontarf, O'Connell climbed down. He and his closest colleagues were sentenced to a year in prison for conspiracy, though the judgment was reversed in the House of Lords.

What would have happened to the cause of Repeal under O'Connell had he lived, and had there not developed a far greater issue to overshadow it altogether, is useless speculation. O'Connell died in 1847 but before this a calamity had struck the Irish people beside which a political issue like Repeal seemed an irrelevant abstraction. This was the Great Famine of the years 1845–9 in which the only consideration for most Irishmen and their families was how to try and stay alive.

For the long-term future what was to be of the greatest importance to nationalism was not only that store of national strength which O'Connell had built up but also the way in which he had done so. For with his great organizational campaigns for Emancipation and Repeal, backed by priests and people, he had successfully channelled the power of the Catholic Church's bond with the people into politics. He himself linked Roman Catholicism and Irish consciousness into a great national movement. He linked them together so firmly indeed that, as one acid modern historian J.C. Beckett has put it, 'succeeding generations have hardly been able to prise them apart'.

No 'uncertainty' about the potato crop. Total failure.

Chapter 5

Famine

No event in Irish history has had a more emotional effect on Irish national feeling than the Great Famine of 1845–9. It was an experience for the Irish people that is sometimes seen as comparable in its impact on popular national consciousness to that of the German 'final solution' on the Jews. Indeed it is not infrequently thought that the Famine was something very like that: a form of genocide engineered by the English against the Irish people. Certainly, the story of what happened in Ireland in those years is deeply disturbing. It provides an emotional legacy in what is experienced in Ireland today. But one needs to retain a few hard facts before starting to examine it.

First: 'the Irish' by this time were a mixture of many races including English. The blood of former English settlers and conquerors ran in the veins even of those whose first language was Irish.

Second: those who *ruled* the Irish were a mixture of many races including Irish. Through intermarriage, Gaelic blood ran through the veins even of some of the most English-seeming members of the House of Lords.

Third: the two populations – British and Irish – had for so long been not only partly racially connected, but also connected politically and administratively that, for all their many differences in characteristics, they could not, then, easily be thought of as belonging to 'separate' countries.

Technically, the British government was no less concerned with the common people of Ireland than it was with the common people of the rest of Britain. Unfortunately in neither case was that concern close enough. Particularly, it was not close enough in the case of the Irish.

The Irish were further away geographically of course: even in the new railway age of the 1840s Dublin itself was at least twelve hours away from London. They were more remote in other ways too: in the different language which half the population spoke before English; and in the Gaelic cultural traditions and ways of life which still remained very much alive though they had not yet given rise to a modern political nationalism.

History, as well as geography, had accentuated differences. It had left most of the Irish, except in the north-east, Roman Catholics in a Protestant state. It had left most of them, except in the north-east, largely dependent for survival on agriculture. More remarkable still, it had left most of them, except in the north-east, largely dependent for survival on one single agricultural crop: the potato.

Travellers in Ireland had long commented on the extreme misery of the poorest Irish peasant. He lived off a tiny piece of land for which he paid a rent such that almost all – and sometimes all – the cereal crops he grew on it had to be sold to pay that rent. He and his family subsisted on a plot of potatoes. And this situation had become increasingly precarious during the first four decades of the nineteenth century which saw a vast population explosion in Ireland. In 1800 the population of Ireland can be estimated at four and a half million. In 1841, the year of the first reliable official census, it was eight million. The pressure of this vast increase in numbers on the land became desperate, and land became subdivided into smaller and smaller plots on which more and more people subsisted mainly on potatoes. The poorest of all simply hired out their labour in return not for a wage, but for a small plot on which to grow them. In these circumstances, if the potato were to fail, the social consequences were not hard to predict. The government in fact knew perfectly well what happened when the potato crop failed because it had already failed for one reason or another a number of times in the first three decades of the century. There was a particularly terrible famine with thousands of deaths in 1817.

In 1824 the government held one of its many thorough enquiries into the state of things in Ireland. One of the parliamentary commissioners asked a witness this question: 'Looking ahead to fifteen years or more, what must this increase in population without employment end in?' 'I do not know,' came the answer. 'I think it is terrible to reflect upon.'

In 1845, terrible it proved to be. As with many great disasters in human affairs there was no unmistakable signal that a disaster was at hand. It had been a hot fine summer, but there was a sudden break in the weather at the beginning of August with showers of sleet, thunder and lightning, and heavy rain. Reports from Counties Galway and Mayo, however, spoke of potato crops of 'the most luxuriant character . . . promising abundant yield'. The *Freeman's Journal* of 20 August wrote: 'The growth of the potato plant progresses as favourably as the most sanguine farmer could wish.' Then, on 11 September 1845 it published this report:

DISEASE IN THE POTATO CROP

We regret to have to state that we have had communications from more than one well-informed correspondent announcing the fact of what is called 'cholera' in potatoes in Ireland, especially in the north. In one instance the party had been digging potatoes – the finest he had ever seen – from a particular field, and a particular ridge of that field up to Monday last; and on digging in the same ridge on Tuesday he found the tubers all blasted, and unfit for the use of man or beast.

All sorts of different reasons were suggested as the cause of the trouble: frost, easterly winds, the moon, guano manure, even electricity, the effect of summer thunderstorms. The cause in fact was a killer fungus, then still undiagnosed: *Phytophthora infestans*, which produces black spots on the leaves themselves with a whitish mould on the underside of the leaf. This mould contains spores which are conveyed to other potato plants by wind, rain and insects. Once the fungus has established itself in the plant, the potato underneath, first blackening round the edges, is doomed to end as rotten pulp.

The potato was hit just as badly in England as in Ireland that summer, but the blight caused no famine there. In England, unlike Ireland, even the poorest could afford food other than the potato, and no other crop except the potato was affected in either country. Moreover, there was hope at first that at least some of the Irish potato crop could be saved. But at the end of the first week of October 1845, the *Cork Southern Reporter* was writing:

The hopes entertained by many appear to be delusive. The potato is apparently sound when dug but on examination small round spots are found running round the tuber and having each the appearance of a running sore or cancer. The potato in this state . . . will within a few days be completely destroyed, necessitating a method of turning it to food as quickly as possible.

This was easier said than done. A report from County Carlow described how there, when they tried boiling potatoes which had been sound when dug, it was impossible to bear the stench they emitted; and a small farmer wrote from County Meath: 'Awful is our story concerning the potatoes. I do be striving to blind them in the boiling. I trust no harm will come from them.'

By the third week in October every post brought in new accounts from all over Ireland of extensive failures in the staple food of the country. But it was the spread of the disease in the west that was most serious, the most ominous report of all being the latest from County Mayo in the extreme west where nine-tenths of the population depended on the potato for survival. A priest wrote from there to the *Freeman's Journal*:

It grieves me much to have to inform you that the rot is making frightful ravages even in the potatoes which about eight days ago were intact. The country hereabouts is in a most melancholy state: despondency and tears are to be seen in almost every face.

The paper's leader columns struck a proper note of alarm:

All other feelings must give way before the paramount obligation of endeavouring to avert the famine with which the poorer class of this country are now threatened. . . . It would be criminal to refrain any longer from demanding from the government active measure for the protection of the lives of the people.

The Prime Minister of the day was Sir Robert Peel who, reading the reports from Ireland, noted that the Irish always had a tendency to exaggerate. (It was said of him that he had a smile like the brass plate on the lid of a coffin.) But he was a conscientious Prime Minister. He knew government sources reckoned that even in normal times, over a quarter of the Irish population spent part of the year in a state of semi-starvation and he admitted he too was now 'alarmed'.

From September he ordered the constabulary to make weekly reports on the state of the potato crop, and in the middle of October he appointed a government scientific commission of enquiry. This now reported in solemn tones that it was baffled and could only recommend a number of laborious and, as we now know, irrelevant precautions for preserving those potatoes which appeared sound when dug. There was for a time still some hope that the very abundance of the 1845 harvest would supply enough sound potatoes to prevent total disaster. But reports like this one from County Limerick in November soon put paid to such hopes:

Though the people here are using every precaution, by carefully separating the sound from the infected potatoes, by making large holes in the sides of the pits to admit air, and by scarcely putting any covering on top of the pits but the dry stalks, still every time they come to examine them they find the rot spread among that portion of the potatoes which but a few days before they believed to be safe. . . . If something be not done in time God knows how this much-apprehended panic will terminate.

In the middle of November 1845 the Archbishop of Dublin, Dr Murray, called for prayers in all Catholic churches 'that God in His mercy would vouchsafe to avert the calamity which seems impending over us.' And the collect '*pro quacumque tribulatione*' ('in times of tribulation') was added to the Mass.

By February 1846 the potato disease had struck every county in Ireland and three-quarters of the country's potato crop had been destroyed. The dreaded fever (typhus) which always tended to accompany poverty in Ireland had broken out in Cork, Kilkenny and other counties and by the beginning of March, together with diarrhoea and dysentery, had been registered in twenty-five counties out of thirty-two.

But no-one had yet died of starvation. So what was to be done? As Daniel O'Connell declaimed in the House of Commons:

The people are not to blame! It has pleased Providence to inflict this calamity on them. It is your business to mitigate it as well as you can. . . . Famine is coming, fever is coming and this House should place in the hands of the government power to stay the evil.

Apart from commissioning reports, Sir Robert Peel had, in November 1845, in fact taken three major decisions:

Firstly, he had ordered from America, on behalf of the government, a large supply of maize, or so-called Indian corn, to be shipped to Ireland, for eventual sale at low cost from government depots there.

Secondly, he had appointed a relief commission in Dublin. One part of its job was to supervise these Indian corn depots; but an even more important task was to co-ordinate and co-operate with the local committees of landlords and other local residents, which were being set up all over the country to try and mitigate distress by providing not only cheap food but, through public works, the employment by which men could earn the money to buy it. The government, through the relief commission, gave matching cash grants to the committees, of two-thirds at first and then fully equal amounts of whatever they were able to raise themselves by private charity. And the Board of Works collaborated with the local committees on the organization of public works such as road-making to provide employment.

Peel's third decision was to remove all the protectionist duties on grain imported into the United Kingdom of Britain and Ireland in order to lower the price of bread. In other words, to repeal what were known as the Corn Laws. In English terms this was a big decision. But lowering the price of bread in Ireland was of little use to people there. One-third of the Irish

ABOVE: Repealing the Corn Laws in the House of Commons – not much use to starving Ireland.

RIGHT: 'One-third of the Irish population depended solely on the potato for survival.' In County Mayo: nine-tenths.

population – those about to be hit hardest by the coming famine – could hardly afford bread at *any* price. That was precisely why they lived off potatoes. Still, by the standards of the day Peel had acted quite imaginatively.

These standards of the day were not, primarily, those virtues of charity and selfless generosity towards the poor and needy of the Christianity then so widely professed, but the principles of another religion altogether known as 'political economy'. Certain almost unshakeable, sincerely held economic beliefs were to underlie all governmental policy towards the Famine. And the greatest of these was that principle of political economy which maintained that you should interfere to the absolute minimum with the market forces of supply and demand because if you *did* so interfere, you endangered the natural flow by which supplies could reach the market.

The State could not *give* people food because, by doing so, it would undermine market prices and thus make merchants withhold food from the market altogether – the last thing you wanted in time of famine. The flaw in this was of course in the supposition that the needy would be able to buy on the market at all.

The foremost guardian of these principles of political economy – a man who, as chief official in charge of relief measures, was soon to assume something like dictatorial powers of life and death behind the scenes – was a British civil servant, Charles Trevelyan, permanent Head of the Treasury of the day. An able, well-bred, cultivated man in his late thirties, he was given to reading chapters from the Bible in a loud sonorous voice.

Now Trevelyan's watchfulness for the rules of political economy had to be particularly sharp. His Prime Minister, Sir Robert Peel, was bending these rules to some extent by bringing any government food into Ireland at all. But firstly, Peel was careful to import a specific commodity for which there had not hitherto been a market in Ireland. Secondly – and this seems almost inconceivable today – it was brought in not primarily as food to be eaten immediately by people who were beginning to starve but only as a gently-applied economic lever. The government would judiciously release Indian corn for sale from the government depots when it judged that prices on the general food market were rising too high. Thus, although Indian corn was stored in the Government Depot at Cork where the poor were dangerously short of food, from the end of January 1846, it was not until two months later that the first government sales took place and a near-riot was the predictable result. Even then such evidence of the strength of the demand was used as an argument for quickly suspending the sales, since it was judged that supplies must be held back for the inevitably greater pressure of the summer.

This was in April 1846. It was not until a month later, in the middle of May, that the government ordered the general opening of depots for the sale of the Indian corn all over Ireland. By then the poor were becoming desperate. Food carts carrying flour or Indian corn or wheat, oats and barley grown for rent, sometimes on its way to market or to the ports for export, were being attacked and there was a noticeable increase in sheep-stealing.

The possibility of such disorders had been long dreaded. Indeed, there were times late in 1845 and early 1846 when it had seemed that respectable British opinion was more concerned with the danger to property resulting from the potato famine than with the danger to those starving. And there was already before the House of Commons a so-called 'Coercion' Bill proposing special police measures including a curfew and punishment of fifteen years' transportation for breach of it.

But in Ireland, priorities seemed very different. The *Freeman's Journal* wrote on 15 April 1846:

There have been attacks on flour mills in Clonmel by people whose bones protruded through the skin which covered them – staring through hollow eyes as if they had just risen from their shrouds, crying out that they could no longer endure the extremity of their distress and that they must take that food which they could not procure. . . . As we pass into summer, we pass into suffering. . . . Every week develops the growing intensity of the national calamity.

The trouble was that the other arm of the government's relief action, the relief commission's subsidizing of local committees to help provide both cheap food and the money with which to buy it through employment on public works, was proceeding very slowly. Special local sessions had been held at which schemes for local public works such as road-building were presented and had money allotted to them, but these then had to be sent to the Board of Works for approval. Long bureaucratic delays often ensued before they could be put into practice.

When a boat-load of flour and Indian meal on its way from Limerick to Clare was boarded by a party of fourteen armed men near Smith's Island, held for six hours and emptied of a hundred sacks of flour and twenty of Indian corn the local paper, the *Limerick Examiner*, commented:

These people had hitherto been kept quiet by the promises that the government would every other day carry into operation the public works so often spoken of; and now when they see no immediate source of relief from that quarter I fear they will resort to means such as the foregoing.

After all, every sort of food except the potato *was* there because the harvest in every other crop but the potato was excellent. Food was leaving the country for export in vast quantities. Even more was coming in. Quite apart from the Indian corn, nearly four times as much wheat was being imported into Ireland as exported. It was just not available to the hungry.

Trevelyan's chief concern was that such cheap Indian corn as was being sold, was going to people suffering from the distress normal to Ireland at that time of year between harvests and not just to people in distress because of the potato failure. And he had come to a severe decision. 'Indiscriminate sales', he wrote with curious logic, 'have brought the whole country on the depots, and, without denying the existence of real and extensive distress, the numbers are beyond the power of the depots to cope with. They must therefore be closed down as soon as possible.' In other words, while hoping for a good potato harvest again in the autumn of 1846, the poor must do what they could on the open market with such money as they could earn from the public works.

By August 1846, some 140,000 were employed on the public works. This meant that with their dependants about 700,000 people were getting some sort of sustenance. But the number of people in Ireland who

Our market this morning, as regards Wheat, appeared to open with a firmer feeling on the part of holders, but the millers being still much on the reserve, the transactions in this Grain were limited. Oats dull, and secondary qualities 1d per bushel lower. Prime cuts of Oatmeal being scarce and in tolerable request, realised a slight advance.

PORT OF LIMERICK.

SHIPPING  INTELLIGENCE.

ARRIVED

Ann Moore, M'Fie, Quebec, timber.
Jane, Mulcahy, St. John's, do.
Moy, O'Grady, do. do.
Expedition, Raymond, Glasgow, railway iron.
Thetis, Hughill, Quebec, timber.

SAILED.

Jane Black, Gorman, Quebec, emigrants.
Cleofrid, Leark, do. ballast.
Moodkee, Viggors, do. do.

Freights to London.—2s 0d per quarter oats; Liverpool and Clyde, 7s per ton.

IMPORTS.

Ann & Elizabeth from Windau—1474 pieces timber.
Earl of Devon from Ancona—899 7-8 rubbers of Indian corn, Harvey Brothers.
Roberts from Miramichi—62 tons timber, 3360 pieces deals, Alexander Brothers.
Governor from Quebec—200 tons timber, 3 M pipe. 4 M bri staves, 39½ hund deals, F Spaight. *Energy* from do.—190 loads timber, 30 3 5 deals, 28 3 26 staves J Harvey & Co. *Bryan Abbs* from do.—186 pieces timber, 26 2 14 staves, 29 0 20 deals, F Spaight. *Oberon* from do. for Clare—220 loads timber, MacNamara & Son; 20 0 1 pieces deals, 15 1 20 staves. *Lady Lilford* from do. for Clare—50 loads timber, 20 3 13 pieces deals, 3 fathom lathwood, MacNamara & Son. *Harriet* from do. for Clare—20 loads timber, 26 2 10 deals, 2 fathom lathwood, James Bannatyne.

EXPORTS.

Ann for London—150 firks butter, Edwards & Barry ; 200 do J Edwards; 200 do. M O'Donnell ; 313 do. 100 firks 10 casks lard, G Christie ; 15° do. J Sheehy ; 250 do. T M'Donnell ; 500 do. C Nash & Son ; 100 do. M Hurley ; 300 do. 3 casks hams, P Ryan ; 63 do. A J Yielding ; 81 bales bacon, 62 firks 3 casks lard. J Harley & Son ; 50 do. 20 casks lard, A Russell & Co ; 52 brls pork, Snaw & Duffield ; 60 bales bacon, J. & P M'Donnell ; 39 puns whiskey, J Sharp ; 76 bales bacon, 21 casks hams, 4 crates hair, J Russell ; 264 brls oats, W Herbert.
Messenger for London—1150 brls oats, T Worrall.
Pelham Clinton for Liverpool—725 brls oats, R Wheeler ; 725 do. M Dawson.
City of Limerick for Glasgow—40 tons flour, J N Russell ; 50 bales bacon, 200 kegs lard, A Russell & Co.
British Queen for Glasgow—500 brls wheat, T Macaulay & Co ; 128 do. T Worrall ; 450 do, oats, J & T Myles.
John Guise for London—1663 brls oats, T M Usborne.
Cambrian Maid for Glasgow—1000 brls barley, J Denniston & Co.
Marianne for Tralee—300 sacks Indian meal. J N Russell.

KILRUSH EXPORTS.

Ellen for Bristol—54 qrs barley, P P Foley ; 630 do. oats, Behen & Bowler.
Eluzai for Tralee—30 tons salt, J MacNamara.
Charles G Fryer for London—658 qrs oats, Wm. Blair.
Mary Elliott for London—400 qrs oats, J Kelly & Co ; 280 do. Taylor & Carey.

TRALEE EXPORTS.

John St. Barbe for London—664 qrs oats, Walker & Gilse.
Spokesman for Liverpool—515 qrs oats, 252 qrs barley, N Riordan & Sons.
Claudia for London—630 qrs oats, 168 do, barley. J Twoomey.
Marianne for Limerick—31 qrs oats, J N Russell.
Queen for London—700 qrs oats, C Murphy.

GALWAY EXPORTS.

Mary for London—550 qrs oats, H Comerford ; 250 do. C Sloper.
Victoria for London—250 qrs oats, 20 tons oatmeal, T M Usborne ; 90 tons provisions, W Grieves ; 50 do. H Comerford.
Swan for Limerick—60 sacks flour, 30 sacks oatmeal, P Regan.
Union for Limerick—10 tons oatmeal, P Regan.
Diligence for London - 940 qrs oatmeal, R D Persse.

STEAM-PACKET COMMUNICATION FOR JULY.

LIMERICK TO KILRUSH.			KILRUSH TO LIMERICK.		
Date.	hs.	ms.	Date.	hs.	ms.
29.. Wednesday,	9 0	Morn	29.. Wednesday,	3 0	Aft
30.. Thursday,	10 0	—	30.. Thursday,	3 0	—
31.. Friday,	11 0	—	31.. Friday,	7 0	Morn

PRICE OF IRISH STOCKS, &c.—TUESDAY.

Bank Stock	..	—
3½ per cent. Debs. (£92 6s 2d)	..	—
Three per cent. Consols	..	93

FAR LEFT: 'Every other sort of food was there. Plenty of it.'

LEFT: No room at the workhouse. 'We're starving! We want something to eat!'

BELOW: Taking matters into their own hands – 'Hitherto kept quiet by the promise of public works'.

depended wholly on the potato for survival was well over two million altogether. So how were the other million and a half expected to survive?

The workhouses of Ireland, maintained on the rates, had room for about 100,000 people. By law they were not allowed to give relief to anyone *outside* them, and the régime inside was made intentionally harsh as a precaution against encouraging scroungers to enter. Even so, in the summer of 1846, the workhouses were filling rapidly. But since they could only take 100,000 the question remained: how were most of the million and a half to survive?

The government had always thought that the main responsibility for relieving Irish distress must rest with the Irish landlords. There was obviously some moral sense in that, since landlords drew their often – but by no means always – wealthy livings from the rents of their tenants. But the landlords' behaviour varied considerably. In many districts they were playing a most active part on the local committees – of which there were over 600 by the summer of 1846. Sometimes too, they took special individual action to help their tenants, allowing them to consume the crops they normally handed in for rent and remitting or partly remitting the rent. Sometimes they would start employment schemes of their own without waiting for the government's public works. A Mrs Power in County Tipperary was reported to be buying up all the bread and meat she could find in the town and distributing it to the people on her estates.

Some landlords on the other hand were said to be contributing meanly to the local committees while others appeared totally unmoved, and were even evicting the poor and starving who could no longer pay their rents. A correspondent of the *Freeman's Journal* gave the following description of one such eviction in County Galway:

It was the most appalling sight I ever witnessed: women, young and old, running wildly to and fro with small portions of their property to save it from the wreck – the screaming of the children, and wild wailings of the mothers driven from home and shelter. . . . In the first instance the roofs and portions of the wall only were thrown down. But that Friday night the wretched creatures pitched a few poles slant-wise against the walls covering them with thatch in order to procure shelter for the night. When this was perceived the next day the bailiffs were despatched with orders to pull down all the walls and root up the foundations in order to prevent the poor people from daring to take shelter amid the ruins.

Clearly it was risky to say the least to leave the fate of most of those now destitute from the potato failure largely in the hands of the Irish landlords, and yet this was exactly what the government was doing: closing those depots that still held food and ordering no more Indian corn for those that were empty. Moreover, in continued expectation of a good new harvest in the late summer of 1846, Trevelyan, whose principal concern was the expense of the whole operation to the Treasury, started to wind up the scheme of public works.

In England, a new government, under a new Prime Minister, Lord John Russell, replaced Peel at the end of June 1846. Trevelyan marked its first week in office by actually rejecting a cargo of Indian corn that was on its way to Ireland, writing officially: 'The cargo of the *Sorcière* is not wanted; her owners must dispose of it as they think proper.'

And a few weeks later as the first signs were already appearing that the new harvest too was blighted, Trevelyan wrote confirming the overall decision to cease relief operations:

The only way to prevent people from becoming habitually dependent on government is to bring operations to a close. The uncertainty about the new crop only makes it more necessary. . . . Whatever may be done hereafter, these things should be stopped now, or you run the risk of paralysing all private enterprise and having this country on you for an indefinite number of years.

Now, the whole argument behind the Act of Union of 1800 between Britain and Ireland had been that the two countries were thenceforth indissolubly bound together for better or worse for all eternity. But if this were not to be so, if Ireland was to be thought of as irritatingly 'on' Britain for an indefinite number of years, the Irish might be forgiven for drawing certain political conclusions for the future. For the present, though, political thoughts were increasingly overshadowed by the more basic consideration of simple survival. There was no 'uncertainty' about the new potato crop. Its total failure was soon all too certain.

A Protestant gentleman farmer of means, personally unaffected by the failure of 1845 and now hoping to grow potatoes as a commercial venture on a hundred acres of mountain ground near Cardtown in Queen's County, described how the total failure of the potato crop of 1846 confronted him:

On 1 August I was startled by hearing a sudden rumour that all the potato fields in the district were blighted; and that a stench had arisen emanating from their decaying stalks. I immediately rose up to visit my crop and test the truth of this report, but I found it as luxuriant as ever, in full blossom, the stalks matted across each other with richness and promising a splendid produce. . . . On coming down from the mountain I rode into the lowland country and there I found . . . the leaves of the potatoes on many fields I passed were quite withered and a strange stench . . . filled the atmosphere adjoining each field of potatoes.

Five days later he went back up the mountain again. Spores of *Phytophthora Infestans* had been up there before him:

My feelings may be imagined when, before I saw the crop, I smelt the fearful stench. . . . No perceptible change except the smell had as yet come upon the apparent prosperity of the deceitfully luxuriant stalks, but the experience of the past few days taught me that all was gone and that the crop was utterly worthless . . . the luxuriant stalks soon withered, the leaves decayed, the disease extended to the tubers, and the stench from the rotting of such an immense amount of rich vegetable matter became almost intolerable.

For him it meant the loss of several thousand pounds. For hundreds of thousands of poor men, women and children it meant that their lives were now at stake.

Only a week later, Lord John Russell announced in the House of Commons the first part of Trevelyan's policy for Ireland in the new season.

It was implacable: 'We do not propose', said the Prime Minister, 'to interfere with the regular mode by which Indian corn and other kinds of grain may be brought into Ireland.'

The process would be left to market forces. The Chancellor of the Exchequer, Sir Charles Wood, expressed it even more bluntly: 'It is not the intention at all to import food for the use of the people of Ireland.'

Something had to be done, however. Trevelyan decided to reorganize the public works scheme of the previous season which he had just closed down. This time the local landlords were to be compelled to accept their share of the burden by paying for most of the works by local rates. The government would advance the money only as a loan, repayable with interest, until the rate could be collected, though it would make an outright grant to the most distressed districts in the west. By and large even this was not ungenerous by the standards of the day.

But events were quickly overwhelming Trevelyan and his orderly attempt to apply the standards of the day. The new public works projects took many weeks to organize, being again subject to rigorous bureaucratic supervision and delay: and in County Mayo, County Tipperary and County Sligo, parties of several hundred men, often carrying shovels, were marching into towns and on to landlords' estates pleading for work. Usually they were almost pathetically peaceful. When several thousand called on the Marquis of Sligo at his house in Westport they were careful not to tread on his grass, and though he had no work for them they were rewarded by being told he would not harass them for their rents.

There were food riots in Galway and Dungarvan, County Waterford, while in Mallow men and women scaled the workhouse walls with cries of: 'We want something to eat! We are starving!'

'Why this delay in starting the public works?' asked the *Freeman's Journal* on 7 October 1846 and again a week later ran a leader: 'The Delay in Employment – Who is at Fault?' Eye-witness accounts of the terrible plight of the people, particularly in the western districts, multiplied daily. A justice of the peace wrote from County Mayo:

The heart sickens at the sight of so many fellow creatures all but dead. Should even public works commence, many, many, many are not able to work, they are so debilitated from want of food. I see hundreds of women and children going through the stubble fields striving to get an old stalk of potato.

Trevelyan, reading his reports, reluctantly decided to change part of his policy and make government purchases of Indian corn available for cheap sale in Ireland after all. But the decision came far too late for any of the new supplies to arrive before Christmas, 1846. And with only 26,000 again employed on public works by the beginning of October, the first deaths from starvation began to be reported: two from Castlehaven, County Cork; one from Macroom, County Cork; two from Ballycastle, County Galway. In Skibbereen people were 'literally falling in the streets from exhaustion'.

The public relief works themselves, when they did gradually start, mostly provided for the construction of roads, sometimes useful, more often unnecessary, or for the lowering of hills, or the filling-in of hollows. Trevelyan had strictly laid down that no individual landlord or farmer should benefit from the work being done, so that no agricultural improvement could be undertaken, no cultivation at public expense of other crops such as oats as an alternative to the potato. A country gentleman wrote from the west:

... the breaking up and rendering impassable at an enormous outlay of unexceptionably good public highways, the commencing of expensive and unnecessary new lines of road at a season of the year very unsuitable to such operations, many of them and most of them, altogether unnecessary for any present or probable future wants of the county, appear to those who, like myself, are unskilled in the mysteries of government as an anomalous mode of meeting a calamity ...

A complaint heard everywhere was that – again in order to comply with the so-called laws of political economy – wages on the public works had to be lower than those hitherto prevailing on the ordinary labour market in order not to undercut it (although in fact of course the ordinary labour market had virtually disappeared). To these complaints *The Times* in London retorted:

Such are the thanks that a government gets for attempting to palliate great afflictions and satisfy corresponding demands by an inevitable but ruinous beneficence. . . . It is the old thing, the old malady is breaking out. It is the national character, the national thoughtlessness, the national indolence.

Worse than the low wages was the fact that, owing to bureaucratic delays, wages quite often were not paid at all. At Skibbereen men were working on the roads, weak and exhausted for want of food, without being paid for a fortnight.

On the morning of Sunday, 11 October the body of a labourer, Jeremiah Hegarty, who had been employed on the public works was found on the road just outside Skibbereen. The coroner's jury found that he met his death for 'want of sufficient sustenance for many days previous to his decease, and that this want of sustenance was occasioned by his not having been paid his wages on the public works . . . for eight days previous to the time of his death.'

Within weeks there were to be hundreds like him. James MacHale, the parish priest of Hollymount, County Mayo, was soon writing:

Deaths, I regret to say, innumerable from starvation are occurring every day; the bonds of society are almost dissolved. . . . The pampered officials . . . removed as they are from these scenes of heart-rending distress, can have no idea of them and don't appear to give themselves much trouble about them – I ask them in the name of humanity, is this state of society to continue and who are responsible for these monstrous evils?

Well, there was no doubt about that: the British government were responsible. And the *Cork Examiner* of 2 November 1846 made an unanswerable political point:

Talk of the power of England, her navy, her gold, her resources – oh yes, and her

enlightened statesmen, while the broad fact is manifested that she cannot keep the children of her bosom from perishing by hunger. Perhaps indeed Irishmen may not aspire to the high dignity of belonging to the great family of the Empire; they may be regarded as Aliens. But when the Queen at her coronation swore to protect and defend her subjects, it is not recollected that in the words of the solemn covenant there was any exception made with regard to Ireland. How happens it then, while there is a shilling in the Treasury, or even a jewel in the Crown, that patient subjects are allowed to perish with hunger?

'Cartfuls' of people were said to be arriving daily at the workhouse in Middleton, County Cork. Numbers doubled during October. At the end of November in Listowel, County Kerry, a party of some 5,000 people attacked the workhouse shouting, 'Bread or blood'. An eye-witness commented:

Their bodies could scarcely be said to be clothed and their pallid visages showed what ravages gaunt famine had already made on their health and vigour. Heaven only knows when these things are to end, for it is to be feared we have yet scarcely seen even the beginning of the misery that awaits our unhappy people.

Although by Christmas 1846 there were 400,000 persons employed on public works in every county in Ireland (fifteen times the number of three months before) the local committees were constantly putting destitute people on the list for tickets to work which the government official in charge of the local works was unable to issue them. Of some 500 people on the committee's list at Islandeady, Castlebar, County Mayo, only thirteen were given tickets. The Revd Richard Henry, the local parish priest, wrote:

Crowds of famished tottering beings that throng round my dwelling afflict and shock me with fearful tales of distress. . . . Groups of those whose names were on the list approved by the committee but to whom labour tickets were refused by Captain Carey, daily besiege my dwelling. . . . On Friday last especially, being the day before the meeting of the committee, they thronged, imploring my interference. When . . . I was compelled to tell them that all that could be done was done already; that it didn't depend on me or the committee and that as tickets had already been refused I could not hold out any certain hopes, the tears of agony and despair gushing from the eyes of hardy and aged men gave evidence of the intensity of their sufferings. Should employment be given them even now the bulk of the people will, I fear, be unable to avail themselves of it. Their strength is enfeebled, their spirits and hopes broken; they become gradually unable to go abroad; they pine within the cabin and may expire there unknown to all, forgotten and unrecorded.

Even if people could get tickets and earn money from the public works, owing to the lateness of Trevelyan's reluctant order for more Indian corn there were still many weeks before the new supply for cheap sale from the government depots could be made available. On the west coast though, where, as in Cork, there were some supplies left in the depots from the previous season, distress had been so great so early on that some local relief officers had, against orders, been distributing small amounts for sale. Sir Randolph Routh, the Commissary General, fulfilling Trevelyan's instructions, reprimanded them for this action which 'undermined market forces' and ordered them to close down at once. There seemed to be an official feeling that the people were somehow not making enough effort to get the food that was undoubtedly in Ireland.

Routh wrote: 'You will find there is no spot so bad that there is not some supply and we must force the people to consume that. . . . The time has come to subject the people to a little pressure.'

There were people in England, and with them *The Times* newspaper, who maintained that as usual the Irish were exaggerating. To verify the situation, an officer of the Government Commissariat was sent to Skibbereen in December 1846 to investigate, and he found that there had been as many as 169 deaths from starvation in that little town alone in the previous three weeks. His report contained the following detail:

On Sunday last, 20 December, a young woman begging in the streets of Cork collapsed and was at first unable to move or speak. After being given 'restorations' and taken home to her cabin she told those helping her that both her mother and father had died in the last fortnight. At the same time she directed their attention to a heap of dirty straw that lay in the corner and apparently concealed some object under it. On removing this covering of straw, the spectators were horrified on beholding the mangled corpses of two grown boys, a large proportion of which had been removed by the rats while the remainder lay festering in its rottenness. There they had remained for perhaps a week or maybe a fortnight . . .

In Ballydehob, not far from Skibbereen, deaths were now so prevalent that 'coffins are not to be had for half of those who expire from want . . . so that in many places the deceased are tied up in straw. The Golleen relief committee have devised a coffin with a slide bottom . . .'

A Protestant clergyman, the Revd F. F. Traill, was soon to describe what were called 'trap coffins' which he saw at Bantry, in County Cork:

. . . the bottom is supported by hinges at one side and a hook-and-eye at the other. In these coffins the poor are carried to the grave, rather to a large pit, which I saw at a little distance from the road, and the bodies are dropped into it . . . But I was told in this district the majority were taken to the grave without any coffin and buried in their rags; in some instances even the rags are taken from the corpse to cover some still living body .

How those 'still living bodies' were faring was made clear by this report from Clonmel on 15 December 1846:

Woe, want and misery are fearfully depicted on the countenance of our people. Sorrow, suffering and mute despair seem to have taken possession of their souls. Their feelings are blunted, their ideas confused and their energies paralysed. Starvation has so completely prostrated them that they have more the appearance of ghosts than living beings.

The 'confusion of ideas' and the 'paralysis of energies' were evidence of the fever, typhus, which, together with relapsing fever (both transmitted by lice), were now spreading throughout Ireland. In fact, *typhus* is the Greek word for mist, the confusion of the brain, which is a classic symptom of the disease.

A justice of the peace, writing to the Duke of Wellington, described how in one hovel which he entered:

. . . six famished and ghastly skeletons, to all appearance dead, were huddled in a corner on some filthy straw, their sole covering what seemed a ragged horse-cloth and their wretched legs hanging about, naked above the knees. I approached in horror and found by a low moaning they were alive, they were in a fever – four children, a woman and what had once been a man . . .

The fever was soon raging as an epidemic through the whole country and did so throughout 1847, even in relatively well-fed towns like Belfast and Dublin. The reason for its spread is contained in the name by which it was popularly known: 'road fever'. It was carried down the roads by people fleeing from the more stricken counties in the west. An eye-witness from County Cork in April 1847 described how:

Crowds of starving creatures flock in from the rural districts and take possession of some hall door or the outside of some public building where they place a little straw and remain until they die. Disease has in consequence spread itself through the town. There are now over 400 afflicted with fever and dysentery. The graveyard has its entrance in the centre of the main street, and in several instances when the gates were closed and parties seeking to bury the remains of their friends, the coffins were placed on the wall and abandoned.

From Macroom in County Cork, a correspondent wrote:

Every avenue leading to and in this plague-stricken town has a fever hospital having for its protecting roof the blue vault of heaven. Persons of all ages are dropping dead in each corner of the town, who are interred with much difficulty after rats have festered on their frames.

With the spread of fever the effects of the famine were now inevitably striking upwards in society. The casualty rate among priests and doctors was especially high because they were in direct contact with the dying and the dead. But at least when the higher classes died they died in their beds, and at least their families could bury them properly.

One priest, reporting how, six months before, his parish had consisted of some 3,000 persons, went on to describe how over 500 of them were now dead, three-quarters of them buried coffinless.

They were carried to the churchyard, some on lids and ladders, more in baskets, aye and scores of them thrown beside the nearest ditch, and there left to the mercy of the dogs which have nothing else to feed on.

And among the endless horrible and tragic details with which the newspapers were filled there was this report from County Cork:

A countryman, apparently almost deranged, entered a shop which was attended by

a respectable female, and asked for money. Not receiving it he took from under his coat a dead child which he cast upon the counter in desperation, telling her he was unable to procure a coffin for it and immediately fled.

Horror succeeded horror; deaths accumulated faster and faster. Consciences in Britain were seriously disturbed, and two major charitable projects had already started dispensing free food from soup kitchens in Ireland and helping local committees financially. One was run by the Society of Friends, the Quakers, and the other by an organization specially formed for the purpose, the British Association. The latter attracted large sums from prominent people in England. Queen Victoria herself gave £2,000 (perhaps nearer £100,000 in today's money). But of course the real responsibility remained with the government, and the principles on which that responsibility was assumed did not primarily include compassion. When at the very end of December 1846, Trevelyan had finally given the order for the Indian corn depots to open, at market prices plus five per cent, even his obedient Commissary General in Ireland, Sir Randolph Routh, asked him to make the price lower. But Trevelyan replied: 'If we make prices lower I repeat for the *hundredth* time that the whole country will come in on us.' And, as for actually giving anything to the starving, Trevelyan wrote:

If the Irish once find out there are any circumstances in which they can get free government grants we shall have a system of mendicancy such as the world never knew.

But that was exactly what they already had. By March 1847 the numbers employed on the public works throughout Ireland had reached the staggering figure of 728,000 or nearly three-quarters of a million, though the extent to which the low wages and the conditions attached to the works actually provided the relief they were meant to was questionable.

Working in terrible wintry conditions people died on the public works, as everywhere else in Ireland, in their thousands. A Catholic priest described the daily scene of the time:

. . . funerals passing and re-passing in every direction, the congregations on Sunday reduced by half, the churchyards like fields lately tilled, without a green spot, constantly visited by processions of a few gaunt figures, carrying with difficulty the remains of some more fortunate relative or friend. . . . From the sad effects of this calamity all classes have suffered severely, but most of all those on the public works, and especially the old and decrepit of both sexes who were exposed without food or clothing to the piercing cold of winter. Indeed, almost all of these are dead. Being secretary to the relief committee of the district I have had a good opportunity of witnessing the dreadful effects of the system . . . on these poor creatures and could at this moment refer to many cases of persons who attended the committee for weeks before they could be admitted on the books, and, when admitted a few days later, had scarcely time to earn themselves the price of a coffin.

And then, at last, under the accumulating pressure of such appalling events, the government undertook a revolutionary change in policy. The outer framework of that policy remained the same, namely that whatever was undertaken was undertaken in the hope that the next potato harvest would be good enough to absolve the government of responsibility altogether. But in the meantime the decision was now taken actually to distribute free food. A Soup Kitchen Act was passed allotting public funds for free soup and other basic rations. And the costly and painful relief works would be wound up. Unfortunately, in the interests of economy, the government relief works were very rapidly wound up and the government-subsidized soup and rations were very slow in appearing.

The Protestant rector of Cong was soon writing:

Eighty per cent of the work people have been dismissed and yet they can't hope to be under the system of relief for ten days yet. All the relief committee funds are expended. Deaths are increasing ten-fold.

In one part of County Mayo in eighteen days only four days' rations were handed out. Even a temporary gap between the issue of rations and the closing of the public works brought an immediate rapid increase of deaths.

Gradually, however, the ration system provided by the Soup Kitchen Act began to take effect. By the middle of July 1847 over three million Irish adults and children, or not far short of half the population of the entire country, were receiving relief. The reaction of Treasury officialdom was predictable. Trevelyan's secretary to the Relief Commissioners in Dublin wrote to each Poor Law Union:

There is much reason to believe that the object of the Relief Act is greatly perverted and that it is frequently applied solely as a means of adding to the comforts of the lower classes, and of assisting the farmers and employers in carrying on their business instead of being, as intended, a provision for the utterly destitute, and for the purpose of warding off absolute starvation . . .

And a similar letter from the same secretary to the Commissioners a week later, 15 July 1847, ran as follows:

The Commissioners cannot but complain of finding the demands for rations from many districts continuously increasing, and sometimes largely, without even a word of explanation to account for it . . .

The remedy for such extravagance at the British tax-payers' expense lay, of course, ready to hand. The harvest of the late summer and autumn of 1847 was a good one as far as it went, though of course relatively little potato ground had been cultivated because there had been little seed available and few cultivators. But in the light of the good harvest an official decision was gladly taken: all government relief under the Soup Kitchen Act would cease at the end of September 1847.

At the same time, new Poor Law legislation would be enacted, enabling the workhouses to take in the able-bodied to be fed in return for work, and permitting workhouses for the first time to provide outdoor relief to those who were not residents of them. The cost of the operation was to be borne on new local Poor Law rates – the government again advancing a grant, repayable with interest until such rates could be raised. There was one exception to the new concession of workhouse outdoor relief: no-one in possession of more than a quarter of an acre of land was entitled to it. Thus the State actually added its own quota to the ever-increasing number of landlord evictions, for anyone starving on just over a quarter of an acre now had to get out of his house and go to the workhouse if he wanted to live.

By the end of September 1847, although the previous relief scheme had not quite been wound up and a million Irish people were still receiving free rations, two million who had been getting them were deprived of them and thrown on the workhouses and the local rates. The *Cork Examiner* wrote in October 1847:

We foresee that the rural population – particularly along the coasts – will pour itself into the workhouses. The necessity will be stronger than last year. Then the people had the government works . . . to look to. Now they have none. The consequences for the Unions throughout the country must be dreadful. The houses cannot contain them all. Nor can the rate-payers pay for them all. We should not wonder if these workhouses became the charnel houses of the whole rural population.

Such predictions immediately began to be fulfilled. On the same day as that leader appeared in the *Cork Examiner*, the following scene was reported from Bantry:

Our town at six o'clock this morning was a scene of unparalleled misery and destitution. At that early hour two hookers arrived at our quay laden with 240 human spectres from Berehaven who had quitted their homes of wretchedness to find shelter in the workhouse. I saw them crawl from where they landed. . . . I saw them cling with tenacity to the outer gates; he who was so fortunate as to grapple with the iron railing kept his place till one of the Guardians arrived who secured admission for the famished applicants. Here even our misery does not terminate . . . the resources of this Union are exhausted and the establishment is in debt to a fearful amount. . . . Let ministers no longer deceive themselves by vainly imagining that the local resources of any Union in Ireland would be sufficient to maintain its poor. If they regard us as fellow subjects and wish to snatch us from the jaws of death let them interfere without loss of time . . .

But, unbelievable as it must now seem, English ministers had already done all they were ever going to do to deal with the Irish Famine. Throwing responsibility for relief onto the rates and the 130 Poor Law Unions of Ireland was the last major positive step the government were to take. Some of those Poor Law Unions, particularly in the west of Ireland, were already bankrupt. All were going to be strained far beyond their resources by the pressure of the starving thrown upon them. Many local landlords who as the largest rate-payers should have been the mainstay of the financial burden were made bankrupt by the weight of it. Quite prosperous farmers, equally ruined by the high rates themselves, sometimes had to become inmates of the workhouses which the rates were levied to sustain. These cruel realities were all too easily lost sight of from Westminster beneath a growing conviction that all that could possibly be done for Ireland had been done and that Ireland must now be left to what Trevelyan in a terrifying phrase described as 'the operation of natural causes'.

'It is my opinion', he wrote, 'that too much has been done for the

LEFT: An American Fenian map of Ireland, with heroes (Father Matthew, temperance reformer, in bold company).

RIGHT: Charles Stewart Parnell. '. . . No man has the right to fix a boundary to the path of a nation . . .' (*Vanity Fair* cartoon.)

BELOW: Gladstone under the influence of the Land League. A revolutionary bill.

·NO HOME RULE·

UNITED WE STAND

DIVIDED WE FALL

PAT · JOHN BULL · SANDY · TAFFY

JOHN CLELAND & SON, LTD BELFAST. IRELAND. ENGLAND. SCOTLAND. WALES.

WE WON'T HAVE HOME RULE

COL. WALLACE · SIR EDWARD CARSON, K.C.M.P. · CAPTAIN CRAIG, M.P.

OUR CIVIL AND RELIGIOUS

LIBERTIES WE WILL MAINTAIN

KING WILLIAM III

No Home Rule

LET OUR FLAG
RUN OUT STRAIGHT
IN THE WIND,
THE OLD RED
SHALL·BE
FLOATED
AGAIN

WHEN THE RANKS
THAT
ARE THINNED SHALL
BE THINNED,
WHEN THE NAMES
THAT ARE
TWENTY ARE TEN.

ULSTER!

people. Under such treatment the people have grown worse instead of better, and we must now try what independent exertion can do . . .' As for himself, it was time he took a rest: '. . . after two years of such continuous hard work as I have never had in my life.' He went off with his family for a fortnight's holiday in France.

In the Limerick workhouse alone deaths were running at over 130 a week.

Dying was one way out of the nightmare. But there had for some time been another: emigration. People were leaving from every port in Ireland. In the course of 1847 alone a quarter of a million Irish men, women and children left Ireland and the rate was to continue at that level and sometimes higher for the next four years. It was a mass emigration which was not only to alter permanently the population structure of Ireland but also, in concentrating the seeds of Irish bitterness towards English government in Ireland in the United States – the separate rich and powerful nation across the Atlantic which most of the emigrants hoped to reach – it was to affect profoundly the future development of Irish nationalist feeling.

Many of the poorest in fact never got beyond the English port to which they sailed. By mid-May 1847 there were over 100,000 Irish wandering, begging and destitute about the streets of Liverpool and other towns in the north of England. But it was by no means only the poorest who were emigrating. The more comfortable class of farmer and his family, well-dressed and with a good deal of baggage on cars, was going too. Not that emigration always enabled them to escape from horror or even death. Conditions on board the emigrant ships were sometimes as appalling as anything in Ireland: airless overcrowding below decks in the steerage, fever, little water, few rations, few cooking or sanitary facilities. Such conditions can be gauged from a few simple statistics of the year 1847.

Although seventy-five per cent of the Irish emigrants went to the United States (and most of them to New York), some of the very worst conditions were experienced on the route to Canada. The emigrant ship *Loosthawk* arrived at Quebec after seven weeks crossing the Atlantic from Liverpool. It had set out with 348 passengers. One-third of them, 117 people, had died at sea or were dead on arrival. The *Larch* sailed from Sligo to Quebec with 440 passengers of whom 108 died at sea and 150 arrived with a fever of which many would undoubtedly have died later. On the *Virginius*, nine weeks out from Liverpool to Quebec, out of 476 passengers 158 died at sea, while another 106 landed sick with fever, or 'more dead than alive' as an eye-witness described them.

Nor, by the middle of 1847, were these particularly exceptional cases. On 12 August the Montreal Board of Health reported that of the 4,427 passengers who had set sail in ten ships (including those last two) from Cork and Liverpool for Canada in the previous month, 804 (just under a fifth) died at sea while another 847 passengers were sick with fever on arrival.

'It may well be supposed', the Board went on, 'that few of the survivors could reach any other than an early grave. Terrible as have been the tales of the slave trade, against which the British nation has so long protested . . . they exceed not in horrors, nor perhaps equal the dreadful realities to which these unfortunate wanderers have been subjected.'

It was Canada, and particularly the green island called Grosse Isle off Quebec in the St Lawrence river, that saw the worst of the horrors when the

LEFT: Lord John Russell: 'I do not believe it is in the power of this House to prevent the dreadful scenes of suffering and death now occurring in Ireland.'

BELOW LEFT: Charles Trevelyan, knighted for his labours. '. . . Too much has been done for the people . . . Ireland must be left to the operation of natural causes.'

Aftermath.

ships arrived. Quarantine regulations were less severe there than in New York and it was at Quebec that some of the poorest arrived, meagrely assisted in their passage by landlords who wanted to get rid of them from their estates. One eye-witness watching boats bringing the sick and the dead from ship to shore described how 'hundreds were literally flung on the beach, left amid the mud and the stones to crawl on the dry land as they could', while another watching them as they crawled said they were 'dying like fish out of water'.

In Ireland itself the autumn and winter of 1847–8 were as bad as anything the country had yet experienced, with evictions increasing and corpses lying unburied even in a town like Limerick for days on end. Even in the kinder weather of June 1848 one inspector of roads near Clifden, County Galway, had to bury 140 corpses he found scattered along his route, while a man from the same district up on a charge of sheep-stealing was saved from imprisonment by stating in open court that his wife, maddened by hunger, had been driven to eat the flesh of her own dead daughter. But the worst was still to come.

In the early autumn of 1848, to an Ireland already reeling under three successive years of famine, came the final blow: news that all over the country the new potato crop was once again almost totally blighted. 1849 was to be the most terrible year of all. And yet it was that very autumn that a list of exports of food from Cork on a single day, 14 November 1848, ran as follows:

> 147 bales of bacon
> 120 casks and 135 barrels of pork
> 5 casks of hams
> 149 casks miscellaneous provisions
> 1,996 sacks, and 950 barrels of oats
> 300 bags of flour
> 300 head of cattle
> 239 sheep
> 9,398 firkins of butter
> 542 boxes of eggs

In February 1849 while the parish priest of Partree, County Galway, was writing simply, 'The great majority of poor located here are in a state of starvation, many of them hourly expecting death to relieve them of their sufferings', the Lady Mayoress held a ball at the Mansion House in Dublin at which, in the presence of the Lord Lieutenant, 'dancing continued until a late hour of the night and refreshments of a most *recherché* description were supplied with inexhaustible profusion . . .'

At Ballinrobe in County Galway, there were dead bodies everywhere. 'Every village has dead bodies lying unburied for many days,' wrote an eye-witness. 'Almost every hovel in the suburb of this town has its corpse. . . . May God forgive our rulers for this cruel conduct towards God's creatures here. . . . The poor are dropping into their graves in multitudes.'

A Protestant clergyman addressed an open letter to Lord John Russell, the Prime Minister. 'My Lord,' he said, 'I have a right to speak for I am a Minister of God. Let me then importune and implore you, my Lord, to stand in the breach between the living and the dead. . . . Tell the assembled Parliament that the people must not any more be left to die.'

But in the House of Commons in May 1849 Lord John Russell had only this to say:

I do not think any effort of this House would, in the present unfortunate state of Ireland, be capable of preventing the dreadful scenes of suffering and death that are now occurring in Ireland. I distinctly repeat that I do not believe it is in the power of this House to do so. . . . I do not feel justified in asking the House for an additional advance of £100,000 which at least would be necessary if the House should say there should be no possible cause of starvation in Ireland.

Deaths in the workhouse of Ballinasloe, County Galway, which had a total population of about 5,000 for the week ending 28 April 1849, had been 226. For the week ending 5 May, the month in which Lord John Russell felt the House of Commons could do nothing, they rose to 490. Someone wrote from Ballinrobe in that month: 'The streets are daily thronged with moving skeletons. The fields are strewn with dead. . . . The curse of Russell, more terrible than the curse of Cromwell, is upon us . . .'

Charles Trevelyan, recently knighted for his labours, had been busy writing a history of the Famine. In his account he made it end in August 1847. But now, over *eighteen months later*, the Dublin *Freeman's Journal* was writing:

We again ask: is it not possible to contrive some means of saving the people from this painful and lingering process of death from starvation? Do we live under a regular or responsible government? Is there justice or humanity in the world that such things could *be*, in the middle of the nineteenth century and within twelve hours' reach of the opulence, grandeur and power of a court and capital the first upon the earth?

Such was the question that Irishmen were to continue to ask themselves for decades. And it was the inescapable answer to that question which, among other later influences was to lead them in the end towards an inescapable political conclusion: that Ireland should in the future, one way or another, run her own affairs. For nothing would ever be able to efface the memory of this monstrous thing that had happened in these years to Irish men, women and children in their own country, in the name of the British government in Ireland.

In 1841 the population of Ireland had been 8,175,124. Given a normal rate of increase it could have been expected by 1851 to have reached 9,018,799. But the census of 1851 gave the population of Ireland as 6,552,385. If the figure of about 1,500,000 who emigrated during the five years 1845–9 is added to the 1851 census total the result is just over eight million – or one million short of the anticipated population figure for that year. Deaths from the Famine years 1845–9 can therefore be estimated approximately at one million. Modern Irish historians whose objectivity is exemplary usually put the figure at around 800,000.

The names of only a few hundred are known. They are known from the inquests held from time to time on their emaciated bodies found in fields, by the side of country roads, in the middle of towns, or at their work-places where they had collapsed. But the vast majority of deaths went unrecorded. There are few monuments to the dead. Irish nationalists would say that their true monument is Irish freedom.

National uprising or Battle of the Widow MacCormack's Cabbage Garden? Scene of James Stephen's debut under Smith O'Brien.

Chapter 6

Bold Fenian Men

In Protestant areas of Northern Ireland the word 'Fenian' is a term of abuse, a six-letter word often supplementing the word 'bastard'. In nationalist areas of Ireland it has a reverential, vaguely mystical connotation, in no way diminished by the fact that many people are imprecise about the historical realities it embraces. It seems to emanate from the world of nebulous Gaelic myth – as indeed it was intended to do when first used for an Irish Republican organization in the 1850s, the word deriving from *Fianna*, a legendary band of warrior heroes. In the United Kingdom as a whole the word is virtually unknown. Yet it is the Fenian tradition from which the Irish Republican Army of our day directly derives.

Fenianism was always more effective as tradition rather than as reality, for the tradition was formed from a sequence of actual events which, however nobly inspired, barely rose above the level of the ludicrous. Karl Marx's dogmatic quip, in the context of Louis Napoleon, about history repeating itself, appearing the first time as tragedy and the second time as farce, could well be inverted in the Fenian context. The Fenian Rising of 1867 was a farce. The successful nationalist uprising which developed between the years 1916 and 1921 in the Fenian tradition, would be seen by some as tragedy.

When, in 1916, Patrick Pearse, first 'Commandant General of the Irish Republic', began that second Fenian uprising, he read a proclamation from the steps of the Dublin Post Office in which he referred to 'six times in the past 300 years' in which the Irish nation had risen in arms to assert its right to national sovereignty and freedom. By the first occasion he presumably meant the great rebellion of 1641 (though in fact this was technically initiated in the name of the king, Charles I); by the second, he presumably meant the Jacobite war of 1689–91, fought for one king of England, Scotland and Ireland against another; by the third, the rebellion of 1798 which degenerated into little more than a peasant's revolt; and by the fourth, that Dublin street riot which was Robert Emmet's ill-fated rising of 1803. But certainly the two last occasions to which he referred were the Fenian Rising of 1867 and the so-called Rising of 1848 which was its prologue. It was a prologue appropriate to the ensuing farce.

The village of Ballingarry in County Tipperary is a place of minor obvious interest except to its inhabitants – little more than a pleasantly populated crossroads on the route from Thurles to Cashel. Yet here, the history books will tell you, was the scene of that 1848 Rising to assert Irish national sovereignty and freedom. It is still remembered in Ballingarry though not exactly in those terms. If you ask in the main street for the location of that farmhouse where the principal incident of the Rising took place, you may be met for a moment with that look of politely disguised bewilderment with which the Irish in their natural courtesy tolerate the apparent idiocy of strangers. But a true folk-memory will eventually surface to meet you. 'Ah! You mean "the War House"!' And this is indeed what you mean, for, directed to a two-storey grey-stone farmhouse on the top of a small hill a couple of miles to the east of Ballingarry, you recognize at once the building which can be found in an *Illustrated London News* engraving of August 1848. A plaque above the door enjoins: 'Remember 1848'.

The Irish people have good reason to remember 1848, the penultimate year of that famine which killed perhaps as many as a million of them altogether and caused another million and a half to emigrate. They have reason to remember it in this particular corner of Tipperary because here was the scene of an attempt by Irishmen to challenge in arms the authority of that government in whose care they were supposed to be.

The challenge was made by a most unlikely character: an upper-class Protestant, William Smith O'Brien, who had been a member of Parliament at Westminster for many years. Educated at Harrow, he had an English accent and what the Irish regarded as the typical stiff and stilted mannerisms of the English gentleman of his day. Yet his name was O'Brien and he could trace his ancestry back to the great Gaelic High King of the eleventh century, Brian Boru. Such, by now, were the complex subtleties of Irish nationality.

Smith O'Brien had been a late convert to Daniel O'Connell's great constitutional movement for Repeal of the Union which abjured physical force. But under the devastating impact of the Famine he had gravitated towards and become the most prestigious member of an impatient young group within the movement, who went under the name of 'Young Ireland'. Under the intellectual leadership of one of them, Thomas Davis, Young Ireland had long been preaching in the columns of their newspaper, *The Nation*, a common nationality which would embrace Protestants and Catholics alike, thus picking up the theory of the United Irishmen in the atmosphere of romantic European nationalism of their own day. Davis had died in 1845 but the others, as the Famine wreaked havoc with O'Connell's movement, became more and more desperate and impolitic. Their words became wilder and their attitudes more menacing. Wildest of all was the son of a Presbyterian minister from Ulster, John Mitchel, who founded a new newspaper, *The United Irishman*, from which he openly preached republicanism and eventual rebellion. When Mitchel was arrested, the mantle of militant leader fell on the gentlemanly and wholly unsuitable figure of Smith O'Brien who, against his better judgement, found himself in the summer of 1848 testing out the spirit of the Tipperary peasantry with a view to confronting the British government in arms. A warrant was soon issued for his arrest too and a party of the Irish constabulary – a paramilitary body of Irishmen armed with rifles – moved on the village of Ballingarry to execute it. Finding, however, that barricades were up there and that large numbers of people, some of them armed, were milling about

OPPOSITE

ABOVE: Arrest of Smith O'Brien on Thurles railway station. Stephens was luckier.

BELOW LEFT: James Stephens, founder of the organization that became the Irish Republican Brotherhood: '. . . implicit obedience to commanders and superiors . . .'

BELOW RIGHT: John Mitchel: '. . . wild and menacing words' in a paper he called *The United Irishman*.

104

in indeterminate mood, they retired temporarily to the grey stone farm-house a couple of miles away to try and sort out problems of valour and discretion. O'Brien, followed by about twenty peasants armed with guns, pistols and pikes, and a large crowd of curious sightseers, then moved after the police to try and make them opt for discretion.

The house belonged to a widow named MacCormack. She was out at the time but her five children were all inside when an Inspector of the Irish Constabulary and forty-six men entered the house chorusing 'The British Grenadiers'. They started breaking up the furniture to put it in a state of siege. After O'Brien had unsuccessfully tried to persuade them to surrender, a sudden cry from the crowd of, 'Slash away boys, and slaughter them!' was followed by a volley of stones and possibly a shot or two at the house.

This was enough for the understandably nervous police. They fired a volley into the crowd, who took shelter behind the surrounding wall, and they continued to fire intermittently for the next hour or so. Two of the besiegers had been killed and several wounded when another force of police arrived to raise the siege, and O'Brien and his lieutenants made off into the countryside as best they could.

Such was the so-called Rising of 1848 which Patrick Pearse was to elevate so prestigiously. It is more truthfully known as 'the battle of the Widow MacCormack's cabbage garden'. And yet in a way Pearse's oratory can be justified, for the Fenian movement itself was to stem directly from it.

One of O'Brien's lieutenants at Ballingarry, who had not been arrested but had managed to make his way to France, was James Stephens, a young Protestant from Kilkenny. In Paris he became involved with radical and revolutionary secret societies and took some part in the popular resistance to that *coup d'état* of Louis Napoleon in 1851 which gave Marx his flawed epigram about history repeating itself. Stephens's contacts with the secret societies gave him ideas for a new approach to the problems of Ireland.

Revolutionary organization had been conspicuously lacking from the experience of 1848. That of the United Irishmen in 1798 had been clumsy, riddled with informers, and ham-strung by its inadequate co-ordination with the peasants' secret society, the Defenders. Stephens gradually set his mind to forming a new professional modern secret society to help establish an Irish Republic. He did so just about the time that another former Young Irelander, Gavan Duffy, gave up hope of furthering Irish national interests altogether and, emigrating to Australia (where he eventually became a prime minister) declared the situation of Ireland to be that of 'a corpse on the dissecting table'.

James Stephens's strongest characteristic, which would be both invaluable and disastrous to his cause, was his egotistical belief in his own powers. The prospect of reviving the corpse was one that he took quite literally in his stride. In 1856 he set out on a 3,000-mile tour of Ireland, mostly on foot, to gauge the country's revolutionary potential. Although he found very little practical evidence to encourage him, and that mainly in the agrarian secret societies known as 'Ribbonmen' whose interests were confined to local agrarian problems rather than nationalist ideals, he did not allow himself to be discouraged. Among labourers, small tradesmen and the sons of tenant farmers he found what he described as a great deal of general 'disaffection' which 'even now would not be hard to stir into insurrection'.

The bad side of Stephens's egotism was displayed in his capacity for bombast, for small-minded jealousy and self-deception; the good side in an extraordinary capacity for hard work, organization and disregard for his own material well-being. To the task of stirring disaffection into nationalist insurrection he was to dedicate the next ten years of his life, and on St Patrick's Day, 17 March 1858, he and a few fellow conspirators in Dublin solemnly swore an oath: '. . . in the presence of God, to renounce all allegiance to the Queen of England, and to take arms and fight at a moment's warning to make Ireland an Independent Democratic Republic, and to yield implicit obedience to the commanders and superiors of this secret society . . .' The society was later to become known as the Irish Republican Brotherhood.

What had finally brought Stephens to take this momentous step was the encouragement he had received from America, where the possibilities of furthering insurrection in Ireland by summoning at least material resources from the embittered emigrants of the Famine and post-Famine years, were considerable. Emissaries had passed backwards and forwards between Stephens and John O'Mahony, a comrade of the 1848 days who had fled to America. Soon after forming his own organization in Ireland, Stephens himself went to America where he and O'Mahony founded a twin American society, named by O'Mahony (a Gaelic scholar) the Fenian Brotherhood, after the ancient warrior élite of legendary times. Because secrecy was imperative under British rule, it was under the name of the American part of the organization, which was able to function openly, that the whole movement was usually referred to in Ireland.

Stephens was determined that his organization should not be broken by informers as the United Irishmen had been, and for a surprisingly long time he was successful in this, principally because of the elaborate system of security which he devised. The secret society consisted of closed 'circles' in which only one member was supposed to know only one member of any other circle. Since much of the swearing-in was to take place in public houses and at public sporting events this was a timely precaution. Indeed the effectiveness of the system was proved not long after its inception when the government discovered a circle in Cork late in 1858 but failed to appreciate the scope of what they had discovered. They caught one of Stephens's young men, named Jeremiah O'Donovan Rossa, swearing in new members to establish an Irish Republic, but he was able to pass himself off simply as one of a band of foolish local young men who had formed a national society of their own named the Phoenix Society. The whole thing blew over when he and the others let themselves be bound over to keep the peace.

O'Donovan Rossa was unstintingly to devote much of his life to the Fenian cause and to endure great hardships in its name but his greatest achievement for it was to be as a corpse. This fact is symptomatic of the nature of the Fenian achievement as a whole. For when Rossa died in the United States in 1915 at a time when most people in Ireland regarded Fenianism itself as defunct, his body was brought back to Ireland by secret neo-Fenians, of whom Patrick Pearse was one, and given a great funeral to refresh public memories. Though Rossa himself had never fired a shot for the cause of Irish republicanism, a military volley was fired over his grave and Pearse himself then made a speech in which he railed at the British

RIGHT: John O'Mahoney, Gaelic scholar and founder with Stephens of the American Fenian Brotherhood. But 'leader of a warrior élite'?

BELOW: American Fenians. '. . . gala days and jolly nights, bunkum and filibustering . . . beakers of fizzling champagne.'

OPPOSITE

TOP: American Fenian certificate of status.

BELOW: 'Recognizable in their felt hats and square-toes boots . . .' Civil War veterans of the Confederate Irish Brigade.

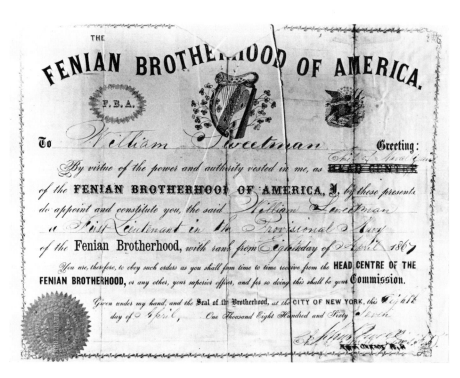

government with the words: 'The fools! The fools! The fools! They have left us our Fenian dead, and while Ireland holds these graves Ireland unfree shall never be at peace.'

It so happened that the first major success of Stephens, Rossa and the rest of the secret society in Ireland was the organization of a funeral on similar lines to that which Pearse and his friends were to engineer for Rossa himself more than fifty years later. A relatively unknown young man who had been 'out' in 1848, Terence Bellew MacManus, had died in San Francisco. The Fenian Brotherhood in the States decided to send his body back to Ireland and Stephens made spectacular arrangements for the funeral in Dublin. More than 20,000 people turned out to view the coffin as, escorted by Stephens's horsemen with black arm-bands and batons with which to keep crowds in order, it wound its way slowly, after lying in state, through the city streets to Glasnevin cemetery. Although Archbishop Cullen, decrying this glorification of a man who had risen in arms in unlawful rebellion, had forbidden the use of the Catholic Pro-Cathedral for that lying in state, Stephens had made effective alternative arrangements and had countered the Church's official disapproval of Fenianism by securing the services of a dissident radical priest to glorify the dead man and his cause at the graveside. As even the constitutionally-minded *Freeman's Journal* willingly conceded: '. . . the demonstration owed its origins and its magnitude to the cause with which MacManus was identified.' By thus advertising that cause so effectively Stephens had given it a new lease of life.

He exploited the new impetus resulting from the MacManus funeral by undertaking a new series of organizational tours through Ireland in the course of which considerable numbers of new recruits were sworn into the organization. And in the summer of 1863, he started a newspaper of his own, the *Irish People*, which, though just keeping within the bounds of legality, went much further than any of the other Dublin newspapers by promoting a total national independence to be won by means other than parliamentary agitation. It kept in front of Irishmen constant reminders of the existence of the open Fenian Brotherhood in the United States, and although the outbreak of the Civil War temporarily overshadowed Fenian activities there, the potential significance of that war for Ireland was periodically stressed, for example in a poem entitled 'An Irish Maiden to Her American Soldier' which ended with the line: 'But stay away if you bear not back your manhood's resolve for Ireland.'

In 1864 Stephens, increasingly critical of O'Mahony's leadership of the American Fenians, himself went to the States to organize Irishmen in the Union armies. He had complained before of American 'Irish tinsel patriots' with their 'speeches of bayonets, gala days and jolly nights, banners and sashes, bunkum and filibustering, responding in glowing language to glowing toasts on Irish National Independence over beakers of fizzling champagne.' It was true that although the United States now contained a vast potential of resources, both in men and money, which could theoretically be deployed actively for the Irish cause, its contribution towards that cause had so far been disappointing. Although millions of Irish men and women had emigrated there since the Famine with a terrible bitterness in their hearts towards Britain as they settled down in the new Republic, finding work and even a relative prosperity compared with what they had left behind in Ireland, this bitterness took on a doctrinaire rather than a practical tone. It gave them status to add to their new roots in America rather than any real very practical incentive to concern themselves with Irish affairs. But as the Civil War moved towards its end, Stephens was able to write to O'Mahony: 'Let no man for an instant forget that we are bound to action next year.'

In Ireland, an aide of Stephens', John Devoy, was undermining the loyalty of British soldiers to the Queen with a new version of the secret oath which now declared the Irish Republic to be 'virtually established'. Drilling of civilians was taking place in halls in towns; mysterious bodies of men were seen or were said to have been seen drilling by night in the countryside. And the lines of a new song ran:

> Pay them back woe for woe,
> Give them back blow for blow,
> Out and make way for the bold Fenian men!

By the beginning of 1865 Stephens reckoned he had 85,000 men organized in Ireland alone, for whom he hoped to get arms mainly from America, together with reinforcements of trained soldiers. The latter at least were beginning to come over as the Union and Confederate armies disbanded, easily recognizable in their felt hats and square-toed boots. At the beginning of September 1865, as Fenian drilling became more and more blatant, Stephens wrote to one of his subordinates: 'This year – and let there be no mistake about it – must be the year of action . . . the flag of Ireland – of the Irish Republic – must this year be raised . . .'

But there had already been mistakes. A Fenian named Nagle, once a schoolmaster and later a folder of parcels and writer of labels at the *Irish People* office, had been giving important information to the authorities about the Fenian organization for the previous eighteen months. And since that organization's activity was clearly moving towards some sort of climax, the authorities struck. The editorial staff of the *Irish People* were arrested, with the single exception of Stephens himself who managed to remain free for a further two months living under an assumed name in a house in the Dublin suburb of Sandymount, which he left only at night. From there he continued to send urgent calls to the American Fenians for men and supplies, stressing that the organization in Ireland remained intact and was ready for action in spite of the arrests at the *Irish People*.

Then, on the morning of 11 November 1865 as he lay in bed, he too was arrested, betrayed by another informer. He was lodged in Richmond Jail (later Richmond – and now Griffith – barracks). His arrest seemed to break the tension in Ireland. Although there were still a number of Irish American veterans of the Civil War hanging around Dublin, the danger of a Fenian rising seemed over. People felt they could sleep more easily in their beds at nights.

However it was from Richmond Jail that Stephens was to carry out his most effective single piece of action to boost the Fenian morale. Two of Stephens's warders were already sworn members of his secret society. With their help, one stormy night two weeks after his arrest, he walked out of his cell to a point on the outer wall, from the other side of which a rope-ladder was thrown over by a pre-arranged escape party commanded by one of the Irish Americans, named Kelly. Stephens got clean away.

The 'Chief Organizer of the Irish Republic' – as Stephens liked to call himself – was now at large again and the danger somehow seemed even greater than before. It was clear that the tentacles of the conspiracy spread everywhere, even into the very heart of Her Majesty's prisons. The only question that remained was: would Stephens still have time to keep his much repeated vow to strike in arms before the year was out? There were only a few weeks left.

But the arrest and escape seemed to have brought Stephens into closer touch with reality. His 85,000 men looked well enough on paper, but control over them by the recently appointed Fenian Military Council, staffed largely by Irish American veterans, was tenuous, and much of their armament still problematical. Though urged to start an immediate rising both by that American colonel, Kelly, who had commanded the escape party, and by John Devoy who had also been with it, he eventually persuaded them and the rest of the military council to agree to a postponement. He and Kelly then slipped off to the United States to try to repair a split that had occurred in the Fenian Brotherhood over the desirability of action against the British in Canada rather than Ireland.

By the middle of 1866 Stephens was again boasting that he would have an Irish army fighting on Irish soil before the end of the year. At the end of the year he was again urging postponement. To put a kindly interpretation on this: he had finally called his own bluff and had realized that preparations were still not sufficiently advanced for a rising. A less kindly interpretation was that his arrest had given him a fright and that he was scared. Certainly this is what the Irish American veterans thought, particularly Colonel Kelly. Late in 1866 Stephens was deposed from leadership of the organization in Ireland and was to play no further effective part in it. Kelly took over control himself and in January 1867 sailed from New York with a number of other Civil War veterans who were all determined to start a Fenian Rising in Ireland at the earliest possible moment.

Though Kelly was now 'acting Chief Executive of the Irish Republic', overall military command of the coming campaign was placed in the hands of a French soldier of fortune named Cluseret who, after service in Algeria, the Crimea and Sicily (under Garibaldi) had ended up in the Union Army under Maclellan in the Civil War. Headquarters were set up in London rather than Ireland (off the Tottenham Court Road) because *habeas corpus* was not suspended in England as in Ireland, and freedom to conspire there was consequently easier.

The general military plan was for guerrilla units to assemble in different parts of Ireland, with a concentration round Dublin and the south-west. Rail and telegraph communications were to be cut, police barracks attacked and the government generally harassed until the Army of the Irish Republic could receive substantial aid from America. Pitched battles were not contemplated. The outbreak was to be signalled on 11 February 1867 by a daring raid on Chester Castle in England where it was hoped a large supply of arms would be captured to be shipped to Ireland for immediate use.

On the morning of 11 February Irishmen with revolvers under their clothes were pouring into Chester by every train. Then at one p.m. came news that the whole plan had been betrayed to the government by an informer. (A man close to the inner councils of the Fenians named Corydon, though his identity was not yet known.) With remarkable deftness the operation was called off in time and the police had to be content with a haul of revolvers and ammunition dumped in the vicinity of the railway station and in the ponds and canals of the town. The postponement of the Rising was effectively conveyed to all units in Ireland except one which made an abortive attack on the police barracks at Cahirciveen in County Kerry. The new date set for the Rising was the night of 5 March 1867.

On the evening of 4 March an Irish American 'General' named Massey (several of the Civil War veterans promoted themselves in rank for the Rising), who had been appointed military commander in the field immediately under Cluseret, set out from Cork by train to Limerick Junction where he was to take up his command. As he stepped from the train onto the platform someone came up to him and tapped him on the shoulder. He was under arrest, betrayed by the informer Corydon together with all the Fenian plans. He immediately turned Queen's evidence and told the authorities everything he knew. Cluseret, on learning of Massey's arrest, packed his bags and left for France.

In the circumstances it is a credit to the Fenians that they had any success at all. In the environs of Dublin they captured two police barracks at Stepaside and Glencullen before news of Massey's arrest came through, though a body of several hundred Fenians were easily driven off by one volley from fourteen men of the Royal Irish Constabulary at Tallaght. At Ballyknockane in County Cork the rebels captured a police barracks and at Knockadoon, also in County Cork, they captured a coastguard station with a quantity of arms. But more symptomatic of the general Fenian experience was that of one of the guerrilla units assembled at a small ancient earthworks named Ballyhurst not far from Tipperary town.

You can see, once you have climbed the short hill to the small circular ditch and mound, just why it was chosen as a position, for it commands a view not only of the main railway line from Dublin to the south but also a number of roads in the area as well. Selecting the place however was about the sum total of the military acumen displayed there.

In command at Ballyhurst was an Irish American Civil War veteran named Bourke, also promoted to the rank of General in the Fenian cause. He had a shrunken leg but that was no immediate handicap because he was mounted on a horse. He and his men had in fact been quite successfully destroying telegraph poles and tearing up railway lines in the district. But they proved better at sabotage than at open fighting. When a party of soldiers who were out looking for them approached the earthworks, the Fenians fired one ragged volley and turned and fled, while Bourke galloped off in a different direction shouting: 'To the mountains! To the mountains!'

To the mountains eventually, pursued by flying columns of soldiers, went the scattered Fenians from Ballyhurst and other areas, with snow falls making their plight more desperate still. Bourke himself did not even get that far. He was brought down from his horse by a soldier with a clever shot at about 300 yards, and was caught soon afterwards limping along by a hedge. (In his pocket was found a Catholic prayer book, photographs of some girls, a prescription for an eye infection, a Bradshaw's railway guide

'No murder at Manchester.' Sergeant Brett killed but Kelly
the Chief Executive of the Irish Republic and his assistant freed
when Fenians attacked a prison van conveying the two to prison.

and a special new sort of oath to be administered to the civilian population in the event of victory, making them swear not to oppose the Irish Republic until relieved of the obligation.)

But Ballyhurst was not only not a victory: it was a total disaster, as was the whole Fenian Rising. None of this, however, stopped the Fenians entering into the heroic national myth. Bourke himself before being sentenced to death (he was later reprieved) could still, from the dock, speak grandly of Ireland having been a distinct and separate nationality for 700 years and express his hope that God would help her retrieve her fallen fortunes and 'raise her in her beauty and her mystery'. A ballad-maker a quarter of a century later could solemnly write that 'Ballyhurst did more that day to raise all England's fears' than all the political talk he had heard 'these five and twenty years'. And, as part of the heroic national myth, the Fenians were after all, some fifty years after their Rising to help bring about a change in the reality of Ireland.

Characteristically, perhaps the most valuable part of the Fenian contribution to the myth took place several months after the Rising itself had ended in débâcle. The Irish American veteran, Colonel Kelly, remained in England undetected, in spite of an intensive search for him. Then on 11 September 1867, the police arrested two men in Manchester acting suspiciously in a doorway. They gave their names as Wright and Williams and were charged with loitering. But on being put in front of the informer Corydon they were immediately recognized as Captain Deasy who had been active in County Cork during the Rising and the Chief Executive of the Irish Republic himself, Colonel T. J. Kelly.

A week later, the most important Fenian action of the year was fought in the streets of Manchester. For, as an unescorted prison van was conveying Kelly and Deasy in handcuffs from the police court to Belle Vue prison, it was stopped and surrounded by about thirty Fenians who had been lying in wait for it. Some of them, armed with revolvers, forced the unarmed police on the outside of the van to get down and kept onlookers at bay while others tried to batter open the locked van and rescue Kelly and Deasy from the cells inside.

Inside the van with the two Fenians and some common criminals was Police Sergeant Brett who, called upon through the ventilator of the locked back door to surrender, refused to do so. Whereupon one Fenian, aware that help for the beleaguered sergeant would soon be on the way, fired his revolver through the ventilator, though whether with intent to kill or frighten the sergeant or simply break open the door will never now be known. In any case the bullet mortally wounded the sergeant and one of the women criminals in the van took the keys out of the dying man's hands and passed them through the ventilator. A minute later Kelly and Deasy, still in their handcuffs, were free and making their way over a wall and across the railway line. They were never recaptured.

It was the sequel that was all-important for the future. Three men were eventually executed for Sergeant Brett's death. Their names: Allen, Larkin and O'Brien. All three had been present at the attack but none had fired the fatal shot. And because of that, and because few people in Ireland believed the sergeant's death to be anything but a justifiable accident, Allen, Larkin and O'Brien have gone down in history as the 'Manchester Martyrs'.

WHETHER ON THE SCAFFOLD HIGH OR IN THE BATTLES VAN THE NOBLEST PLACE FOR MAN TO DIE IS WHERE HE DIES FOR MAN

Larkin

Allen

O'Brien

IRELANDS LATEST MARTYRS.

EXECUTED AT MANCHESTER ENG.^D NOV. 23RD 1867. THEIR LAST PRAYER
"GOD SAVE IRELAND."

DESIGNED & PUBLISHED BY J. T. FOLEY 118 NASSAU ST N.Y.

PRINTED BY G. SCHLEGEL 97 WILLIAM ST N.Y.

Statues to them are to be found all over Ireland and their deaths are still commemorated there annually.

They also provide a link with a man who, though himself never a Fenian and ostensibly at least a Parliamentarian, was not above using the Fenian tradition for his own very effective purposes when it suited him. One day in the House of Commons in 1876 a reference was made by the Chief Secretary for Ireland of the day to 'the Manchester murderers'. A cry of 'No! No!' from the Irish benches stopped him in his tracks. Turning towards them he said with some hauteur: 'I regret that there is any Honourable Member in this House who will apologize for murder.' Whereupon the member for County Meath, a Protestant landowner who had been educated at Cambridge, rose in his seat and replied: 'The Right Honourable Gentleman looked at me so directly when he said that he regretted that any member should apologize for murder, that I wish to say as publicly and as directly as I can that I do not believe, and never shall believe, that any murder was committed at Manchester.' His name was Charles Stewart Parnell, and he was about to bring the cause of Irish nationalism to the very forefront of British politics.

Chapter 7

Parnell

No one man has ever disturbed the scene of British democratic politics so profoundly or for so long as the Irish Protestant landlord, Charles Stewart Parnell. In the 1880s he dominated British parliamentary life. No British prime minister could rule without taking into account how he might next exercise his power. He helped bring about a great social revolution in British history: the change in relations between landlord and tenant in Ireland. He also raised popular Irish national feeling to the most effective level it had yet achieved, in a demand for Home Rule for all Ireland under the Crown. All this Parnell had done by the age of forty, in little more than ten years of active political life.

His rise had been meteoric; his fall was equally so. Overnight he lost his power after one of the greatest sexual scandals in the history of politics. Fighting back with all the skill and strength at his command he died suddenly at the age of forty-five, leaving the political world stunned by his absence. If he had lived, the later course of British-Irish relations could only have been different. But on one point he never wavered. Speaking in the House of Commons at the end of his maiden speech in 1875 he asked: 'Why should Ireland be treated as a geographical fragment of England as I heard an ex-Chancellor of the Exchequer call it some time ago? Ireland is not a geographical fragment but a nation.'

Towards the end of the 1870s the appalling realization broke on Ireland that once again a danger of Famine threatened on something like the scale of the terrible disaster of 1845–9. That disaster, apart from bringing death to perhaps as many as a million of the Irish people had started a flow of emigration from Ireland, principally to America, which had continued for many years. In the ten years after the start of the Famine some two million had left – about a quarter of the entire population of Ireland in 1845.

In one way this emigration had, at least temporarily, improved the agricultural situation in Ireland by easing the pressure of population on the land. There had been a decline in the number of small farms and an increase in the prosperity of the larger farmer. But the small tenant farmers, though reduced in numbers, still lived very much as they had lived at the time of the Famine, which meant that they were still dependent for survival, very largely, on the potato crop. This was particularly true of the west of Ireland, where good times meant times in which you survived without difficulty. The mid-1870s had seen particularly good times, with farm prices

Charles Stewart Parnell, 1846–91. 'Ireland is not a geographical fragment but a nation.'

high and even the small tenant farmer enjoying a greater measure of well-being than that to which he was traditionally accustomed. This made any prospect of another famine all the more unbearable.

Towards the end of the 1870s two shock waves hit the Irish social system. First, the opening up of the corn-growing areas of the American west, together with the development of efficient transport by rail and fast steamship across the Atlantic, had begun to flood Europe with cheap grain, which meant that farm prices dropped. The small Irish tenant farmer in particular was soon unable to pay his rent. Second, a disastrously wet season in 1877 began a series of failures of the potato crop, so that by 1879 only about a quarter of the normal quantity of potatoes were available for consumption. Unable to pay rent, the small farmer, particularly in the west, began to be evicted, deprived even of the small plot of land on which he could grow a bare minimum of potatoes necessary for survival. Scenes grimly reminiscent of the terrible 1840s began to be re-enacted. By 1879 a real famine threatened. The annual number of evictions had doubled in the year before and now doubled again. Famine was only prevented by a massive charitable operation mounted on behalf of the starving Irish on both sides of the Irish Sea on a scale far greater than anything seen in the 1840s. But there was also a new factor at work and this was to lead to a sensational development in the political field and influence the whole future of Irish nationalism.

A former Fenian named Michael Davitt, released after many years in British prisons for the nationalist republican cause, began early in 1879 to concern himself with the more practical cause of his starving fellow Irishmen threatened with eviction in his home county of Mayo. After helping to organize a meeting of tenants which demanded, and secured locally, a reduction of rates by twenty-five per cent, he was instrumental in setting in motion a whole new land agitation for a national reduction of rents, an end to evictions and finally, as a long-term aim, a transfer of the ownership of the land from landlord to tenant.

The immediate necessity was the organization of the peasantry to demand reduced rents and an end to evictions. Standing ready to help him place this new land agitation on a national political basis was the young Member of Parliament for County Meath, Charles Stewart Parnell. Davitt had already had some contacts over the future of Irish nationalism with Parnell and he persuaded him to come and make a speech to a meeting of tenant farmers of Westport in the summer of 1879. At that meeting Parnell set the whole subsequent tone for the movement which Davitt was soon to launch through a new organization to be known as the Land League. What Parnell said that day went straight to the heart of the matter:

A fair rent is a rent the tenant can reasonably afford to pay according to the times, but in bad times a tenant cannot be expected to pay as much as he did in good times. . . . Now, what must we do in order to induce the landlords to see the position? You must show them that you intend to hold a firm grip of your homesteads and lands. You must not allow yourselves to be dispossessed as your fathers were dispossessed in 1847. . . . I hope that on those properties where the rents are out of all proportion to the times a reduction may be made and that immediately. If not,

OPPOSITE

ABOVE: Parnell's home, Avondale, County Wicklow. A personal background calculated to make him difficult.

BELOW LEFT: The Fenian who turned to Parnell for help: Michael Davitt – inspiration of the Land League.

BELOW RIGHT: A Land League poster 1881. A dangerous game with extremists which Parnell played off and on throughout his life.

THE LAND WAR!

NO RENT!

NO LANDLORDS GRASSLAND

Tenant Farmers, now is the time. Now is the hour.
You proved false to the first call made upon you.
REDEEM YOUR CHARACTER NOW.

NO RENT

UNTIL THE SUSPECTS ARE RELEASED.

The man who pays Rent (whether an abatement
is offered or not) while PARNELL, DILLON &c.,
are in Jail, will be looked upon as a Traitor to his
Country and a disgrace to his class.

No RENT, No Compromise, No Landlords' Grassland,
Under any circumstances.

Avoid the Police, and listen not to spying and delu-
ding Bailiffs.

NO RENT! LET THE LANDTHIEVES DO THEIR WORST!

THE LAND FOR THE PEOPLE!

you must help yourselves, and the public opinion of the world will stand by you, and support you in your struggle to defend your homesteads.

Who was this young Charles Stewart Parnell, thirty-three years old at the time, whom Davitt had so aptly chosen to give political life to the new land movement on behalf of the tenants?

The first surprising thing about him was that he was himself a Protestant landlord, owning some 5,000 acres in County Wicklow. This included some of the most beautiful country in Ireland. In the solid eighteenth-century house of Avondale dominating the estate, Parnell had been born and had spent his early childhood. In it his mother and father had entertained in style the grand Protestant gentry of the neighbourhood, many of whom were their relations.

But Parnell had in no way embarked on some classical revolt against his parental background. The very reverse was, in a way, the case, and this accounts at least in part for the extraordinary, single-minded personal drive which he put into his political career. For the strength of his attitudes derived partly from an earlier Protestant tradition than that of the nineteenth-century Unionist – namely, that eighteenth-century Protestant tradition of independence which had preceded the Union and at first opposed it. Parnell's own great-grandfather had been one of those to oppose it most strongly. Colours of the old Volunteer regiments still hung in the hall at Avondale in Parnell's day.

This hereditary streak of natural opposition to English government in Ireland was hardly diminished by the influence of his maternal side. His mother, who was a strong, forceful personality in any case, was an American, and Americans, then a century closer than today to their own Declaration of Independence, still carried within them a positive awareness of the lack of any special relationship with Britain. Mrs Parnell's own father had been a famous naval commander who had 'whipped the British' in the war of 1812.

There was thus in Parnell's inherited political make-up at least a pre-disposition to detachment from loyalty to British government. Given the beautiful Irish background of his home this could only be an Irish detachment. An early childhood experience possibly added to this a personal element of indignation. He was sent to boarding-school in England at the age of six and – this may have made the experience particularly traumatic – to a girls' school at which he was the only boy.

His natural resentment of this early separation from home may have helped develop that bellicosity which seemed often to rule him in youth and which he was to turn to powerful political advantage in his maturity. After nearly four years at Cambridge he was sent down before the end of the summer term for taking part in a brawl in the street for which a judge fined him £20 (about £1000 in today's money). Later the same summer he was involved in a fight in a hotel in County Wicklow, though there it was his opponent who was fined, presumably because Parnell was a close friend of the local magistrates. When he entered the House of Commons, mainly because he could think of nothing else to do, he soon made a name for himself with his awkward aggressiveness at Question Time and became one of a small group of extremists among the otherwise gentlemanly Irish members who routinely pleaded for a domestic Irish Parliament or Home Rule. One English parliamentary correspondent wrote of him in 1876:

Mr Parnell . . . combines in his person all the unlovable qualities of an Irish member with the absolute absence of their attractiveness. . . . Something really must be done about him. . . . He is always at a white heat or rage and makes with savage earnestness fancifully ridiculous statements.

Michael Davitt summed him up more succinctly when he described him with his English education and accent as 'an Englishman of the strongest sort moulded for an Irish purpose'. In October 1879, when Davitt formally founded the Land League of Ireland to carry on the campaign against the landlords, Parnell became its president.

This campaign was now being fought with increasing bitterness and violence – the violence being used not only against landlords themselves and their agents but also against those tenant farmers who disobeyed the Land League's orders, and particularly against those who took land from which another had been evicted. Officially the Land League did not approve of violence. Violence was publicly deprecated by its president, Parnell, and other members of the Irish parliamentary party at Westminster, though sometimes on an ambiguous note – Joseph Biggar, the member for Cavan, for instance, saying that the shooting of landlords was wrong because the assailant frequently missed and hit someone else.

However, the League's rank and file operators included members of the agrarian secret societies who had long been practising rough and ready methods of persuasion at a local level. Even more important, many of its top officials, as well as rank and file, were former Fenians. Accepting that the likelihood of achieving an Irish Republic by force of arms was at the moment a remote one, they lent their energies to the more practical objectives of the Land League convinced that they were thus laying the foundation for more positive Irish national thinking among the farmers and peasantry. Such men were not squeamish about the use of violence to attain objectives of any sort.

Parnell knew quite well that the top officials of the Land League were all former Fenians. He had had some clandestine contacts of his own with members of the Irish Republican Brotherhood, though he himself declined to join it. What precisely these officials may sometimes have been up to he was careful not to know, allowing the campaign itself to benefit from methods from which he was thus scrupulously able to dissociate himself. It was a dangerous game, but the sort which any skilled politician needs to be able to master, and Parnell played it masterfully off and on throughout his life. In any case he was now about to add his own dimension of bitterness to the 'Land War', as it came to be called, specifically deprecating violence while at the same time inviting people to a course of action which could be almost as unpleasantly intimidating.

'Now what,' he asked a big outdoor meeting at Ennis in 1880. 'What are you to do with a tenant who bids for a farm from which his neighbour has been evicted? Now I think I heard somebody say "Shoot him" – but I wish to point out a very much better way, a more Christian and more charitable way . . .' And he went on to outline the principle of what came to be known as the 'boycott' after the name of the land agent in County Mayo against whom it was first applied:

You must show what you think of him on the roadside when you meet him, you must show him in the streets of the town, you must show him at the shop counter . . . even in the house of worship, by leaving him severely alone, by putting him into a sort of moral Coventry, by isolating him from the rest of his kind as if he were a leper of old, you must show him your detestation of the crime he has committed.

In the House of Commons Parnell's vitality in the land war brought him to leadership of the Irish Party soon after the death of the much less aggressive figure of the lawyer Isaac Butt, who had first given the Irish members some parliamentary cohesion though little real force. Now, under Parnell, the question of the land in Ireland, the question of Ireland itself, was to be at the forefront of the British political scene. How would the British government under its prime minister of the day, William Gladstone, deal with it?

Gladstone, who in an earlier ministry had tentatively begun to introduce legislation to protect the Irish tenant farmer, had long regarded the problems of Ireland with a sympathetic eye, but was determined that, before any further change in the land system should be legislated for, law and order must be restored. He introduced a severe, so-called 'Coercion' Bill, giving special powers to the police and military and suspending some normal civil liberties. Parnell and his followers fought it bitterly in the House of Commons, forcing the House into a continuous session of forty-one hours before the Speaker had to suspend it. Parnell and thirty-five of his MPs were themselves suspended and escorted out of the House of Commons by the sergeant-at-arms.

At the same time Gladstone introduced a bill to reform the Irish land system. This put Parnell into a difficulty. As the Land League's 'war' became more and more violent Parnell found himself temporarily a prisoner of his more extreme supporters. The bill did introduce considerable reforms for the tenant farmer, but because it did not go very far towards the longer-term goal, which Parnell shared, of an eventual transfer of land to the tenants he had to show greater opposition to the bill than he felt was right. It did after all actually tell the landlord that he no longer had a right to do what he willed with his own land and set up Land Courts or rent tribunals to decide what a fair rent in given circumstances should be. It also guaranteed the tenant fixity of tenure provided he paid the rent and gave him the right to sell his holding together with any improvements he had made to it, to an incoming tenant.

The bill became law, but although Parnell knew that these were excellent long-needed reforms he could not, in the climate of the time and given the aggressive mood of his Land League followers, accept it gracefully from a British prime minister. Particularly he could not afford to antagonize those former Fenians in Ireland and America (source of much Land League money) who had entered into the Land War with ultimate nationalist aims. And he began to make increasingly belligerent speeches in Ireland in which he denounced Gladstone and the British government

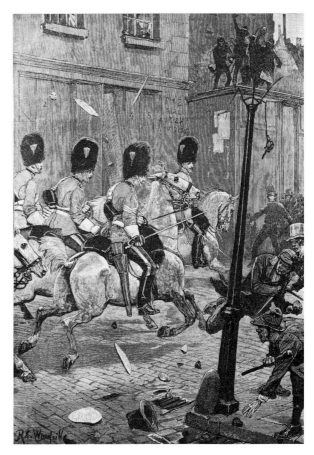

ABOVE: The shooting of landlords wrong 'because the assassin too often missed and hit someone else.'

RIGHT: Land War not only in name. Dragoons charge in the streets of Limerick, 1881.

in general terms, reminding them that behind all this lay Ireland's national aspirations.

He had already, while on a visit to America in 1880, shown recklessness in committing himself to the sort of nationalism his audience wanted to hear about. 'When we have undermined English misgovernment', he said at Cincinnati, 'we have paved the way for Ireland to take her place among the nations of the earth. And let us not forget that is the ultimate goal at which all we Irishmen aim. . . . None of us, whether we are in America or Ireland, or wherever we may be, will be satisfied until we have destroyed the last link which keeps Ireland bound to England.'

And though he was later to deny that he had used those exact words, in the late autumn of 1881 he went far enough to dismay the government when he declared at Cork that what Ireland wanted was for the Crown to be the *only* link. He had just held in Dublin, to the accompaniment of similarly provocative speeches, a great meeting with torchlight processions, said to be the largest held since the Monster Meetings of O'Connell nearly forty years before. The clash between Parnell and Gladstone was coming to a head, and in a speech at Leeds Gladstone attacked him outright for the combined militancy and ambivalence of his language:

O'Connell professed unconditional and unanswering loyalty to the Crown of England. Mr Parnell says that if the Crown is to be the link between the two countries it is to be the only link; but whether it is to be the link at all is a matter on which he has not, I believe, given any opinion whatsoever.

And looking at the state of Ireland with its boycotting which Parnell had instigated and outrages which he professed to deplore, Gladstone went on:

If there is still to be fought in Ireland a final conflict between law on one side and sheer lawlessness on the other then I say, gentlemen, without hesitation, the resources of civilization are not yet exhausted.

To which Parnell replied viciously:

It is a good thing that this masquerading knight-errant, this pretending champion of the rights of every other nation except those of the Irish nation, should be obliged to throw off the mask today, and stand revealed as the man who, by his own utterances, is prepared to carry fire and sword into your homestead, unless you humbly abase yourselves before him and before the landlords of the country.

Gladstone put the resources of civilization to the test. As a contemporary Irish ballad-maker put it:

It was the tyrant Gladstone and he said unto himself,
I never will be easy till Parnell is on the shelf,
    So make the warrant out in haste
    And take it by the mail,
    And we'll clap the pride of Erin's isle
    Into cold Kilmainham jail.

Parnell was arrested and lodged – pretty comfortably as it turned out – in Kilmainham. It was the best possible thing that could have happened to him in the circumstances. He had the best of all worlds: he was a martyr to the cause of extremism on the land, from which he wanted to withdraw in any case. At the same time he was absolved of all responsibility for the continuing violence which was increasingly out of touch with the mood of those tenant farmers in whose interest the cause was proclaimed. For the new Land Act was working well. The rents fixed by the land courts were reasonable and though there was a problem for those already in heavy arrears with rents, the return of better potato harvests meant that the crisis on the land was temporarily easing. Parnell could now turn his mind to a new wider political campaign to satisfy Irish nationalist aspirations, in particular that for an all-Ireland parliament in Dublin which was his party's ultimate objective.

There was, however, another matter to which he could turn his attention, of much more personal concern to him, though it was one which in the course of time would invade his political life and bring about the gravest crisis in the Home Rule party's political history.

In 1880 Parnell had met in London and started a passionate love affair with Katharine O'Shea, the wife of one of the Irish members of parliament. William O'Shea, a dashing but feckless character who had once been an officer in the Eighteenth Hussars, was now hoping to achieve through politics that worldly wealth and influence which had so far eluded him in bloodstock breeding and company promotion. He was on close friendly terms with his wife but they had two separate establishments and it was he who had encouraged her to make much of Parnell and even invite him to visit her in her house at Eltham. Obviously he hoped it would further his political career to be in favour with the star of the Irish Parliamentary party, though whether he expected his wife to go as far as she did is by no means clear.

In October 1880 after a number of formal, if sometimes slightly coy, letters from Parnell to her beginning 'My dear Mrs O'Shea . . .', there is a complete change of tone after they had met privately one day at Parnell's lodgings in London: 'My own love. . . . You cannot imagine how much you have occupied my thoughts all day and how very greatly the prospect of seeing you again comforts me . . .'

By the following year, at the height of the Land League crisis, and just before Parnell was arrested and sent to Kilmainham he was writing to her: 'My own Wifie – I know that you must have been worried by my failure to send you a few words, but my beauty will forgive her own husband . . .'

But Katharine O'Shea was still firmly married to Captain William O'Shea as she was to be for the next nine years. The terms 'wife' and 'husband' were simply figures of speech, a lover's metaphor, as were the words later in the same letter: 'Your King thinks very often of his dearest Queen, and wishes her not to be sad but to try to be happy for his sake.'

Yet the notion that he was the only man with whom Mrs O'Shea enjoyed sexual relations, clearly fostered by Mrs O'Shea herself, though of questionable accuracy was clearly very important to Parnell and reassuring to the impeccably moral stance which he contrived for himself in the role of adulterer. At the time he entered Kilmainham he knew that she was

LEFT ABOVE: An IRA flying column of 1920–21 (painting by Sean Keating).

LEFT BELOW: Appealing today to a successful tradition of violence: 1916 . . .

RIGHT ABOVE: Communicating with IRA prisoners, Dublin 1920 (painting by Jack Yeats).

RIGHT BELOW: Rebel leader Michael Collins. '. . . Sure – they won't shoot me in my own county . . .' (painting by Sir John Lavery).

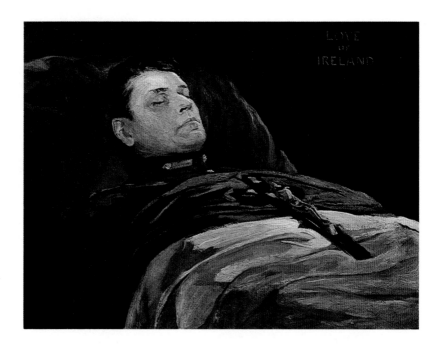

RIGHT: Orange Day parade, Belfast. Above all: the right to hold what they have.

BELOW: Posters in Nenagh, County Tipperary, '. . . to break the connection with England, the never failing source of all our political evils . . .'

pregnant by him and wrote to her from there just before Christmas: 'My own darling Queenie. . . . Nothing in the world is worth the risk of any harm or injury to you. How could I ever live without my own Katie? – and if you are in danger, my darling, I will go to you at once.'

Parnell thus had a strong personal reason for wanting to get out of jail. He also had a good political reason by that time, for the extremists' campaign on the land, which involved an attempt to get tenants to pay no rent at all, had been a failure. Tenants were taking advantage of the land courts, whose decisions on rents were proving acceptable to them. There was thus every reason for coming to some sort of agreement with Gladstone by which if he, Parnell, undertook to cool the situation in Ireland, Gladstone would look with a sympathetic eye on the remaining difficulties on the land. In particular Gladstone might begin to look sympathetically on Ireland's national aspirations for which ultimately Parnell and his party were in business.

Certain tentative oblique negotiations were carried on between Parnell and Gladstone while he was in Kilmainham, the emissaries on Parnell's side being none other than the Member of Parliament for County Clare and his wife, Mr and Mrs William O'Shea. In February 1882 Parnell was released on parole from Kilmainham officially to attend the funeral of a nephew who had died in Paris. He did go to Paris but on his way there stopped at Eltham to see his first child, a daughter, to whom Mrs O'Shea had just given birth but who died almost immediately. He was eventually released from Kilmainham in May under the tacit agreement which came to be known as the Kilmainham Treaty, though there was no written document of any sort. All seemed set fair for a course of co-operation with the Liberal Prime Minister whom Parnell hoped before long to be able to convert, together with his party, to the cause of Home Rule for all Ireland. Then, out of the blue, something happened to devastate the mood of incipient hope.

Because the Chief Secretary for Ireland, William Forster, had disapproved of Parnell's release he had resigned and a new Chief Secretary was sent to Dublin a few days after Parnell left Kilmainham. He was Lord Frederick Cavendish, a nephew of Gladstone's by marriage. One of Parnell's lieutenants, Tim Healy, said of him scornfully: 'We will tear him to pieces within a fortnight.' He spoke more truly than he realized.

At about half-past seven on the evening of his arrival in Dublin, Lord Frederick Cavendish was walking across Phoenix Park to the Vice-Regal Lodge with his Under-Secretary, a Catholic Irishman named Thomas Burke, when they were set upon by a gang of men armed with twelve-inch long surgical knives. Lord Frederick had a go at them with his umbrella but it did him no good. Both he and Burke, who was the primary target, were soon lying hacked to death in the roadway. The gang, who were caught some time later and tried and executed, were former members of the Irish Republican Brotherhood organized in a new secret society called the 'Invincibles'. They had acted with the connivance at least of high officials of the Land League of Great Britain which had shared an office at Westminster with the Parliamentary party. The surgical knives for the deed had actually been bought in Bond Street, London, and brought over to Dublin by the pregnant wife of the Land League's secretary, in her skirts.

ABOVE AND BELOW: 'Ulster will fight and Ulster will be right' (postcards of the time).

129

MURDER of LORD. F. CAVENDISH & Mr. BURKE

ESCAPE OF THE ASSASSINS

SCOVERY OF THE BODIES

ABOVE: Murder of Chief
Secretary for Ireland in
Phoenix Park, May 1882.
Disastrous for Parnell.

FAR LEFT: New personal
considerations: Katharine
O'Shea 'My own Wifie . . .'

LEFT: But her husband was the
dashing but feckless Captain
O'Shea, Irish Member of
Parliament.

The murder was disastrous for Parnell, setting back all his hopes for closer co-operation with Gladstone on the national question for a long time. In any case, mistrust among the Liberals about the exact nature of Ireland's national demand – did it, or did it not mean eventual separation? – was greatly increased by the knowledge that however moderately Parnell himself might express it, dark deeds such as the Phoenix Park murder could also be committed in its name. And after all Parnell himself had been ambiguous enough in the past.

He was to become less so when, after the necessary interval following the Phoenix Park murder had elapsed, he began to return to the theme. The General Election of 1885, fought on a new wider franchise which included the agricultural labourer, strengthened his party in the House of Commons and at the same time gave it the balance between Liberals and Conservatives. In such circumstances Gladstone eventually came round to endorsement of Home Rule, or a parliament for all Ireland with powers to legislate on Irish domestic matters only, under the overall sovereignty of Westminster. Was this really all that Parnell stood for in the way of a national demand?

He was far too instinctive a politician to commit himself permanently to an inflexible approach on a matter of principle. 'They will do what we can make them do,' he once said of British government and that sums up his basic political maxim. In explicitly Irish nationalist terms his view is best expressed by a quotation from his speech at Cork in 1885 which is today engraved on his statue in Dublin:

No man has a right to fix the boundary to the march of a nation. No man has a right to say to his country: thus far shalt thou go and no further. We have never attempted to fix the *ne plus ultra* to the progress of Ireland's nationhood and we never shall.

Or, as he put it more gently, also at Cork:

I do not pretend to predict in what way the rights of Ireland will be ultimately gained . . . but a man in my position ought to consider that in anything that he does, or in anything that he says, he ought not to hamper the people in their march for their liberties . . . although our programme may be limited and small, it should be such a one as shall not prevent hereafter the fullest realization of the hopes of Ireland.

And yet none of this detracted from the impression of sincerity that he gave in his speech in the House of Commons on the Home Rule Bill in 1886, with its limited domestic freedom for Ireland when he said: 'We look upon the provisions of this bill as a final settlement of the Irish question and I believe that the Irish people have accepted it as a settlement.' He added with accuracy: 'Not a single dissentient voice has been raised against the bill by any Irishman holding national opinions.'

The bill was opposed in the House by a significant section of the Liberal party and also, of course, by the Conservatives. But the strongest opposition came from outside Parliament altogether, from the Protestants of Northern Ireland, where drilling had been taking place. (In the House of Commons the Conservatives were, in the words of Lord Randolph Churchill, simply 'playing the Orange card'.) This external opposition was not so menacing as it was to become a generation later because at this stage in Parliamentary history the House of Lords still had a veto on all legislation and everyone knew that there was no question of a Home Rule Bill getting through the House of Lords. Yet Gladstone went out of his way to reply to the Ulster opposition in terms which sound almost provocative in the context of a modern British government's utterances on the subject almost a century later:

I think the best compliment I can pay to those who have threatened us is to take no notice of the threats, to treat them as momentary ebullitions which will pass away with the fears from which they spring. I cannot conceal the conviction that the voice of Ireland is constitutionally spoken. I cannot say it is otherwise when five-sixths of its lawfully chosen representatives are of one mind on this matter. . . . I cannot allow it to be said that a Protestant minority in Ulster, or elsewhere, is to rule the question at large for Ireland. I am aware of no constitutional doctrine tolerable on which such a conclusion could be adopted or justified . . .

Parnell himself went out of his way to be placatory to Ulster:

We cannot give up a single Irishman. . . . The class of Protestants will form a most valuable element in the Irish legislature of the future, constituting, as they will, a strong minority, and exercizing a moderating influence in making laws. . . . The best system of government should be the resultant of what forces are in that country. . . . We want all creeds and classes in Ireland.

Though the Home Rule Bill of 1886 was lost in the House of Commons as a result of the Liberal defection, the defeat was not as depressing to Irishmen as, looking back today from a much more highly developed Irish nationalism, one might expect. Indeed, the fact that a Home Rule Bill had been sponsored by a British government at all and was now inscribed, nominally at least, on the banner of one of the two main British political parties seemed a triumph. Parnell now bided his time until political fortune should once again give the Irish party the balance between Liberals and Conservatives in the House of Commons. Meanwhile other more personal considerations dominated his life.

His liaison with Katharine O'Shea had indeed by now cemented itself into a sort of marriage. The only trouble with this 'marriage' was that Mrs O'Shea was legally married to someone else and from 1886 onwards, the date of the rejection of the Home Rule Bill, her legal husband – however much he may or may not have condoned the liaison earlier – was making more and more strenuous efforts to persuade her to give it up. As a result, in order to be able to be together as much as they wanted, Parnell and Mrs O'Shea had to have recourse to a number of standard devices appropriate to their situation. They lived from time to time together at Eltham but also took a number of rented houses together on the south coast and elsewhere, Parnell sometimes giving his name as Fox and sometimes as Preston.

But if O'Shea objected to the liaison why did he not take the standard action and sue for divorce? The answer is related to O'Shea's permanent need for money. Mrs O'Shea had a very rich, very old aunt whose favourite she was, a Mrs Benjamin Wood. 'Aunt Ben' was ninety-three in 1886 and was expected to leave Mrs O'Shea her fortune when she died. This, in the course of nature, could not be long and O'Shea was prepared to wait and get his share of the money rather than risk losing it by scandalizing the old lady with a divorce suit. Aunt Ben did not die until 1889 and O'Shea soon afterwards brought his action for divorce. He did so at a moment when Parnell's political reputation stood higher than ever, not only in Ireland but also in England.

Two years earlier *The Times* had published a sensational letter apparently signed by Parnell in 1882 and addressed to someone closely in touch with the Phoenix Park murderers of Lord Frederick Cavendish and the Under-Secretary for Ireland, Thomas Burke. The letter ran as follows:

Dear Sir,

I am not surprised at your friend's anger but he and you should know that to denounce the murders was the only course open to us. . . . But you can tell him and all others concerned that though I regret the accident of Lord F. Cavendish's death I cannot refuse to admit that Burke got no more than his deserts.

You are at liberty to show him this and others whom you can trust but let not my address be known. He can write to the House of Commons.

Yours very truly,
Chas S. Parnell

No-one maintained that the body of the letter was in Parnell's handwriting – it was normal for a secretary to provide this before the days of typewriters – but the signature appeared to be his.

That same night he told a colleague in the House of Commons that he had not written an 'S' like that since 1878 and denounced the latter in the Chamber as 'a villainous and bare-faced forgery'.

Some time later *The Times* produced another letter allegedly written by Parnell in 1882 which looked like evidence of actual instigation of the Phoenix Park murder. This ran:

What are these people waiting for? This inaction is inexcuseable. Our best men are in prison and nothing is being done. Let there be an end to this hesitency. Prompt action is called for. You promised to make it hot for old Forster and Co. Let us have evidence of your power to do so . . .

Yours very truly,
Chas S. Parnell

It contained curious spelling mistakes in the words 'inexcuseable' and 'hesitency' and the style had a racy touch which few would have associated with Parnell. Eventually a Special Commission was appointed by Parliament to look into the question of these letters and the general activities of the Land League during that period, and Parnell was overwhelmingly cleared at least over the letters when a hard-up nationalist journalist named Richard Pigott confessed to having forged them. He had been trapped in court by Parnell's counsel into writing down the word 'hesitancy' with an 'e' instead of an 'a'.

Parnell received a standing ovation when he next entered the House of

Commons and overnight won great sympathy from British public opinion as a much maligned man of essential decency and repute. The O'Shea divorce case put an end to all that.

Although Mrs O'Shea put in a defence that O'Shea had condoned the relationship and a counter-charge of her husband's adultery with her sister, neither she nor Parnell appeared in court, apparently in the belief that long before it ended they would be able to buy the impecunious O'Shea off with part of that fortune which Katharine had by now duly inherited from Aunt Ben. But the family disputed the will and the £20,000 O'Shea seems to have wanted was not yet available. Since neither Parnell nor Katharine appeared in court, the case – which in those days was heard in front of a judge and jury – became an opportunity for the plaintiff husband and his witnesses to make all manner of embarrassing charges which could not be challenged.

Evidence of Parnell and Mrs O'Shea's intimacies and subterfuges over the years quickly made them the laughing-stock of the Press and the butt of the music-halls. Perhaps the most damaging piece of evidence of all was the unsubstantiated story of a maid at the O'Sheas' rented house at Medina Terrace, Brighton. She described how one day Parnell and Mrs O'Shea had been closeted in an upstairs room when Captain O'Shea himself arrived at his own house. Parnell, she said, quickly nipped out of the window onto a balcony and down the fire-escape to reappear with a ring at the bell some time later as if he had only just that moment arrived. O'Shea was granted his divorce.

The effect of this sort of thing on Catholic Ireland and, just as important, on that nonconformist opinion in England which was the backbone of the Liberal Party's support, was devastating. The immediate question was whether or not Parnell should remain leader of the Irish Party. Characteristically he never for a moment seems to have doubted that he should. But there were those in his party who thought it would be disastrous while Gladstone added force to their argument by declaring that if Parnell were to remain leader he, Gladstone, could not answer for the effectiveness of his own leadership of the Liberals.

In the end, in December 1890, a stormy and traumatic meeting of the Irish members of parliament took place on the subject in Committee Room 15 of the House of Commons, the climax to which went as follows:

One member was arguing that if the party rejected Parnell it would in effect be placing itself under Gladstone's leadership. Someone called out: 'Gladstone is not a member of the Irish party!'

To which someone else replied: 'He is the master of the party!'

Whereupon Tim Healy, the member for South Londonderry who had known of the liaison with Mrs O'Shea for some years and had often resented Parnell's aloof and autocratic conduct of the leadership called out viciously: 'Who is to be mistress of the party ?'

There was uproar. Parnell rose white-faced and furious, looking as if he were about to hit someone. A voice cried: 'I appeal to my friend the Chairman!'

At which Parnell, glaring at Healy shouted: 'Better appeal to that cowardly little scoundrel who dares in an assembly of Irishmen to insult a woman!'

The meeting voted by 45 votes to 29 to depose Parnell. The party, in the House of Commons and in Ireland too, split into Parnellites and anti-Parnellites. The national issue of Home Rule fell back into second place before the all-important question of whether, in a country where the influence of the Catholic Church was so powerful, an adulterer could be allowed to lead the nation's party. And the fact that he subsequently married Mrs O'Shea made him no less an adulterer.

Now began the fiercest and most tragic struggle of Parnell's life, as he fought in Ireland a losing battle against that Church's power. It drove him to desperate methods as, in a succession of bye-elections, he tried to force the issue away from his own fitness to lead. Was the Irish party really to be dictated to by an English statesman, Gladstone? He suddenly produced unsubstantiated 'evidence', which he had never mentioned before, that in his last private meeting with Gladstone before the divorce Gladstone had tried to get him to agree to a watering-down of Home Rule next time the Liberals put it forward. And he turned, in his desperation, more and more to his old doubtful allies of the Land League days, the Fenians or 'hillside men', who could be relied on to see nationalism as a more important abstract cause than morality. The year before he had been 'the Uncrowned King of Ireland'. Now he lost three bye-elections in a row, at one of which lime was thrown in his eyes.

His health deteriorated. Physically it was an exhausting time. He had married Katharine after the divorce and was living with her in a house at Walsingham Terrace, Hove, which he left every weekend to make the laborious journey to Ireland via Euston station in London and Holyhead before speaking at bye-election meetings and returning to Hove to come back to Ireland again the next weekend. On Sunday, 27 September 1891 he spoke at a meeting in County Galway, bareheaded and with one arm, crippled by rheumatism, in a sling. The change of clothes which Katharine had packed for him was somehow mislaid and he sat about for several hours in his wet suit. He then went to Dublin where he spent a few days before leaving for England on 30 September, saying he would be back on 'Saturday week'. He was a few hours out in his forecast. He died of a heart attack at Hove with his wife by his side on 6 October, and his body was brought into Kingstown Harbour on Sunday morning, 11 October and buried in Glasnevin cemetery.

It is possible to see now that any hopes for Home Rule as 'a final settlement' of Ireland's national aspirations were buried with him.

'Men to be reckoned with' (*The Times*). Ulster Unionists will not
have the Second Home Rule Bill, 1892.

Chapter 8

We Will Not Have Home Rule!

It had only been after the General Election of 1885, when the Prime Minister, Gladstone, found his Liberal Party dependent in the House of Commons on the support of the eighty-six-strong Irish Nationalist Party, that he had finally decided to introduce a Home Rule Bill. Lord Randolph Churchill, a Conservative, father of Winston Churchill, soon afterwards made a famous private remark that was to achieve public fame. Looking around for a new effective identity for his own party, he decided that the best hopes lay in outright opposition to Home Rule, declaring judiciously: 'The Orange card is the one to play'. By this he meant that the best way of opposing Home Rule was to use the energies of the Protestant Orange Order Lodges in the North of Ireland with their traditional fears of the Catholic majority in Ireland. He added that he hoped the card would prove to be the ace of trumps and not the two.

Both Liberal and Conservative positions reveal an habitual aspect of English policy towards Ireland which Irish nationalists have never been slow to point out: namely, that it was primarily in the interests of English politics rather than those of the Irish people that Westminster was prepared to concern itself with Ireland. In this instance though, politicians at Westminster were embarking on a course which was to endanger the entire constitutional structure of the United Kingdom and bring it closer to Civil War than at any time since the days of Charles I.

The original Orange Society, founded in 1795 and taking its name from that Protestant king, William of Orange (William III), who had rescued Irish Protestants from the 'tyranny' of the Catholic king, James II, had been simply a reorganization with Masonic overtones of an agrarian and working-class secret society called the 'Peep O'Day Boys'. This was so named because it was much given to terrorizing Catholics out of their homes at dawn, 'papering' their doors with notices saying 'To Hell – or Connaught', an injunction to remove themselves south and west which they were inclined to obey when they saw the barbarous punishments, such as knee-capping, inflicted on those who did not.

At the time of the United Irishmen and their attempt at rebellion in the years 1797–8 – a confusing time because it was a group of Presbyterian radicals who originated the idea of bringing Protestant and Catholic Irishmen together in one national denomination – the authorities, while disapproving of the Orangemen's wilder excesses, had also seen the advantages of exploiting sectarian prejudices to the full. One magistrate of the time had almost pre-echoed Lord Randolph Churchill when he spoke of the Orangemen as 'a rather difficult card to play'.

This ambivalent attitude of respectable opinion in Ireland towards the Orangemen persisted for much of the nineteenth century. In the 1830s the Society was actually officially banned after a conspiracy in which it had become part of a British political design to put the Duke of Cambridge on the throne in place of William IV. But it had been reconstituted under the respectable leadership of the earl of Enniskillen in the next decade when the success of O'Connell's campaign for Repeal of the Union seemed to threaten the established order of Irish society. The Orangemen's official constitution spoke in unexceptionable terms of brotherly love, toleration and loyalty to the Crown, but as a Royal Commission looking into it after sectarian riots in Belfast in the 1850s commented, in spite of this: '. . . the uneducated and unrefined, who act from feeling and impulse, and not from reflection, cannot be expected to restrain the passions excited by the lessons of their own dominancy and superiority over their fellow subjects whom they look upon as conquered foes.'

Divisions within Ulster Unionism had been exposed clearly at the time of the disestablishment of the Protestant Church in 1868 – Gladstone's first optimistic attempt finally to solve the Irish problem. 'We will fight,' declared one Presbyterian Minister, 'as men alone can fight who have the Bible in one hand and the sword in the other . . . and this will be our dying cry, echoed and re-echoed from earth to heaven and from one end of Ulster to the other – "No Popery, no Surrender!"' But a highly respectable Protestant Defence Association spoke only of the entitlement of people of social position and wealth in Ireland to consideration and protection of their interests in all legislation affecting their property and religion; and it went out of its way to dissociate itself from the provocative activities of Orange Lodge members. Nevertheless it was in the Orange Lodges that the vitality of any movement concerned to defend Protestant interests in Ulster lay. When the Grand Master of County Down was sentenced to a month's imprisonment for marching with twenty thousand Protestants with drums beating and orange flags flying in defiance of the Party Processions Act of the time, and respectable opinion widely deplored his action, special trains of working people were run to Belfast to celebrate his release.

A crude Marxist interpretation of Northern Ireland today would define the fears and prejudices of working-class Protestants there as the product of indoctrination and exploitation by landed and capitalist interests. Any truly scientific study of the history of the last two hundred years in Ulster shows that this has not been the case. It is true that the landed and capitalist classes made use of those crude Protestant prejudices that existed, but the prejudices existed on their own account. Complaints by the working classes against the landed and capitalist classes have been not generally to the effect that their prejudices were exploited but that they were not sufficiently indulged. This attitude was to reach its climax in the Ulster Workers' Strike of 1974.

There was however to be little discrepancy in mood between the two wings of Ulster Unionism during the period of opposition to Home Rule which began in the 1880s. An intensifying harmony of spirit reached its

OPPOSITE: Prime Minister Gladstone applying his mind to Ireland, 1886.

own climax on the eve of the First World War. Upper- and middle-class Irish Protestants, together with the English Conservative Party, played the Orange Card with a vengeance. And it proved to be the ace of trumps and not the two.

Even before the Home Rule Bill of 1886 had been introduced there were threats of civil war from Ulster. A Loyal and Patriotic Union was formed and advertisements began to appear in newspapers asking for rifles and for men to instruct in military drill. There were reports of drilling with and without arms. 'Ulster,' cried Lord Randolph Churchill, 'Will Fight, and Ulster will be right.' Ulster did not have to fight, but when the Home Rule Bill was defeated in the House of Commons there were celebratory riots in the streets of Belfast in which people were killed.

Soon afterwards the Liberals went out of power for six years, but when they came back again in 1892 their majority was plainly sufficient, this time, for them to carry a Home Rule Bill through the House of Commons. Preparations in Ulster to prevent Home Rule were more thorough. A vast Ulster Unionist Convention had already been held in the Botanical Gardens in Belfast in the summer. The 12,000 delegates – of whom a third were tenant farmers and the remainder business men – assembled in a specially constructed pavilion on the walls of which hung the slogan: 'If necessary we must shed blood to maintain the strength and salvation of the country.' And after a resolution to take no part in the election to, or the proceedings of, any Dublin parliament, the Chairman, the Duke of Abercorn, declared in ringing tones, with upraised arm: 'We Will Not Have Home Rule!' Another speaker, who was cheered to the echo, cried: 'In the last resort we will be prepared to defend ourselves.' The correspondent from *The Times* decided that 'These were men to be reckoned with.'

Nor did the Ulster Unionists and their supporters mince words in Parliament. In the House of Lords the Marquess of Londonderry said that they would be justified in shedding blood to resist the disloyal Catholic yoke, while in the Commons, Colonel Saunderson, who had joined the Orange Order early in the 1880s to organize military style opposition to the first Home Rule Bill, said that before the government could count on the army to shoot down Irish Loyalists in an attempt to force obedience to Home Rule they must have a British majority behind them. He meant one that did not rely on the Irish content in that majority.

It was at this time that it became fashionable for Irish nationalists and their Liberal supporters to dismiss such utterances as bluff. That there was, in 1892 and 1893, a considerable amount of bluff involved is undeniable. Everyone knew that even if the Home Rule Bill passed its third reading in the House of Commons, as it did, the House of Lords still had the power to veto it, which they did. But this defiant tone set the pattern for Ulster thought and action should that veto ever be removed and the danger of Home Rule become real. This was not to happen for another seventeen years.

A popularizing history may perhaps use its licence for crude hindsight to look at a gap of seventeen years like this as if it had seemed a gap at the time. Certainly it is useful to do so because while the greatest British constitutional crisis of modern times was waiting in the wings, things were happening in southern Ireland which, though in themselves unrelated to attitudes in the North, were in their effect to help add to the gravity of that crisis.

As with the famous Sherlock Holmes case involving the significant dog in the night, the significance of which was that it did not bark, so with this period of seventeen years in southern Ireland: politically not much happened. The Irish Nationalist Party simply spent the years preparing to bid again for Home Rule next time the English parties should be so finely balanced as to enable it to call the tune with the Liberals. But such a situation was not to arise until 1910. The party slipped into squalid political doldrums in which its will and energies were perhaps permanently damaged by continued quarrelling between the two sections that emerged from the Parnell 'split'. The nationalist goal became obscured by discussion of the personal merits of the two sets of politicians involved. And the ghost of poor Parnell himself was allowed small rest.

In a sermon in the early 1890s at a church near Parnell's old home of Avondale a priest had said:

Parnellism is a simple love of adultery and all those who profess Parnellism profess to love and admire adultery. They are an adulterous set, their leaders are open and avowed adulterers, and therefore I say to you, as parish priest, beware of these Parnellites when they enter your house, you that have wives and daughters, for they will do all they can to commit these adulteries, for their cause is not patriotism – it is adultery . . .

The disgust which many nationalists felt about this sort of comment, and the low level to which it reduced nationalist politics turned their minds to other aspects of Irishness altogether, principally the ancient origins of Irish identity: the fast dying Irish language, and Gaelic legend and folktales. A 'Gaelic League', founded in 1893, specifically dissociated itself from politics while at the same time it waged a war against what one of its founders called 'this awful idea of complete Anglicization'. Not only was the Irish language to be learned and encouraged, but Irish clothes, Irish dances, Irish poetry and song, every cultural detail that could be found to distinguish Irishness from Englishness was to be sought out and made the inspiration of the Irish people. A 'Gaelic Athletic Association', founded earlier, was doing the same thing for Irish games. An Irish literary movement, using the English language but Irish literary traditions, eagerly embraced by the poet and dramatist Yeats, concerned itself with the heroes of ancient Gaelic legend – a remote but more ennobling mythology than anything the Parliamentary National Party was in a position to offer.

Largely middle class and lower middle class in its appeal, this wide Irish-Ireland movement even made available an Irish as opposed to an English snobbishness. It opened new avenues of self-respect to those who had been hitherto only able to demonstrate narrow social superiority by aping an ascendency which took its standards from London. It became possible to feel equal to that ascendency by being different, by the assertion of an Irish difference. Non-political as the movement declared itself to be, there was an obvious political potential in all this. And there was a small minority of extreme political nationalists who took an active part in the movement who were fully aware that this potential might one day become available for their own ends. Among such was a poet and schoolmaster Patrick Pearse who was to found a school, St Enda's, Rathfarnham, near Dublin, where the young were to be indoctrinated with the Irish-Ireland spirit. Along with a romantic consciousness of the disappointments of Irish history, it was to lead many of them including their headmaster into eventual membership of the Irish Republican Brotherhood. This latter clandestine organization, after years of moribund torpor, was revived in the first decade of the twentieth century by a new generation of young men encouraged by an old Fenian named Tom Clarke, who having served fifteen years in British jails, operated after 1907 in the shadows of Irish political life from his tobacconist shop in the centre of Dublin.

A more open attempt to combine the new mood of Irish social and cultural consciousness with political impetus was made by a young journalist, Arthur Griffith, who through two successive newspapers, *The United Irishman* and *Sinn Fein* (Ourselves Alone), tried to interest the Irish people in a scheme by which duly elected Irish Members of Parliament should not go to Westminster but meet as an Irish Parliament in Dublin and there form a government and administration which, while sharing a joint Crown with Britain, would otherwise be independent of her. The idea was not new; it had first been proposed in the 1840s by the Young Ireland movement. In Griffith's presentation it was based on two rather precarious analogies: the action of Hungarian nationalists in withdrawing from the Viennese Parliament though not from the Austro-Hungarian Empire, and the Protestant Irish 'Patriots' of the eighteenth century who had won for their parliament a sort of independence under a joint Crown. Though such ingenuity of thought did interest some of those already pursuing alternative roads to Irish identity through the Irish-Ireland movement, it commanded no wide support among the Irish population as a whole, and the political organization which Griffith eventually formed, called Sinn Fein, lost the only bye-election in which, before the First World War, it challenged the hold of the Parliamentary party on Irish political life.

The truth was that the party was able to keep its routine hold in these years of hiatus because, quite aside from the national question, Parliament had been completing a great social revolution on the land, begun by Gladstone's Land Acts. By a series of so-called Land Purchase Acts the Irish tenant was being enabled to become the owner of the land he farmed. 'Land Purchase' meant that the State bought out the landlords, advancing mortgages to the former tenants over a long period, to be paid off by annual instalments which with interest usually amounted to less than the previous rent. As a result of two further great Land Purchase Acts in 1903 and 1909, the latter of which introduced the principle of compulsory sale by landlords, eleven million acres had, by 1920, changed hands and the sale of a further two million acres was being negotiated – by far the greater part of the land of Ireland. In such circumstances the failure to make progress on the national question could seem temporarily of secondary importance.

Only in the towns and particularly Dublin was there serious discontent and this took an industrial rather than a political form. The slums of Dublin were the worst in Europe and the wages of those who lived there were extremely low. Just before the First World War the city witnessed the first major self-assertion of protest by the Irish working class. The Irish

On the perimeter in the South: Jim Larkin, socialism and the Citizen Army.

Arthur Griffith, economic conservatism, non-violent nationalism and *Sinn Fein*.

Transport Union, a movement which had been organized in the first decade of the century by James Larkin, a Liverpool Irishman, and James Connolly, an Edinburgh Irishman, took on, in the summer of 1913, the owner of the Dublin tramways in a confrontation which turned to strike, lock-out, and six months of even more intense hardship for the Dublin poor. It ended in a return to work without any gains for the workers, except that the employer, Walter J. Murphy, had failed to break the Union.

This labour struggle, though not directly related to any nationalist demand, was in the end to have an influence on the Dublin working classes' approach to nationalism – much as the Irish-Ireland movement was indirectly to influence the approach to nationalism of other classes. Not only were the owners of some of the worst slum properties orthodox supporters of the Parliamentary Nationalist Party, but Murphy himself was a pillar of the Home Rule movement. The inference had to be that if the opponents of the workers were wedded to a nationalism that accepted Home Rule as adequate, then that nationalism must be inadequate for the workers.

Larkin and Connolly had already formed an armed and uniformed workers' Irish Citizen Army for self-defence. And bitterness at defeat on their own ground began to turn to bitterness against the Parliamentary party as, in the new situation in which the Home Rule movement found itself as a result of two General Elections in 1910, the party showed itself ready to accept compromise on the full Home Rule nationalist demand. For the Conservatives, in opposing the Liberal government of Asquith, had been playing the Orange card with a vengeance.

The results of the two elections in 1910 were almost identical: the Liberals and Conservatives were equally balanced and the eighty-two Irish Nationalist members held that balance. In one sense the Irish were in a stronger position than they had ever been before. Not only was their support indispensable to the Liberals but also, because one of the main issues on which the elections had been fought was the abolition of the veto of the House of Lords, the first major legislation of the Liberal government duly abolished that veto with the Parliament Act of 1911. The way was clear for a Home Rule Bill to pass through Parliament and become law. This very strength of the Home Rule position, however, meant that Northern Protestant resistance to Home Rule would also be stronger than ever before; and so it proved to be.

Against such a day as this an Ulster Unionist Council had been formed as long ago as 1905 and it had now acquired a formidable leader in the Irish Protestant barrister and senior Member of Parliament for Dublin University, Sir Edward Carson. On the passing of the Parliament Act in 1911 he had written from London to the most active member of that council, a self-made whiskey millionaire named James Craig, that before assuming full leadership of the new movement to oppose Home Rule he wanted to satisfy himself that 'the people over there really mean to resist. I am not for a game of mere bluff.' In September 1911, even before the Home Rule Bill had been introduced, Craig organized for Carson a vast demonstration of some 50,000 Orangemen and Unionists at his own home, Craigavon, near Belfast. Carson addressed them, telling them that 'with the help of God you and I joined together . . . will yet defeat the most nefarious conspiracy that has ever been hatched against a free people.' If the Home Rule Bill were to pass, he said, they must be prepared the same morning to become the government of the Protestant province of Ulster.

Drilling began and two days before the bill was introduced in the House of Commons in April 1912 an even larger demonstration was held at Balmoral, a suburb of Belfast, at which 100,000 men marched past a saluting base while what was said to be the largest Union Jack ever made was unfurled in an only moderate breeze from a ninety-foot flagstaff in the grounds. On that saluting base stood the leader of the English Conservative Party, Bonar Law, who pledged that 'There will not be wanting help from across the Channel when the hour of battle comes.' Later in 1912 at a great Unionist meeting at Blenheim in England he proclaimed: 'There are things stronger than parliamentary majorities . . . I can imagine no length of resistance to which Ulster will go, in which I shall not support them.' The Ulster Unionist Council could be in no doubt that the English Conservatives, who at the last election had had as much support in the country as the Liberals, were right behind them.

The third Home Rule Bill, like its two predecessors, was a fairly modest business, setting up an all-Ireland Parliament with an executive responsible to it for most domestic matters but excluding from it all matters affecting the Crown, peace and war, the army, navy, international treaties, the imposition of most taxation in the first instance and even, for a period of six years, control of the Royal Irish Constabulary. The final absolute supremacy of the Westminster Parliament over that in Dublin on all matters was affirmed. Nevertheless the passage of the Bill's third reading through the House of Commons in January 1913 was hailed in Ireland as a great national triumph with much blazing of bonfires and tar barrels and the singing of 'A Nation Once Again'.

Ulster's determination had already hardened in advance. Drilling of men parading with wooden rifles to the sound of fife and drum was taking place all over the province. On the 28 September 1913 over a series of days nearly a quarter of a million Ulstermen signed a 'Solemn League and Covenant' to resist Home Rule at a Union-Jack-covered table in the Belfast Town Hall, many signing in their own blood. Nearly a quarter of a million women signed a parallel declaration supporting them. Perhaps the surest indication that they really meant business was a preparedness to accept that they could no longer block Home Rule for the greater part of Ireland but that they must concentrate on obtaining exclusion for Ulster.

While demanding in the House of Commons that all nine counties of Ulster should be excluded from the Home Rule Bill's operation, Carson had already in fact revealed his minimum demand: the exclusion of the six counties of Derry, Antrim, Down, Tyrone, Fermanagh and Armagh. And this apparent attitude of compromise was a further effective weapon in undermining the Liberal government's will to force the full measure through. At the same time the Northern Protestants were taking no chances, and as the Irish Home Rule Bill went through the House of Lords unamended, the Ulster Unionist Council organized an Ulster Volunteer Force of 100,000 men through the local Orange Lodges. This still only had dummy rifles in the main, though some real ones purchased by wealthy members of the movement were already appearing. The most sinister feature of all about the new body was that command of it was taken by a recently retired English General of the Indian Army, Sir George Richardson. His appointment had been arranged by Field Marshal Lord Roberts. There seemed little doubt on whose side the English Establishment stood. When Richardson held a review of 10,000 of his men at Balmoral in September the brilliant young English Conservative lawyer, F. E. Smith, acted as his 'galloper' on the parade ground.

In the face of all this the Liberal nerve was showing signs of failing. Asquith was preparing to look at the exclusion of at least some of the Ulster counties from the bill as an acceptable compromise. It was time for the Irish Nationalist Party under the leadership of John Redmond to become alarmed. Secret meetings had been taking place between Asquith and Bonar Law. Redmond declared: 'Irish nationalists can never be assenting parties to the mutilation of the Irish nation; Ireland is a unit. . . . The two nation theory is to us an abomination and a blasphemy.'

But it was too late. Suddenly the party's apparently strong position was seen to be built on sand. For although the Liberals had needed Irish parliamentary support to form a government and had paid the price for it with a Home Rule Bill, if the Irish now withdrew that support because they did not like what was being done to the bill they would be no better off, for the Liberals and Conservatives were moving towards agreement over the exclusion of Ulster. The Irish were being squeezed out.

It was in this situation that Home Rulers in the south of Ireland, without waiting for further leadership from Redmond, were soon flocking to join a new body dedicated to the defence of the full Home Rule measure and acting as a counter-balance to the Ulster Volunteer Force. This was known as the Irish Volunteers. The initiative for its formation had in fact come from a small group of republican extremists of the revived Irish Republican Brotherhood who saw in the Volunteers a useful front organization which could one day be manipulated for their own ends. But the great majority of the rank and file who joined it were faithful if apprehensive followers of Redmond determined to insist that the British government should keep its word and pass the Home Rule Bill through Parliament unamended. Redmond himself was caught by surprise by the strength of feeling and only assumed official control of the movement in June 1914, to the dismay of those extremists who hoped to keep control of it for their own more revolutionary purposes.

By this time, however, the organization of the Ulster Volunteer Force in the North was formidable indeed and far superior to that of the Irish Volunteers in the South. Above all the Ulster Volunteer Force were better armed, as the result of a brilliant feat of gun-running executed with all the skill of professional staff work when some 24,000 rifles and 3,000,000 rounds of ammunition were landed at the northern ports of Larne and Bangor on the 25 April 1914. Police and military had been physically prevented from interfering and the arms were successfully distributed throughout Ulster bringing the total number of rifles available there to more than 40,000. An 'Ulster Provisional Government' was formed, ready to take over the administration of the province at a moment's notice.

By this time too a drama had been played out within the British army in Ireland which revealed all too clearly just how dangerous the whole crisis

Ulster Gun Running. "Bravo Ulster."
The mystery Ship "Fanny" unloading at Larne Harbour.
Alongside are the Motor Vessel and "Roma" receiving their cargoes
for Bangor and Donaghadee.

ABOVE: Gun-running. Arms for the Ulster Volunteers: 24,000 rifles, 3,000,000 rounds of ammunition.

LEFT: Arms for southern Irish Volunteers: 1,500 rifles and 40,000 rounds of ammunition.

had now become for the constitutional structure of the United Kingdom. Confronted by the obvious effectiveness of the Ulster Volunteer Force, the Government had to ask itself whether or not it was prepared to use force to insist on acceptance of an Act of Parliament. Subsidiary to this question, and almost unasked, so frightening were its implications, was the question whether or not the army in Ireland would obey Government orders to 'coerce' Ulster. There was the awkward fact that the Director of Military Operations at the War Office, Sir Henry Wilson, an Irishman whose family had been in Ireland for two hundred years, was passionately opposed to every form of Irish nationalism and was actively intriguing both with the Conservative opposition and the leaders of the Ulster Volunteer Force to prevent any attempt by the Government to use the army to enforce a Home Rule law.

The commander-in-chief of the British army in Ireland, Sir Arthur Paget, had already been to London to ask what he was to do if his officers should refuse to obey orders to move against the Ulster Volunteer Force. It would have been an odd question for any self-respecting professional officer to ask in normal times but the times were not normal. The reply he got made this clear enough. For he was told that should the eventuality arise in which the army had to move against Ulster those officers who lived in Ulster could be allowed to 'disappear'; any other who refused to accept orders would be dismissed.

On his return to Ireland Paget most foolishly asked those officers not domiciled in Ulster outright whether, if asked to move against Ulster, they would obey orders or choose to be dismissed. Sixty of the officers of the Cavalry Brigade at the Curragh camp, including its commanding officer, Sir Hubert Gough, replied that they would prefer to be dismissed. This is the event popularly known as the Curragh Mutiny.

Clearly there was technically no mutiny. After this there was no need for one. Few governments and particularly not one run by a man so given to playing things by ear as Asquith would have forced the issue in the circumstances. To make matters worse the commander-in-chief at Aldershot, General Douglas Haig, made a point of coming up to London to tell the Prime Minister that his own officers strongly supported Gough. Gough himself, who had been summoned to London, was actually able to return to Ireland carrying a written reassurance from the Chief of the Imperial General Staff to the effect that the troops under his command would not be called upon to enforce the Home Rule Bill on Ulster and that he could tell his officers so.

The effect of all this on moderate Home Rulers who had hitherto been satisfied with the moderation of Home Rule as fulfilment of Irish national aspirations can well be imagined. They had no alternative but to remain loyal to Redmond, but Redmond's position had been immeasurably weakened. Two questions were now out in the open. The first was: what was the precise compromise over exclusion of some counties of Ulster that Redmond would have to accept? The second: would his supporters accept it?

In May 1914 a secret undertaking on behalf of the Irish Volunteers had been set in motion very largely thanks to the efforts of two unusual figures, Roger Casement, a Protestant from the Glens of Antrim who had been knighted for his work as a British Consular official, and Erskine Childers, a British civil servant, son of an English father and an Irish mother, who had enthusiastically embraced the Home Rule cause. The undertaking was to secure arms for the Volunteers who were still restricted to wooden rifles or such real ones as could be purchased by individuals. While the arms and ammunition were being purchased from Germany and preparations being made for their landing by private yacht in Ireland, the final negotiating positions of the two parties, which Asquith was trying to bring to agree on an amended Home Rule Bill, crystallized.

Redmond's position up to the last moment – and one in which he was reluctantly backed by his supporters – was that he was prepared to offer any Ulster county the right to opt out of a Dublin Parliament for six years, after which time, unless the Imperial government intervened, it would automatically come under Dublin. At the last moment he made the further concession of dropping the six-year limit thus leaving the duration of any Ulster county's exclusion imprecise. Under these arrangements four of the nine Ulster counties, Down, Derry, Antrim and Armagh, would for certain have opted out, remaining outside Home Rule.

The final position of Carson and the Conservatives was a demand for the permanent exclusion of Down, Derry, Antrim, and Tyrone, together with north Fermanagh and north and mid Armagh. It is worth noting in passing that if Redmond could have accepted this it would have amounted to a better 'partition' deal than that for which more violent and extreme men who superseded him as Ireland's national leaders were eventually to settle. But to Home Rulers at the time even this concession of permanent exclusion of the substantial nationalist population in Tyrone or indeed the permanent exclusion of any Ulster county was unthinkable and unacceptable.

On the 26 July the arms which Casement and Childers had procured from Germany and which Childers had brought skilfully across the North Sea in his yacht, the *Asgard*, were landed at Howth near Dublin into the arms of Volunteers and boys of the Fianna, the youth movement of the Irish Citizen Army. On their way into Dublin an attempt to disarm them was made by the police supported by about a hundred men of the King's Own Scottish Borderers regiment. The attempt was a failure thanks to the Volunteers who got away with all but nineteen of the fifteen hundred or so rifles that had been landed. But the contrast between this interference with Home Rule Volunteers and the total failure of the authorities to prevent the shipment of a far greater quantity of arms by the Ulster Volunteers at Larne could hardly help being observed by nationalist Irishmen. Then later in the day the detachment of the King's Own Scottish Borderers which had been continually harassed by a following crowd on its journey back to barracks in Dublin finally turned and fired into it on one of the quays of the Liffey named Bachelor's Walk. Three civilians were killed and some thirty-eight wounded. The bitterness this caused at the very moment when nationalists were being thwarted over the fulfilment of their aspirations which the Government had promised them, made the two conflicting attitudes to the Ulster problem more irreconcilable still.

Only the outbreak of the European war a few days later appeared to transform the situation. In the interests of national unity the Conservatives and Carson agreed not to press immediately for an Amending Bill to the

Home Rule Act though they made the formal gesture of walking out of the House of Commons when it went onto the Statute Book on the 18 September 1914. In return Asquith and Redmond had agreed that Home Rule should be immediately suspended for twelve months or until the war ended, whichever period should prove the longer. (Since people then thought that the war would be over quickly this meant that they thought that Home Rule would come into force in twelve months.) An Amending Bill was then to be introduced to deal with Ulster. In other words the insuperable difficulties had merely been shelved.

There was, however, one new element in the situation which Redmond and the great body of nationalist Home Rulers thought would work to their advantage and genuinely transform the problem. By dedicating themselves to the British cause in the war, as they now did, transferring from the Volunteers to the British army in tens of thousands, they believed that they were thus earning Ireland's right to have Home Rule introduced as originally promised, without any Amending Bill, when the twelve months ended. It was on this basis that Redmond pledged the Volunteers for war service in a speech welcomed by all but that small minority of extremists within the Volunteer body who had in fact engineered its formation for revolutionary purposes in the first place. These now seceded – some 13,000 out of 180,000 taking with them the name 'Irish Volunteers' while the main body was called 'National Volunteers'.

Morally attractive, even justifiable, as the Redmondite argument might be, it ignored the most important element of all in the situation. It was unlikely that it would appeal to the hard hearts of the Orangemen in the North. In May 1915 Carson actually joined Asquith's cabinet.

As the full horrors of the greatest war the world had ever known unfolded, men's minds became clouded. But it should have been clear enough that trouble in Ireland was not simply going to go away.

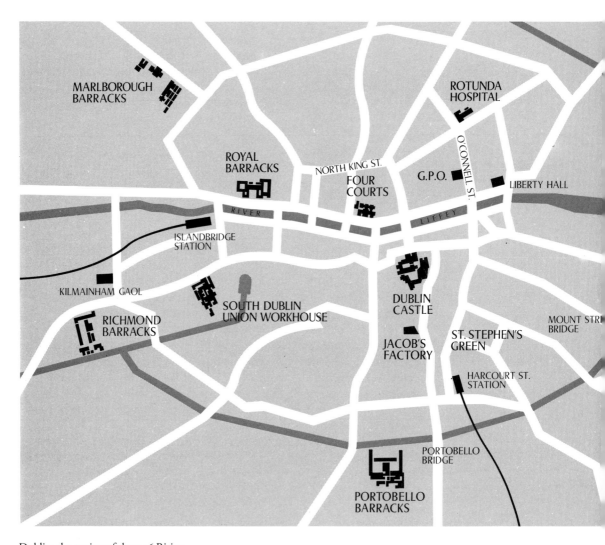

MARLBOROUGH
BARRACKS

ROTUNDA
HOSPITAL

O'CONNELL ST.

ROYAL
BARRACKS

NORTH KING ST.

FOUR
COURTS

G.P.O.

LIBERTY HALL

RIVER

LIFFEY

ISLANDBRIDGE
STATION

KILMAINHAM GAOL

SOUTH DUBLIN
UNION WORKHOUSE

DUBLIN
CASTLE

MOUNT STR
BRIDGE

RICHMOND
BARRACKS

JACOB'S
FACTORY

ST. STEPHEN'S
GREEN

HARCOURT ST.
STATION

PORTOBELLO
BRIDGE

PORTOBELLO
BARRACKS

Dublin: the setting of the 1916 Rising.

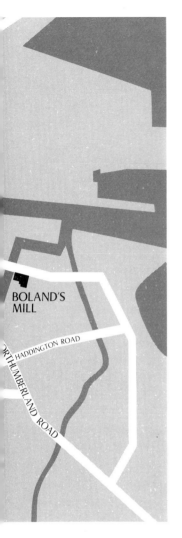

BOLAND'S
MILL

HADDINGTON ROAD

NORTHUMBERLAND ROAD

Chapter 9

1916

The Dublin Rising of 1916 was such a surprising, dramatic occurrence, and such great changes in the relationship between Britain and Ireland were eventually to flow from it that to view it as it was viewed at the time is even more difficult than in examining most important historical events. Nor has it often been so viewed. In Ireland there was too long a political interest to be served by presenting the Rising as if it had been the spontaneous uprising of the Irish people which its protagonists claimed it to be. In England the need to accept the decline of Empire has induced a too ready acquiescence in Irish politico-historical clichés. In fact the most effective way of paying tribute to the Irish heroes of 1916 (and some were heroes by any standard) is to show how unheroic, or even ridiculous, the milieu from which they emerged appeared at the time.

The men and women of the 'Irish Volunteers' and 'Irish Citizen Army' who took part in the Rising had long been regarded, with good reason, by the British authorities in Dublin Castle as so unrepresentative of the Irish people as a whole that there seemed no need to take them seriously. They were allowed to march in uniform and with arms through the streets of Dublin even in wartime, since it was judged better to treat them as a joke than risk turning them into minor Irish martyrs by prosecuting or disarming them. And decades later people still remembered them with phrases like 'they meant nothing to us at all, we thought they were just funny . . .', or 'I thought they were just awful'.

The same witnesses would concede that, after the rebels had acted as amazingly as they did, they thought: 'If a man is prepared to give up his life for something, there must be something he wants very badly.' And the poet Yeats, no friend to the rebels politically at the time, went so far as to say that, after their action, all was 'changed utterly', and 'a terrible beauty' born. But the historical point to make is that, until about twelve o'clock on Easter Monday, 1916, there seemed to the outside world not the remotest possibility of them ever changing anything.

Early in 1914 an artistically-minded film-camera operator moved his camera in a slow and impressive pan from left to right across the top of O'Connell Street (then officially Sackville Street), bequeathing to us today a moving inconsequential picture of ordinary life on any ordinary day in those apparently tranquil times. Historically what is most significant about

Oglaigh na hEireann.

ENROL UNDER THE GREEN FLAG.

Safeguard your rights and liberties (the few left you).

Secure more.

Help your Country to a place among the nations.

Give her a National Army to keep her there.

Get a gun and do your part.

JOIN THE

IRISH VOLUNTEERS

(President: EOIN MAC NEILL).

The local Company drills at_____

Ireland shall no longer remain disarmed and impotent.

this gentle shot is that the camera operator chose to shoot it through a cardboard cut-out of a shamrock, stressing the traditional tourist's harmless view of Ireland. Inside this shamrock world the camera slowly reveals the great thoroughfare named after the parliamentary nationalist, Daniel O'Connell, whose statue stands at the head of it. Tucked in behind this statue and to the left of the tall pillar to Admiral Nelson which was then still there, can be seen the triangular roof of the General Post Office, at the time a building of no particular significance. If you could have then told passers-by that the Post Office would before long be the headquarters of an Irish Republican rebellion they would have thought you mad. For Southern Ireland seemed at this moment, more than at any other in her history, loyal to the British Crown.

There was a straightforward political reason for this. The Liberal British government of the day was then in the process of passing through Parliament a bill for domestic Home Rule for all Ireland under the Crown. Admittedly, this was being done against strong opposition from Ulster and the Conservative party both inside and outside Parliament. But to most nationalist Irishmen such opposition seemed largely a bluff and at any rate a secondary feature to their own elation at the fulfilment of the great political dream which Irish nationalists had been nursing for over a quarter of a century. A few weeks after the First World War broke out in 1914, Home Rule for all Ireland finally passed into law. The Act was signed by the king and placed on the Statute Book, to come into force at the end of twelve months or at the end of the war, whichever should be the longer period. That an 'Amending Bill' to accommodate Ulster's fears was also projected seemed, by contrast, unimportant, a matter that would take on quite a different complexion in different times when nationalist Ireland would have done her bit to help Britain win the war.

All over Ireland nationalist Irishmen were flocking to the British army's colours feeling that they were making Ireland at last one of the small nations of Europe. Men of the great Southern Irish regiments – the Connaught Rangers, the Munster Fusiliers, the Dublin Fusiliers and the rest – now marched, together with Irishmen from Ulster, to slaughter on the battlefields of Europe, a source of pride to most Irish nationalists and an inspiration, it seemed, to the younger generation. When the first Irishmen to win the VC in the war arrived back in Ireland in 1915 they came home to a tumultuous welcome.

There was however in Ireland a quite different, extreme, tradition of patriotism altogether. Implacably opposed to any form of British rule, it regarded Home Rule as a sell-out. At this time, early in the twentieth century, this extreme tradition of Irish patriotism was almost forgotten, although it was still embodied in Dublin by the old Fenian and Republican, Tom Clarke, who owned a tobacconist's shop in the centre of the city. Clarke had spent his fifteen years in jail for trying to set off bomb explosions in British cities and after his release had gone to America for some years. But he had returned to Ireland in 1907 and at his shop in Dublin there congregated a hard core of those minority extremists who had led the minority breakaway of Irish Volunteers from Redmond and his co-operation with the British war effort. Several of them were, like Clarke, members of the old Irish Republican Brotherhood, which had been almost defunct for many years, but which now was being actively revived under his influence with the help of a young nationalist from Ulster named Sean MacDermott.

Just after the outbreak of war the leaders of this group called a meeting to discuss what the IRB and those who thought like them should do during the war. It had been an old Fenian axiom that 'England's difficulty was Ireland's opportunity.' In spite of the fact that the great majority of Irishmen saw England's difficulty as an opportunity to display Ireland's good faith now that Home Rule was on the Statute Book – and thus, it was hoped, ensure England's good faith in return – the decision was taken at that meeting to rise in arms against the British government before the war was over. Others present at that meeting as well as Clarke and MacDermott included Patrick Pearse, the poet and schoolmaster, increasingly obsessed with the need for a blood sacrifice for Ireland; and James Connolly, the trade union organizer and socialist republican who had already formed a workers' 'Irish Citizen Army' to protect workers from the police in labour troubles, and who was the most impatient of all to strike for Ireland's separation from the British Crown and the formation of an Irish Republic.

These conspirators now activated a number of front organizations for propaganda purposes, among them a 'Neutrality League' and the long-standing 'Wolfe Tone Memorial Committee'. And it was the latter which organized in 1915 a great public event on the occasion of the funeral of that old Fenian, Jeremiah O'Donovan Rossa, who had died in America where he had been exiled forty years before, after serving a hard term in British jails for his part in the Fenian conspiracy of the 1860s. He had helped organize for a time a dynamite campaign against British cities in the 1880s, but latterly had been a supporter of Redmond's Home Rule movement. However, it was his revolutionary past that lent itself to exploitation by new conspirators now. His funeral turned out to be a triumph both for their propaganda instincts and their powers of organization.

Thousands of ordinary moderate-minded people filed past the coffin of this man whose extremist patriotism in other times seemed something to which it was now quite fitting to pay respect. An armed guard of honour was provided by the minority Irish Volunteers, though very few of their rank and file guessed that their leaders were already planning to use them for a rising. Redmond's Volunteers were also present that day, marching in long columns but unarmed. Believing as they did that the Home Rule Act fulfilled all Ireland's national aims and that they existed to defend it at home and abroad against any amendment, it seemed perfectly appropriate to pay a qualified martial respect to a patriot who had favoured other methods in other times. That new men were planning to use such extremist methods in the near future and had organized this occasion subtly to condition public opinion towards them again, was a thought that can have entered very few heads that day, on what seemed simply to be a great historic occasion – a memorial to Ireland's sad past on the eve of a better future.

But the Irish Republicans who had organized the arrangements for the funeral made sure that it struck a firm military note. A volley was fired over the grave. And as the coffin was lowered into the grave one of those Republicans most deeply involved in the secret planning of the Rising,

Patrick Pearse, in the uniform of the minority Irish Volunteers, took a paper from his pocket and delivered his speech stating that the true future for Ireland lay in inspiration of the past. Railing against the British government he cried: 'The fools! The fools! The fools! They have left us our Fenian dead, and while Ireland holds these graves Ireland unfree shall never be at peace.'

The O'Donovan Rossa funeral was effective proof of the Irish Volunteers' ability to organize when secretly directed by the inner councils of the Irish Republican Brotherhood. But the other private army in the south was preparing too. Outside the Irish Transport Union's headquarters at Liberty Hall, Connolly's small Irish Citizen Army, with its proud boast of total independence for Ireland, paraded regularly under the watchful eye of its commandant, James Connolly. Indeed, it was Connolly's impatience for a rising and mistrust of the IRB's resolve to act as well as talk that had finally brought Pearse and the secret group in the Volunteers to agree to rise in arms at Easter 1916. A few weeks before, on St Patrick's Day, 17 March 1916, the minority Volunteers held a big parade in the centre of Dublin at which some 2,000 of them marched past Pearse and other officers. James Connolly, in character, that day took his own Irish Citizen Army on a prospective tour of key sites in Dublin. He stopped at Portobello Bridge to demonstrate the vantage-point of the big public house there which commanded Portobello Barracks, and marched round St Stephen's Green to the Shelbourne Hotel which, he said, would make a fine barracks with plenty of food and plenty of beds.

The general plan for the Rising in Dublin was to take over such strategic strong-points in the centre of Dublin as would command the site of army barracks and/or approach routes into the city including railway stations. A garrison at the Four Courts would command access from the Marlborough Street and Royal Barracks. A garrison at the South Dublin Union workhouse would block access from Richmond Barracks and Kingsbridge station. Garrisons at Jacob's Biscuit Factory and on St Stephen's Green would block access from Portobello Barracks and Harcourt Street station. And a garrison at Boland's Mill would command the access routes of reinforcements from England via Kingstown harbour. The headquarters were to be the General Post Office in O'Connell Street.

But there was another vital part of the plan, on which the possibility of extending the Rising in Dublin to other parts of the country would much depend. A consignment of arms, chiefly some 20,000 rifles, was, in the week before Easter, on its way by sea to Ireland from Germany. These arms were coming under German naval command in a 'neutral' ship, the *Aud*. Arriving at the same time, in a German submarine that was also already at sea, was Sir Roger Casement, the former British Consular figure who had long been an ardent Irish nationalist and who had been instrumental in getting the Germans to send the ship. He was in fact deeply disillusioned with the extent of German help and hoped, on landing, to reach the leaders and warn them that if they were dependent solely on these arms they should not go ahead with the Rising.

Just before landing Casement shaved off his beard on board the submarine to make himself less recognizable. He landed from a rubber boat on Good Friday morning on a lonely beach of County Kerry known as Banna

Strand and was almost immediately arrested and identified, for all his precaution. His arrest touched off a most dramatic series of events.

The secret group planning the Rising were already in some trouble, and paying a price for having had to keep their plans so secret. One of the people they had had to keep in the dark was the official leader of the minority Irish Volunteers himself, a distinguished professor of early Irish history and co-founder of the Gaelic League, Eoin MacNeill.

MacNeill, though he had disapproved of Redmond and the co-operation of the majority with the British war effort, had always been of the opinion that his own Volunteers should only take to arms in self-defence if some government attempt were made to disarm them. On being told in the week before Easter that the 'manoeuvres' planned for Easter Sunday morning were in fact a cover for the outbreak of armed rebellion against the government, he was appalled, and determined to do everything in his power, short of informing the authorities, to stop it. But on being further informed that a government attempt to disarm the Volunteers was in the air, and not only that but that arms were already on their way to Ireland from Germany and that nothing could be done to stop them (the German ship had no wireless), he reluctantly agreed that the Rising should go ahead. Then came news not only that Casement had been arrested but that the arms ship, the *Aud*, had been intercepted by the Royal Navy and the German crew had scuttled her. MacNeill reverted to his former position and refused to sanction a rising. He did more. He placed an advertisement in the Sunday newspaper, the *Sunday Independent*, signed by himself, to the effect that the 'manoeuvres' planned for that day were cancelled.

The resulting confusion among the Irish Volunteers themselves, most of whom thought that the manoeuvres were only manoeuvres anyway, was considerable. And although Pearse, Connolly and the other leaders eventually decided to go ahead with the Rising on the next day, issuing orders on their own account to the effect that the 'manoeuvres' planned for Sunday would go ahead twenty-four hours later at twelve o'clock on Easter Monday, those men who actually turned out on Easter Monday were far fewer than would otherwise have been the case. They numbered rather less than 1,000 altogether, to be joined by another 800 or so in the course of the next few days.

The British attitude of tolerance towards the antics of the Irish Volunteers and the Irish Citizen Army had continued into 1916. When, however, the Castle heard from Naval Intelligence, which had succeeded in breaking the German naval code, that some sort of rising by these men was planned for Easter and that arms were on their way from Germany to help it, the situation took on a much more serious aspect. On the Thursday of the week before Easter an official decision was taken to disarm the Volunteers and the Citizen Army and arrest the leaders.

Then Dublin Castle heard the news that Casement had been caught and that the arms ship had been scuttled. It seemed impossible that any sort of rising could go ahead in such circumstances, and this impression appeared to be conclusively confirmed when the announcement of the cancellation of 'manoeuvres' appeared in the *Sunday Independent*. In this way MacNeill's insertion of the advertisement in fact did Pearse, Connolly and the rest something of a good turn after all. For, although the decision to arrest the leaders was held to, it was decided, on the assumption that there could now be no immediate rising and because the next day was a Bank Holiday with popular races at Fairyhouse, to postpone any action until the following day.

On that Bank Holiday morning, however, not everyone was on their way to Fairyhouse races. Those Volunteers and Citizen Army men whom the leaders had been able to summon were on their way early to their rallying-points, the principal one being at Connolly's Trade Union headquarters, Liberty Hall.

One young Volunteer, Vinny Byrne, a working-class boy of fifteen, on his way to St Stephen's Green, was sent home by a Volunteer officer because he seemed too young. Halfway home, in tears at not being allowed on parade (though he had no idea there was going to be a rising), he met an older friend who told him to take no notice of the order and go along with him. He ended up in the garrison at Jacob's Biscuit Factory. He didn't fire a shot there all week. But four years later he was to be killing British officers in cold blood as they rose from their beds, on Bloody Sunday, 1920.

Another man on his way that morning was Michael O'Rahilly, the O'Rahilly who, like MacNeill, had been opposed to the idea of a rising. However, he had been one of the prime movers in the foundation of the Volunteers and a prominent member of that group that had split away from Redmond rather than take part in the British war effort. When he heard that the Rising was definitely going to take place he decided, that 'having helped to wind the clock he must come to hear it strike' (words that Yeats was later to put into his mouth). He wound his puttees round his legs, and, waving to his pregnant wife and son of four, drove off to battle in a fine De Dion Bouton car of which he was the proud owner.

Tom Clarke, the old Fenian, was also saying goodbye to his wife. As she said afterwards, when you reach that point your only real concern is to see that you don't break down; you make your good-byes as casual as possible. She wasn't sure whether they even shook hands.

One group of Fenian-minded Irishmen who had been living in Britain and had returned to Ireland in recent weeks in the belief that a rising might be imminent had been living in a special camp at Kimmage on the outskirts of Dublin. There were over fifty of them altogether and they were under the command of George Plunkett whose brother had helped to plan the Rising. With a long march ahead of them to Liberty Hall they stopped a tram, held the driver at gun-point until they had all boarded, and then told him to drive straight into Dublin. George Plunkett came up the stairs of the tram in place of the conductor to count the numbers accurately, and then paid for all their fares in full. The incident is symptomatic of the strange mixture of amateurism and deadly intent that characterized so much of that first spasmodic day of the Rising.

At Liberty Hall itself all the officers of the Volunteers and Citizen Army, including Pearse and Connolly, were assembled with their men, together with members of the Youth Organization, the Fianna (named after the ancient Gaelic élite guard from whom the Fenians themselves had taken their name) and *Cumann na Mban*, the women's organization. Some of the Fianna boys were armed only with pikes. The first party to leave for their allotted post was a Citizen Army contingent of twenty-eight men and eight Fianna boys who headed for St Stephen's Green. Later, one sixteen-year-old

Volunteer, Jack Flynn, marching on his way to the bakery at Boland's Mill, passed his mother standing in the doorway of their home. She was horrified to see him with a gun on his shoulder even though she imagined he was only going on parade. Not long afterwards he was marching into the bakery, telling the astonished workers there that the baking had to stop. 'They couldn't make head or tail of it,' he was to say later, 'any more than some of ourselves could.'

The main body of men marched with Connolly, Pearse and Clarke from Liberty Hall to the building in the very centre of Dublin which had been chosen as headquarters for the Rising: the General Post Office. There, a bewildered public was turned out and a little later was even more bewildered to hear an Irish Republic proclaimed by Patrick Pearse from the front of the building.

'In the name of God', ran the Proclamation which Pearse read out, 'and of the dead generations from which she receives her old tradition of nationhood Ireland through us summons her children to her flag and strikes for her freedom.'

While mentioning the support of gallant allies in Europe (the Germans) the Proclamation said that Ireland depended first on her own strength, and was striking in full confidence of victory.

The first victory was over a party of Lancers jingling down O'Connell Street, apparently unaware of what was happening. Some Volunteers assigned to the General Post Office were still on their way there as the firing broke out. They noticed that the Lancers seemed to be taken wholly by surprise. Four Lancers were killed.

Inside the Post Office the chief activity was the breaking of windows and the filling of mailbags with coal, nails, paper and any rubbish to hand to form makeshift 'sandbags'. Some of the windows were barricaded with wax effigies taken from a waxworks show in Henry Street nearby – King George V, Queen Mary and Kitchener were pushed into the windows.

Another vantage-point had been taken over at Jacob's Biscuit Factory which, together with the garrison at St Stephen's Green, commanded a field of fire against Portobello Barracks. But here immediate opposition to the Rising came from quarters other than the British army. The Volunteers occupying the factory were jeered by a hostile crowd waving Union Jacks calling them 'fucking slackers' and telling them if they wanted to fight, they should go out and fight in France. One man made a grab at a Volunteer's rifle. A Volunteer lieutenant told him to keep his hands off or he would be sorry. The man did not take his hands off and was shot in the leg.

Another early casualty was the Irish policeman on duty at the gate of Dublin Castle, the very centre of British rule in Ireland. Volunteers shot him dead as they attacked the Castle, but though it was virtually undefended at the time they did not press home the attack.

The same Monday afternoon a column of elderly part-time soldiers, known from the words 'Georgius Rex' on their belts as 'the Gorgeous Wrecks', had been out on a route march in the Dublin Mountains, unaware of events in Dublin since they had left their barracks in Northumberland Road early that morning. They all had rifles but no ammunition and as they were marching back, tired and in columns of four, they were suddenly fired on at close range. Five of them fell dead and eight were wounded.

FAR LEFT: James Connolly, impatient Citizen Army leader. 'The Shelbourne Hotel would make a fine barracks . . .'

ABOVE CENTRE: Tom Clarke, fifteen years in jail for trying to blow up British cities, and an appointment in Kilmainham. 'You make your goodbyes as casual as possible . . .'

ABOVE: Patrick Pearse (right) with his brother Willie: '. . . increasingly obsessed with the need for a blood sacrifice.'

LEFT: 'The fools! They have left us our Fenian dead . . .' Pearse (in uniform to left of priest) with his speech at O'Donovan Rossa's graveside, 1915.

In the centre of Dublin the chief event had been not military at all but civilian: looting. Swarms of people appeared from all over the side streets crossing O'Connell Street and made their way into a department store called Clerys, 'the Harrods of Dublin' as one surviving witness of the scene describes it. People filled sacks with anything they could find. Women were carrying and wearing fur coats and men were bent double under great bales of tweed and other materials. One man walked off wearing a dress-suit in the middle of the day, and carrying a golf club. There was hair-pulling, and snatching of sacks and a series of punch-ups. But as one witness was to put it, 'although it was horrifying to see, the poor people of Dublin really had a ball.'

But while the poor were having this strange ball what exactly were the British authorities doing? Rebels were in command of a number of strong-points in the centre of Dublin with headquarters at the General Post Office, and were sitting there apparently quite unchallenged. They only numbered about 1,000, though of course the authorities did not know that.

Based in Dublin there were altogether just under 2,500 British troops. Of these, many, on this sunny Bank Holiday, had taken themselves off to Fairyhouse races and other suitable Bank Holiday delights. At each of the four main barracks at which the troops were based – Marlborough, Richmond, Royal and Portobello – there had been for several days a special picket of 100 men each at permanent readiness in view of the earlier alert over the German arms and the known possibility of a rising. But since it was now known that the German arms shipment had failed, and that the Rising was presumably off after MacNeill's cancellation, their state of readiness by that Monday morning must have seemed something of a formality. These 400 men were the only troops immediately available when the attack on Dublin Castle made it clear that the authorities had been caught napping after all.

From that moment onwards though – with one disastrous exception – the British were wide awake. (Many of the 'British' troops based in Dublin were incidentally from Irish Regiments.) Once the four pickets had been sent to secure the Castle against further attack, the British plan concentrated on first bringing in reinforcements, and then establishing a cordon round the centre of Dublin which would be gradually and methodically tightened round the rebel headquarters in the Post Office.

The first reinforcements – 1,600 men of the Third Cavalry Brigade – arrived from the Curragh on Monday afternoon. Artillery was brought in from Athlone. And after an urgent wireless message to London the 176th and 178th infantry brigades of the 59th North Midland Division were embarked on Tuesday to arrive at Kingstown Harbour on Wednesday morning, ready to march on Dublin. It was this day which was to see the heaviest action of the whole Rising.

But it also saw one small, ugly incident. A well-known Dublin figure, the pacifist writer Sheehy Skeffington, had been arrested with two other civilians by an over-zealous, and (as later officially described) 'mad' British officer, and taken to Portobello Barracks. There, that Wednesday morning, another British officer in the barracks heard some shots, and witnessed three stretchers being carried out of the porch of the guardroom on which were obviously dead bodies. On the third stretcher was a body with a

Daily Express

Late War EDITION

EXCELDA HANDKERCHIEFS
For Soldiers and Sailors.
Genuine and Reliable. Price 6½d. each
ASK FOR EXCELDA SOFT COLLARS AND FRONTS.

NO. 5,007.   LONDON, TUESDAY, APRIL 25, 1916.   ONE HALFPENNY.

Invasion of Ireland: Notorious Traitor Captured.

S SECRET O-DAY.

AIR RAIDER DRIVEN OFF.
AEROPLANE'S FUTILE VISIT TO KENTISH

THE KUT RELIEF FORCE.
ALL DAY BOMBARDMENT AT SANNA-I-YAT.

GERMANY'S OLD GAME.
EFFORT TO PLAY FOR TIME WITH

SIR ROGER CASEMENT CAPTURED.

NOTORIOUS IRISH TRAITOR.

ATTEMPT TO LAND ARMS AND AMMUNITION IN IRELAND.

MYSTERY SHIP AIDED BY GERMAN SUBMARINE.

The sensational announcement was made by the Admiralty last night that during an attempt to land arms and ammunition in Ireland Sir Roger Casement, the notorious renegade, was captured. The attempt was made in an auxiliary ship under neutral guise, in conjunction with a German submarine.

The following is the Admiralty statement:—

ADMIRALTY, Monday, 10.25 p.m.
During the period between p.m. April 20 and p.m. April 21, an attempt to land arms and ammunition in Ireland was made by a vessel under the guise of a neutral merchant ship, but in reality a German auxiliary, in conjunction with a German submarine.

The auxiliary sank, and a number of prisoners were made, among whom was Sir Roger Casement.

RENEGADE'S LIFE STORY.

SIR ROGER CASEMENT.

Sir Roger Casement, who is fifty-one years of age, was a distinguished British public servant before he became a renegade. What turned him into a traitor can only be surmised. Sir Arthur Conan Doyle, who knew him well, suggests that his mind was affected by tropical hardships. At any rate, his pro-German sentiments existed long before the war, so she allowed herself to be deceived by Sir Roger Casement's absurd promises of stirring up rebellion in Ireland. He was promptly repudiated by the Nationalists and by the United Irish League in America—he had never been connected with the Home Rule movement—but the "Manchester Neueste Nachrichten" regarded him as the most eminent Irish leader." It is stated that the Kaiser paid him a retainer of £2,500, with a promise of much more if his plans were successful.

GERMAN GOLD.

His proposition was that he should go to America, form a secret organisation there, and send emissaries well equipped with German gold to stir up trouble in Ireland. Unfortunately for his scheme, British warships were "active" in the North Sea, and he preferred not to trek that route. The British Government had set a price of £1,000 on his head, and Germany swallowed even this.

A chance, which he eagerly seized, came when a large number of captured Irish soldiers were assembled in the Limburg Camp—men who had won glory in the retreat from Mons and in other battles. Sir Roger Casement travelled to the camp and addressed his fellow-countrymen. He persuaded them from Home Rule for Ireland, a German farm, a German wife, and 30s a day for life for each man, or a free passage to America after the war, with a grant of £20 and assured employment. Then he asked them to forswear their allegiance to King George and join the "German Irish Brigade." The men heard him in silence. At the

BRITISH PENSION.

ABOVE: Fenians of a feather: Roger Casement (left) and John Devoy (a '65 man) in New York, 1914.

RIGHT: The news that reassured the British authorities.

BELOW: The news that caught them napping. Stop press and the last news for over a week.

BELOW RIGHT: MacNeill trying to disentangle Pearse's web two days before the 1916 Rising.

OFFICIAL.

SINN FEIN RISING IN DUBLIN.

Yesterday morning an insurrectionary rising took place in the City of Dublin.

The authorities have taken active and energetic measures to cope with the situation, which is proceeding favourably.

WOODTOWN PARK, RATHFARNHAM, CO. DUBLIN

22 apl 1916
Volunteers completely deceived. All orders for tomorrow Sunday are entirely cancelled.
Eoinmacneill

blanket thrown over it and a bowler hat placed across the face. From either side of the stretcher hung down one hand dripping blood. This was Sheehy Skeffington. The firing party had done its work so badly that a second party had had to be summoned to finish him off.

It was to be a bloody day. British reinforcements had arrived at Kingstown Harbour just after five o'clock and started to march into the city. The first thing that took the troops by surprise was the arrival of dozens of Irish women bringing them tea and cakes and biscuits. 'They were just like one of us,' one soldier recalled in amazement. 'They seemed as pleased as could be that we'd arrived.' The troops were showered with bars of chocolate and fruit; they felt they 'could have had ten breakfasts a day' if they wished.

These troop reinforcements from England now set off for Dublin in two columns. One column – the 5th and 6th battalion of the Sherwood Foresters – met no opposition and marched round the city to bivouac safely on the western side at Kilmainham. There they joined the cordon that was being methodically drawn round the rebels in the centre of the city. But while they waited in position, with action in the centre of Dublin still only sporadic, the other column of the Sherwood Foresters ran into deep trouble. Proceeding from Northumberland Road towards the centre of Dublin, they ran into small outposts of the rebel strong-point at Boland's Mill, placed in a few houses round Mount Street bridge. There were only seventeen men in these houses altogether. Number 25 Northumberland Road had a garrison of two.

It was about one o'clock that the local inhabitants heard the sound of marching men and looking out saw what looked like the whole British army coming in. They were marching along quite unconcernedly when the two men in number 25 Northumberland Road opened fire on them from the bedroom windows as they reached the junction of Northumberland Road and Haddington Road. Some of the soldiers fell dead or wounded; others threw themselves on the ground not knowing where the firing was coming from, but creeping warily along the road on their stomachs. Then the British officer in charge, Colonel Fane, gave orders for a direct attack on the house across open ground. Although soon wounded himself he was seen to try to rally his men with a sword or stick, arousing admiration even among those onlookers in some of the windows who were in sympathy with the rebels. The rebels' fire was so good and accurate that the British imagined themselves to be confronting two or three hundred men in the area instead of seventeen.

It was not until about seven o'clock in the evening that they finally stormed the doorways with hand-grenades. British casualties at Mount Street bridge amounted to 230 killed and wounded altogether – more than half those of the entire Rising.

Meanwhile British artillery had already started fires in Dublin, and by the next day, Thursday, the infantry were moving steadily in towards the centre. What made progress difficult apart from concentrated sniping were the barricades that had been put up everywhere, constructed largely of household goods, pianos, bedsteads, mattresses, tables and chairs. At the end of the week, making their way through North King Street towards the centre, the South Staffs Regiment gave the civilian population some rough treatment, killing twelve civilians in a number of houses there.

On the whole, the main rebel garrisons spent the greater part of the week in a state of alert inactivity. It was possible for instance to be a member of the important garrison at Jacob's Biscuit Factory and to have 'never fired a shot'. Apart from the action at Mount Street bridge, there were only two concentrated scenes of fighting lasting several hours: one in the area of the South Dublin Union workhouse, and the other in the North King Street district controlled by the Four Courts garrison. No rebel was killed inside the Post Office during the entire week – only after evacuating it in the final withdrawal.

Much of the rebels' time was spent in listening to rumours: in Jacob's Biscuit Factory it was believed for a time that the Germans had landed, those 'gallant allies in Europe' of the Proclamation, and there was cheering for about half an hour before it was realized, in the words of one of them later, that 'it was all a great con . . . no such thing had happened'. They believed the same rumour in the Post Office for a while, even thinking that the heavy shelling which the British artillery was increasingly concentrating on the centre of Dublin was the sound of German guns. There were rumours too, apparently hardly discouraged by leaders, that the rest of the country was rising to support Dublin – though virtually all that happened elsewhere was as follows: one ambush action against the Royal Irish Constabulary at Ashbourne in County Meath, in which sixteen loyal Irish policemen were killed; an assembly of rebels in County Galway dispersed by naval gunfire; and the 'take-over' of the town of Enniscorthy by Irish Volunteers, though this required no aggressive military action, since the police withdrew prudently to their barracks and remained there for the rest of the week.

In these circumstances, many decades later, small incidents of the week remained vivid in survivors' minds. One night towards the end, the garrison in the GPO heard a strange and terrible clanking at the end of the street and were dimly able to make out what looked like some sort of lorry with a boiler stuck on top of it coming towards them. This was in fact exactly what it was: an engine locomotive boiler with an entrance through the firebox on the back, rigged up at Guinness's brewery as an improvised armoured car. Slots had been cut in the side for observation, together with a number of dummy slots. Joe Sweeney, later a General in the Irish National Army, who was at a look-out post on the roof of the Post Office with another Volunteer when it first appeared, fired at one of the slots while his companion fired at the other. Between them they brought the vehicle to a halt, wounding one of the inmates, presumably the driver, because later another armoured monster came along and towed it away.

The most important military action of the week was an ostensibly undramatic one: the slow tightening of the British cordon round the rebels in the centre of Dublin. But it had some dramatic accompaniments, principally the artillery fire which did much damage to the centre of the city. As the British moved closer to the Post Office they even brought into action an armed fishery vessel, usually rather fancifully described as 'the gunboat *Helga*', from the River Liffey.

Much of the damage was done by two eighteen-pounders firing at close range in the streets. By Friday evening the Post Office itself was uncontrollably on fire – the whole scene a most awesome sight to the civilian

RIGHT: 'Because I helped to wind the clock I came to hear it strike' – Michael O'Rahilly (*The* O'Rahilly).

BELOW: After the striking of the clock: O'Rahilly's De Dion Bouton car among the Dublin ruins.

population. The sky was an enormous mass of flame and it seemed as if the whole centre of the city was being destroyed by fire. The end was indeed close at hand. That same evening Pearse, Connolly, Clarke and the other leaders had evacuated the burning Post Office which had been their head-quarters. One party managed to cross safely to the other side of the adjoining street, where they broke their way through the walls of houses to set up new temporary headquarters further away. Connolly was carried on this arduous journey on a stretcher in great agony, having been hit by a bullet in the ankle where gangrene had set in. The rest of the GPO garrison made a sortie headed by O'Rahilly, the man who had been against a rising but who, having been a founder of the Volunteers and a supporter of its extreme minority wing, had felt honour-bound to take part in it once it had started. The sortie charged down Moore Street, with O'Rahilly well in front and had got as far as the corner of Ridley Road and Moore Lane when he was hit. He was seen to turn on his left side in great pain, make the sign of the cross, drag himself forward a few yards further and die. Among the debris found afterwards in the wreckage of Dublin was that De Dion Bouton motor-car in which he had driven to the fight.

Towards evening on the Saturday, word began to go round among the rank and file in the headquarters garrison that Pearse had gone out to surrender. The man who had waxed lyrical about the need for a blood sacrifice for Ireland had been appalled by what he had seen of the slaughter of civilians in the fighting. He had finally gone out after receiving a note from the commander of the British forces in Dublin, General Lowe, in reply to an emissary sent in to make enquiries – a nurse named Elizabeth Farrell. This note had been written at General Lowe's dictation by his son John, destined – as John Loder – to become a film star of the 1930s. It invited Pearse to meet him and surrender, and a photograph was taken of him doing so in front of Lowe and his son, who was dressed in light cavalry-twill breeches. John Lowe, on his father's instructions, then drove Pearse to Kilmainham jail.

In some of the garrisons where men had hardly been tested in the fighting the news of Pearse's surrender caused dismay. And in the South Dublin Union workhouse where they had successfully held off British attacks all week, their leader, Kent, called his men together to ask them what they thought about it. Some were dissatisfied, but Kent pointed out that Tom Clarke was among those surrendering, and added: 'If Tom Clarke, who served fifteen years in British dungeons, has surrendered, then I don't think it's any shame on us to surrender too.' However, Kent later put on record his own personal feeling that to surrender, as he thought prematurely, had been a mistake.

Reluctantly the other garrisons surrendered too. The leader of the garrison at Boland's Mill was Eamon de Valera, a virtually unknown mathematics teacher. A better-known Dublin figure, Constance Markiewicz, born Constance Gore-Booth, daughter of an upper-class Protestant landowner in the west of Ireland, surrendered with Michael Mallin at the head of the Citizen Army garrison at St Stephen's Green. Many of the prisoners were taken to open ground in front of the Rotunda Hospital. There they were addressed by Sean MacDermott who praised them for holding out so long. He forecast that he and the other leaders would be executed but urged the others 'to carry on the struggle'.

Those who had been marshalled in front of the Rotunda Hospital were kept out in the open all night. During that time a British officer, Captain Lee Wilson, earned the dislike of many of the prisoners for his forthright insults. He had Clarke and Willie Pearse and others stripped and searched and was heard to say of Clarke, 'This old bastard's been out before – he's got a tobacconist's shop across the way' – understandable enough language in the circumstances perhaps, but it was much resented by the prisoners and to be the cause of his later 'execution' by the IRA in 1920. The next morning the prisoners were marched down O'Connell Street to Richmond Barracks and, seeing the tricolour still flying over the portico of the Post Office, they raised a great cheer which exacted further abuse from their escorts, though more than once such parties of prisoners being marched through the streets were happy that their escorts were there to protect them against the abuse and even attempted assaults of indignant Dublin citizens.

Once the prisoners were in Richmond Barracks, the G-men or special political detective branch of the Dublin Metropolitan Police visited them, and known leaders and trouble-makers were separated from the rest. Film of the period makes clear how many of the rank and file were drawn from the Dublin working class, and that some were little more than boys. These were treated with reasonable leniency. One later IRA man – the boy who had cried when he thought he was not going to be allowed on the Easter Monday 'parade' – simply had his finger-prints taken and was told to run on home. Paddy Buttner, a Fianna Boy who had been out with the Citizen Army, was brought with others in front of high-ranking officers and told : 'You are thoughtless youths. . . . You've been led by madmen . . . maniacs. Go home and get your mothers to wipe your noses.'

Even many of the more mature members of the rank and file were treated with what, in the context of the time, could be regarded as some leniency. They had, after all, taken up arms against their government in time of war, claiming as allies that very nation with which the government was at war. But court martials were reserved only for a fairly small proportion. The majority were simply marched off through the streets of Dublin down to the quays for internment in Britain. And once again the rebels were reminded of their unpopularity with many of the citizens of Dublin. 'Shoot the bastards!' the escort was told on one occasion, and the former rebel who recalls this later added: 'The Rising in Dublin was not popular in 1916; I can say that without fear of contradiction.'

Yet that impression of a young man who had just been through an intensely bewildering experience, though itself accurate, is only a shallow part of the historical truth. The Rising had not been popular, yet Ireland's history had been too sensitive and complex for rebels to be dismissed easily, on reflection, as madmen. And reflection was what was going on as crowds strolled endlessly up and down O'Connell Street, staring at the ruins while dust and smoke from partly-shelled buildings still filled the air. The rubble which the crowds watched workmen clearing was still smoking. The centre of Dublin at least was 'changed utterly'. Casualties were counted: 300 civilians, 60 rebels and 130 British troops had been killed.

Nothing like this had happened in Ireland for well over 100 years. Irish rebels had held the British army at bay for nearly a week, and though in

that British army many regiments were Irish, it was Irish rebels of one sort or another who were the heroes of Irish history. People began to turn their attention to these Easter rebels and, however much they might deplore their action, to feel at the same time some pride in them.

The immediate question was what would be done with those being tried by the court martials which were now proceeding. From Dublin, one of the Irish Parliamentary leaders, John Dillon, wrote to Redmond who was in London that so far the feeling of the population was against the rebels, but 'if there were shootings of prisoners on any large scale the effect on public opinion might be disastrous'.

Three days after the surrender it was announced that three leaders had been shot: Tom Clarke, the old Fenian who had done so much to bring about the Rising; Thomas MacDonagh, a poet and one of the rebel commandants; and the poet and Commandant-General of this, the twentieth century's first Irish Republican Army, Patrick Pearse. If the executions had stopped there future history might have been different. But they did not stop there.

Willie Pearse was executed on 4 May, apparently for no reason other than that he had been Pearse's brother. He had certainly made no display of belligerency at his court martial. With him were shot Joseph Plunkett, who had indeed helped plan the Rising; Edward Daly, the Volunteer commandant of the Four Courts garrison; and Michael O'Hanrahan, a Volunteer headquarters clerk.

Of the seventy-seven death sentences passed, most were to be commuted, but all the public knew for sure was that seven had now been carried out. And they were wondering with ever-increasing dread how many more would be carried out.

Then on 5 May came another execution: that of John MacBride. He was in no way a leader of the Rising but, sixteen years before, he had fought for the Boers, and there may well have been some retrospective vindictiveness about his sentence.

The Irish Home Rule Party, which most of the Irish people still supported, drafted a resolution condemning the Rising but also condemning the executions and again stressing that any more executions would have the most disastrous effect on the future loyalty of the Irish people.

On 8 May there were four more executions: Cornelius Colbert, an organizer of the Fianna, the Youth movement; Eamon Ceannt, a rebel commandant; Michael Mallin, commandant at St Stephen's Green, and Sean Heuston, also of the Irish Citizen Army. On 9 May, Thomas Kent, a Volunteer from County Cork, who had killed a policeman while resisting arrest, was executed. An Irishwoman was later to write: 'It was like watching a stream of blood coming from under a closed door.'

During Easter Week itself there had been many Irishmen who, while basically of Redmondite Home Rule sympathies and condemning the rebels, had found some sneaking sympathy for them developing in spite of their condemnation. One such, Edward MacLysaght, wrote in his diary at the time: 'My heart is with them and my mind is against them.' The executions made him 'completely and absolutely pro them . . .'

On 12 May, Sean MacDermott, the man who had done so much to help organize the Rising, was shot; and, last of all, though no-one knew he

ABOVE LEFT: The burnt-out shell of the Dublin GPO rebel headquarters. What had it all been about?

LEFT: The Boland's Mill garrison with de Valera (marked X in photograph) surrender and prepare for abuse in the streets. 'The Rising was not popular in 1916 . . . I can say that without fear of contradiction.'

would be the last, James Connolly – shot, because he could not stand on his wounded ankle, in a chair.

The newspapers and the public called it the 'Sinn Fein' rebellion because, although the constitutionalist Sinn Fein movement of before the war had had nothing to do with it, so little was known of the Rising's real leaders and their motives that identification with Sinn Fein seemed the only available explanation. But what had really been the motives of the rebel leaders other than mere affirmation of their belief in an almost mystical 'Irish Republic'?

Pearse had in the past talked of a blood sacrifice needed to purify Ireland, and at times had used the analogy of Christ sacrificing himself for humanity in a way that might almost seem blasphemous. It was hardly a complete coincidence that Easter was chosen as the date for the Rising. Tom Clarke made a similar point in more secular terms when his wife visited him the night before his execution. Talking to her in front of a British soldier in a cell lit by candles in jam-pots he said the leaders believed they had struck the first blow for Ireland's freedom. Freedom was coming and Ireland would never lie down again. But, he added, 'between this moment and freedom, Ireland will go through hell.'

The dreaded 'Auxies' (Auxiliary Division of the Royal Irish Constabulary). Few in number, courageous, ruthless, a law unto themselves. Colloquially lumped together with black and khaki uniformed RIC as 'Black and Tans'.

Chapter 10

Michael Collins
and the Black and Tans

Of all the many rebel leaders who shine out of Irish history only one stands out as a really effective revolutionary: Michael Collins. Except for the fact that in his short public career he was too busy with practical matters to concern himself with social ideas, he was a sort of Irish Lenin. He took hold of a potentially revolutionary situation in Ireland and made it work.

Born in the country in West Cork in 1890, he emigrated like many enterprising young men of his background to England to find a job when he was sixteen, working in the Post Office and finally with the London branch of the Guaranty Trust Company of New York. Early in 1916 he returned to Ireland, because, as a member of the Irish Republican Brotherhood, he probably had an indication of the coming Rising. He took part in that Rising in the rebel headquarters in the General Post Office and was afterwards simply interned as one of the apparently less important rank and file in a prison camp at Frongoch in North Wales.

In Frongoch, using as a nucleus other prisoners he already knew from West Cork, Collins set up an efficient Irish Republican Brotherhood network, seeing to it that those in charge of the huts and others holding key camp administrative positions were all IRB men. He organized classes, some purely educational, others on military matters – particularly guerrilla warfare. Since there were people from all parts of Ireland in the camp he was able, while still there, to build up contacts from all over the country and – what was to be all-important for the future – to obtain information about friendly members of the Royal Irish Constabulary who had helped people in trouble after the Rising.

Meanwhile those Volunteers who had been in the Rising and had managed to escape arrest had been keeping a skeleton network together in Ireland through bogus branches of the Gaelic League, one of the few organizations not suppressed. When, at Christmas 1916, the British government in a good-will gesture released all those who had been interned without trial, including Michael Collins and his friends from Frongoch, a basic undercover structure existed for him to take over and expand.

The most immediate task of the reorganized Volunteers was to work on Irish public opinion. There was already growing retrospective sympathy for the republican rebels, particularly as a result of the executions of the leaders and of the British government's continued failure to implement the Home Rule Act without excluding Ulster. But few questioned the still

dominant hold of the constitutional Parliamentary party under its leaders, John Redmond and John Dillon. It was this hold which the Volunteers and their supporters now challenged in a crucial series of bye-elections during the first half of 1917.

A group including both militant republicans like Collins and supporters of the non-violent pre-war Sinn Fein of Arthur Griffith, put up the father of the executed Joseph Plunkett as a candidate at a bye-election at Roscommon in February. The extent of his victory amazed Ireland. He won nearly twice as many votes as his Parliamentary party opponent. In May, at a bye-election at Longford, the same group put up one of the sentenced prisoners still in jail in Britain and again shocked the Parliamentary party by winning. In both these elections Collins had used the Irish Republican Brotherhood network within the Volunteers to provide a body of campaign workers to rival the traditionally efficient machine of Redmond's party. The extent to which Collins's 'machine' was effective can be gauged from the fact that at the very first bye-election fought after the Rising, at West Cork and before he was freed in November 1916, a Sinn Fein candidate came easily bottom of the poll behind two rival Parliamentary party candidates.

These 1917 bye-election victories in themselves swayed Irish public opinion still further in the direction of a new political movement. And when, in July 1917, the British government, again as a gesture of goodwill, released all the remaining prisoners of the Rising including those sentenced to life imprisonment, thousands waving republican tricolour flags jammed the streets of Dublin to welcome them. This was a very different reception from the booing and jeering they had received on their way to prison a year before.

Among the released life-sentence prisoners was the senior of the commandants of the 1916 Rising not to have been executed: Eamon de Valera. He now stood as a candidate in the third bye-election of the year at East Clare, with Collins's IRB machinery at his disposal. An equally important support of a new sort, significant in its implications, was beginning to come from the clergy, formerly solidly behind Redmond's Parliamentary party. One East Clare parish priest at a campaign meeting suddenly asked de Valera to give him his hand, and raising it in the air declaimed to the audience: 'Valera, you have given me your hand; in return I give you the hearts of my people!' De Valera had an amazing triumph, more than doubling the number of votes for the Parliamentary candidate.

The new movement was soon officially banded together under de Valera's leadership with the old name Sinn Fein. But what it stood for precisely was still rather obscure. Certainly it stood for an independent sovereign republic, though many recognized that this was simply the best tactical way of trying to get a wider measure of Home Rule for all Ireland than that which was on the Statute Book but still unimplemented. How the Republic was to be achieved was what was vague. At the bye-elections, some speakers had preached the classical Sinn Fein doctrine that elected members should stay away from Westminster and form their own parliament in Dublin, though how exactly they were going to bring the British government to recognize that parliament was not clear. Other speakers made no reference to this but spoke of appealing above the heads of the British government to the International Peace Conference which would sit at the end of the war. Some spoke of appealing to the American people. Michael Collins had different ideas.

In September 1917 a grim event brought a wave of popular sympathy to the new movement. A Volunteer, Thomas Ashe, who had been out in the Rising and was a prominent colleague of Collins in the IRB, had been re-arrested during the summer for a seditious speech. He died in prison through forcible feeding while on hunger strike. Collins turned his funeral into a great national demonstration with Volunteers in uniform and rifles reversed flanking the coffin, and another 9,000 Volunteers following it together with more than 30,000 other mourners through the crowded streets. A volley was fired over Ashe's grave in the cemetery and Collins, standing by it in uniform, delivered the funeral oration: 'That volley which we have just heard is the only speech which it is proper to make over the grave of a dead Fenian.'

Although the London *Daily Express* commented that Ashe's death and funeral had made '100,000 Sinn Feiners out of 100,000 constitutional nationalists', it would be wrong to think that the new movement had already totally captured Irish public opinion. The imprecision of its policy and above all the fear that it might lead Ireland into violence once again kept many constitutional nationalists loyal to Redmond's party. And when John Redmond himself died and his son fought the bye-election in his old seat in Waterford wearing the British army uniform of 'an Irish officer', as he put it, he defeated the Sinn Fein candidate. But another external event was about to swing more support to the Sinn Fein cause.

The Great War was going badly and although tens of thousands of Irishmen from North and South were fighting side-by-side as volunteers in the British army, the government began to consider extending conscription to Ireland. (It had applied to the rest of the United Kingdom since 1916.) The threat of conscription was deeply resented by all shades of nationalist opinion and Irish Volunteers and Sinn Fein supporters exploited this new wave of national resentment to the full. An anti-conscription pledge was started and signed at mass meetings in vast numbers. The project was dropped by the government but the damage had already been done.

A military viceroy was appointed to Ireland: General French who, acting on inaccurate information that Sinn Fein was involved in a 'pro-German' plot, had most of the leaders arrested. Collins, through his network of friendly police had advance warning which he passed on to his colleagues, but he himself was one of the few to make sure he avoided arrest. Thus, by the time the General Election took place in 1918 a few weeks after the Armistice, he had been able to gather many of the threads of the new movement still further into his own hands.

It was the first General Election in the United Kingdom for eight years and Irish national feeling had been transformed in the meantime. The electoral register had changed out of recognition too. It was three times larger than in 1910 and included for the first time women over thirty and all men over twenty-one.

A number of factors favoured Sinn Fein. The constitutional Parliamentary party was seen to be on the defensive from the start, not only because they had lost a number of sensational bye-elections but also because they suffered a number of public defections to Sinn Fein while the campaign was in progress. The Parliamentary party was actually unable even to raise a candidate for a quarter of the Irish seats. Then again, many Irish soldiers in the British army – a large proportion of whom were likely to vote for the Parliamentary party and were entitled to a postal vote – never received their ballot papers. Less than a third of the soldiers' votes were cast altogether. The very imprecision of the Sinn Fein programme also helped it with the electorate. Home Rule nationalists could feel that by voting for a theoretical Republic they were simply putting the maximum pressure on the British government. Finally there was another factor which helped Sinn Fein at the polls to an immeasurable degree: the rigging of the vote by Sinn Fein supporters. In at least one constituency a hut was used as a wardrobe for a selection of men's and women's clothing in which Sinn Fein supporters could disguise themselves and go to the polls several times to vote in the names of people who were dead, ill or away. The polling lists had been studied very carefully for the purpose beforehand. Some people were later to recall voting for Sinn Fein as many as twenty times in this way.

The result of the election was an overwhelming victory for Sinn Fein. The old Nationalist Parliamentary party was virtually annihilated. Sinn Fein had won nearly three-quarters of all the Irish seats. Many of those elected were still in jail after the 'German plot' arrests earlier in the year, but the rest met in Dublin as Dail Eireann, the Irish Parliament, and declared a sovereign independent Irish Republic. They were permitted to do so by the British government which thus by implication called their bluff; for to declare independence did not mean they had got it. The release of the rest of the elected members only emphasized that fact. So, how, against the might of the British Empire, was this theoretical independence to be made real?

When the Dail met for the first time at the Dublin Mansion House American flags were waved together with the republican tricolour by the crowds outside, symbolizing the hope many felt that at the Peace Conference in Paris, the American President Woodrow Wilson would insist on the recognition of the rights of all small nations including Ireland. But it turned out that Wilson had no intention of disturbing this moment of allied triumph by quarrelling with the British Prime Minister, Lloyd George.

What, then, was Sinn Fein to do? Campaigners at the bye-elections and at the General Election had often made a point of stressing that there was no question of using violence. De Valera himself had said this. And in the middle of 1919 de Valera went to New York to try to reinforce the appeal to America. He was received with rapturous enthusiasm by the American Irish, collected money for the republican cause but came nowhere near obtaining official US recognition of an Irish Republic. So both the Peace Conference and America had failed Ireland. But there was another way and a pointer had already been given in that direction.

On the very day the Dail met in Dublin in January 1919 two Irish constables of the Royal Irish Constabulary had been escorting a cart carrying gelignite to a quarry at Soloheadbeg in County Tipperary when they were set upon by masked Volunteers and shot down with revolvers at point-blank range. The killing had been carried out by two young Volunteers named Dan Breen and Sean Treacy who had received no orders for this from Collins or anyone else. 'If we were to have waited for orders from headquarters or Dail Eireann', Breen said later, 'nothing would ever have happened.'

The terror that was gradually to overtake Ireland had begun. Two girls being driven down the Soloheadbeg road just afterwards saw the two policemen lying there dead, but the driver looked neither to right nor left and drove straight on.

Some weeks later Collins, at a meeting of the Sinn Fein executive and to the unease of some of its members, forecast what, in his view, was the only policy now open to it: 'The sooner fighting is forced and a general state of disorder created throughout the country', he said, 'the better it will be for the country. Ireland is likely to get more out of a general state of disorder than from a continuance of the situation as it now stands.'

This was the policy which he was now to orchestrate with relentless single-mindedness and efficiency. A reign of terror began against Irish policemen selected by Collins through his intelligence network as being dangerous or obnoxious to the Volunteers. By January 1920, fourteen Irish police had been shot down and killed in just over a year and more than twenty others wounded. Strict military régimes came into being for Tipperary and other parts of Ireland, but the sort of measures on which Collins was relying to create a strong nationally anti-British mood throughout the country were still to come.

Collins himself, during this time, led a double life. As Minister of Finance in the Dail he organized a vast loan for the Irish Republic which he successfully administered through hidden bank accounts which the British authorities were unable to trace. At the same time he was directing in Dublin and co-ordinating throughout the country the activities of the Volunteers or, as they soon came to be called, the Irish Republican Army.

He was a man of great energy and organizing ability, a natural leader with a dominating personality yet much loved by almost everyone he worked with. Dan Breen, who was later to become his political opponent, said he would willingly have laid down his life for Collins at any time. Boyish, full of enthusiasm and jokes, he was at the same time utterly ruthless, the sort of man, as someone who knew him said, 'who would never give you a second chance'. He was personally fearless and although 'on the run' from the latter part of 1919 onwards seldom bothered to disguise himself, riding freely about Dublin on a bicycle and relying on the efficiency of his intelligence system and his hand-picked 'squad' to protect him.

One young colleague with whom Collins was working was surprised to be told by him one night around midnight that they were going for a walk together. Suppressing the thought that midnight was an odd time to be going for a walk, he set off with Collins who took him through the streets of Dublin to a police station. There they were met by the sergeant in charge, named Broy, who was one of Collins's IRB men. They were taken upstairs to the inspector's office where they went systematically through the files to discover which of the detectives were on political work. Their names and addresses were noted and they were first sent a warning to change their job. If they ignored the warning, someone like Dan Breen was sent along to, as he put it, 'rub them out'.

On 15 March 1920, an event occurred which signalled a new development, one which was to set the pattern of conflict between the British

POLICE NOTICE.

£1000 REWARD

WANTED FOR MURDER IN IRELAND.

DANIEL BREEN

(calls himself Commandant of the Third
Tipperary Brigade).

Age 27, 5 feet 7 inches in height, bronzed complexion, dark hair (long in front), grey eyes, short
cocked nose, stout build, weight about 12 stone,
clean shaven; sulky bulldog appearance; looks rather
like a blacksmith coming from work; wears cap
pulled well down over face.

The above reward will be paid by the Irish Authorities, to any
person not in the Public Service who may give information
resulting in his arrest.

Information to be given at any Police Station.

S.O. 14591. (G. 40). 5,000. 11.20.—A. T. & Co., Ltd.

authorities and Irish national feeling for the next sixteen months. The Lord Mayor of Cork, Thomas MacCurtain, an ardent nationalist, was shot dead by a masked gang dressed in civilian clothes. But the gang was made up of policemen of the Royal Irish Constabulary, who were beginning to hit back. This in itself was perhaps not surprising after so much provocation. What was curious was that the gang, which a few days before had tried to murder another prominent Sinn Fein supporter in Cork, spoke with English accents.

Reinforcements for the RIC were now being recruited in England. With the expansion of the force there were not enough of the traditional bottle-green uniforms to go round and some of the new recruits were now equipped with khaki additions to their uniforms – trousers or tunics – and being thus seen, first in County Tipperary, received a nickname after a famous pack of hounds there called the Black and Tans. They were not a special force, being there simply to swell the ranks of the RIC, but their nationality and the fact that they had often been attracted to the job simply by the money, made them a distinctive element within it. There were eventually to be about 7,000 of them altogether.

Soon afterwards a special Auxiliary force was also recruited for the RIC in England composed of former officers, often with experience in the Great War, who were paid at twice the rate of the Black and Tans. They were less than 1,000 in strength until the end of 1920 and never to be more than 1,500 altogether, yet they made up for their lack of numbers by their courage and aggressiveness and, moving about the Irish countryside in the big Crossley tenders of the time, were to become a formidable force against the IRA.

In these circumstances the British government's belated attempt at a political gesture, with a new bill simply for Home Rule and that partitioned between two separate Parliaments in Belfast and Dublin, was understandably to prove irrelevant to the immediate issue. And when, after this bill's passing as the Government of Ireland Act of 1920, elections were eventually to be held for these Parliaments, Sinn Fein would simply use them as elections for the Dail (an all-Ireland Dail) and the British 'Southern Parliament' would have only temporarily nominal existence as an empty shell.

By late 1920, Sinn Fein's attempt to assert the Irish Republic politically, and the British government's attempt to solve the Irish problem had deteriorated virtually into a guerrilla warfare between two increasingly vicious bands of armed men, the 'Tans' – a term colloquially often extended to cover the Auxiliaries too – and the IRA. The Irish people were in the middle.

Of course the very vigour and ruthlessness with which Black and Tans and Auxiliaries operated had soon begun to have an important political effect, just as Michael Collins had calculated it would. If these men, who were tough and often brutal in their searches for arms and suspects, were the British government's only response other than the Government of Ireland partitioning bill to a demand for an Irish Republic, then the Irish people inevitably identified more and more closely with that Irish Republic. The IRA often dealt ruthlessly with fellow Irishmen. But if there had to be a choice between the two sides there could be no doubt on whose side the Irish people would in the end come down.

Apart from killing individuals – police and civilian informers – the IRA

dug holes in the roads to catch police and military transport (often ambushing the occupants afterwards), destroyed bridges and generally interfered with British communications all over Ireland. Both sides felt justified in being ruthless and when suspects were brought in for interrogation by the Black and Tans or Auxiliaries, often after an ambush in which the Crown forces had suffered casualties, the methods of interrogation were by no means in accordance with judges' rules. Often too, the police simply posted notices on the trees to the effect that for every member of the Crown forces shot, two 'Sinn Feiners' would also be shot. Rather as in 1798, reprisal and counter-reprisal followed each other in a cycle of apparently unending horror.

The burning of houses became a standard police form of reprisal. Twenty-five houses were burned in the small town of Balbriggan and the occupants driven from their homes. Co-operative dairies, or 'creameries', were burned down as a means of hitting, through their jobs, at more people than could be burned out of a house. But, of course, such measures simply made it easier for the Irish people to see this as a war between England and Ireland. Only the regular army, now in Ireland in considerable numbers, continued to be regarded with a certain amount of respect or even sometimes, by contrast with the Black and Tans, affection, though there were occasions on which even army discipline broke down.

The IRA developed flying columns of between twenty and thirty well-armed men who lived on the countryside, emerging from it to ambush Crown forces and melting back into it again, elusive, unpredictable and tough.

'On the 28th day of November,' runs a famous song, 'outside of the town of Macroom, the Tans in their big Crossley tenders were hurtling away to their doom . . .' The song celebrates the most successful of all the IRA's ambushes in this 'war': the destruction of an entire patrol of eighteen Auxiliaries at Kilmichael by a Cork flying column under the command of a former soldier of the British army, Tom Barry.

He and his men had marched all night in pouring rain through open country to take up their position by the road at eight o'clock in the morning. They had waited there all day without food, hardly daring to raise their heads and were just about to give up the ambush when at four o'clock in the afternoon, just as it was getting dark, the Crossley tenders with the Auxiliaries were signalled coming down the road. Tom Barry himself induced it to slow down by standing up in the ditch in his Volunteer officer's uniform, sufficiently indistinguishable from a British uniform to make them wonder what he was doing there. Bombs were then thrown and rifle fire started from the column's hiding-places at the side of the road. Nine Auxiliaries were killed for the loss of one IRA man. The rest of the Auxiliaries then called out that they were surrendering, and some of the column stood up and came forward to take them prisoner. The Auxiliaries, who had thrown their rifles away, fired at them with their revolvers, killing two of them, whereupon Barry gave the order to keep firing and take no prisoners. Only one wounded Auxiliary survived. The whole experience had been so unnerving for the IRA column that Barry drilled them for some minutes on the road afterwards among the dead to restore morale.

The 'war' was in the streets of Dublin too, where whole areas of the city

ABOVE: Twenty-four of them altogether in eight months. But 'prisoners of war'?

LEFT: 'Armed men at the Custom House, sir!' British files ablaze but the IRA's worst defeat.

LEFT: Ireland watched and prayed – Dubliners waiting for the result of the Truce conference, July 1921.

BELOW LEFT: Truce but 'a political settlement would be far harder to come by.' De Valera back in Dublin from his first attempt.

BELOW: Some of the men he sent to negotiate without him. Arthur Griffith (centre) and Erskine Childers and Robert Barton (to his right). But the key man was Collins.

were cordoned off from time to time as round-ups of suspects and searches for arms proceeded. Gun battles made life dangerous for civilians. In Talbot Street, Dublin, a British intelligence officer named Price cornered the IRA man Sean Treacy who, together with Dan Breen, had started the whole 'war' off at Soloheadbeg. Both Price and Treacy were killed and their bodies dumped like meat onto the back of a waiting army lorry while bystanders watched. This incident too has been immortalized in song: '. . . our lovely Sean, Is dead and gone, Shot down in Talbot Street . . .'

An equally heroic spectacle of death was provided by Terence MacSwiney, the arrested Mayor of Cork, who died in Brixton prison in London after seventy-three days on hunger strike. His body was brought back to Cork and his funeral there, at which Arthur Griffith headed the mourners, was a massive display of national solidarity. MacSwiney's ordeal had attracted attention to Ireland from all over the world.

In Dublin the street ambush of an army bread lorry in which a British soldier was killed led to the arrest of an eighteen-year-old student member of the IRA named Kevin Barry. The police who took him into the nearest army barracks, beat him up, and the army sergeant-major turned out the guard to rescue him from them. He was rescued to be hanged, in spite of massive protests in the Dublin streets where women paraded with huge banners: 'England Executes Prisoners of War'. But this was a war without nice conventions. Barry was the first of twenty-four IRA men to be executed in the next eight months.

The 21 November 1920 was the first Irish Sunday in the twentieth century to become known as 'Bloody Sunday'. It started at nine o'clock in the morning with a spectacular coup by Michael Collins. He had located the hide-outs of a number of undercover British intelligence officers in Dublin, some of them posing as Sinn Fein supporters. He had fourteen of them shot that morning by picked members of his 'squad', some of whom had been to Mass beforehand.

That afternoon there was to be an important football match between Dublin and Tipperary at Croke Park named after a great nationally-minded Irish archbishop. The whistle had just gone for a penalty against Dublin and one of the Tipperary players, Tommy Ryan, was about to take it when machine-gun and rifle-fire broke out from one end of the field. Ryan, being incidentally a senior officer in the IRA, recognized at once that these were live bullets and fell flat on the ground for cover. He was luckier than one of the other Tipperary players who was hit in the head and died immediately, one of the twelve people killed altogether.

But Bloody Sunday was still not over. In a further reprisal for the killings that morning, two senior IRA men who had been arrested by the police the night before, together with an innocent Sinn Fein supporter from County Clare, were murdered in the guard-room of Dublin Castle. Their funeral, which in the long tradition of Irish political funerals was turned into a mass demonstration of popular support for 'the cause', was distinguished by the extraordinary appearance of the most wanted man in Ireland, to lay a wreath: Michael Collins himself. He was there quite without disguise. A woman spotting him at the graveside called out inadvertently: 'Look! There's Mick Collins!' He glared at her and muttered: 'You bloody bitch!'

The next month there took place the largest of all the acts of reprisal

187

carried out by Crown forces: the burning of the centre of the city of Cork in reprisal for an ambush in which the Auxiliaries had suffered eleven casualties. Led by the commanding officer of K company of the Auxiliaries, about twenty-five men who formed a particularly tough group within the company stormed into public houses where they helped themselves to drink and started looting and burning. When the blaze became really dangerous they tried to prevent the fire brigades from reaching the scene and even cut the hoses of those who were courageous enough to proceed to it. An official British inquiry into the event was never made public.

By now this sort of thing was causing considerable embarrassment and disgust in England as well as in the rest of the world. Liberal pressure began to mount for some sort of political compromise. But the spring of 1921 came and the two sides seemed locked in deadly stalemate, while Lloyd George declaimed confidently: 'We have murder by the throat!'

Late in May 1921, the IRA launched their biggest operation of all from Dublin: the burning of the beautiful eighteenth-century Custom House on the quays of the Liffey, now the all-important centre of British administration in Ireland. The Dublin Brigade of the IRA, consisting of more than 120 men, surrounded the building during working hours and pushed their way into the offices to turn out the civil servants. Two of these, a man and a woman, were sitting quietly enjoying their cup of office tea when they suddenly found themselves confronted by a strange civilian who told them he was turning them out.

'You can't do that,' answered the woman. The intruder, though she was not to know this, was one of the men who had killed British officers in cold blood on the morning of Bloody Sunday. He now showed her his gun.

'Can I get my hat and coat?' she asked.

'You'll be lucky if you get your life,' he replied and proceeded to empty the contents of filing cabinets onto the floor, pour petrol over them and set the place ablaze.

At about the same time an Auxiliary due to return to England that evening at the end of his tour of duty was enjoying a farewell lunch with his commanding officer in Dublin Castle. Suddenly an orderly came in and said: 'Armed men at the Custom House, sir!'

The man who was due to leave decided 'to have one more trip with the boys' and arrived at the Custom House to find smoke belching out of it and rifle fire being directed at him by the Dublin IRA. But now it was the IRA's turn to be surrounded; the Auxiliaries and other Crown forces had arrived in the nick of time. One or two IRA men were shot dead and the rest, over 120 altogether, surrendered. It was not only the biggest operation the IRA had launched but also the greatest disaster they had yet experienced.

Where did this leave the IRA as a whole? They were still powerful and active in the countryside and organization and morale were good; but in Dublin, Collins had lost almost all his men as well as a considerable quantity of badly needed arms. The IRA's shortage of ammunition at this time was such that after a man had fired six shots from his revolver it was difficult for him to get any more.

The two sides in the stalemate had already begun to put out feelers towards each other. Now they did so with more realistic intent than before. On 9 July 1921, de Valera and other representatives of Sinn Fein and the IRA met British representatives including the commander-in-chief in Ireland, General Macready, and the Under-Secretary, Andy Cope. Two days later a truce was signed between all the Crown forces and the IRA. Not long before *The Irish Times* had written: 'All Ireland streams with blood.' Now, quite suddenly and almost unbelievably, it was over.

But a political solution which would turn the truce into a peace was going to be harder to achieve. There had been little opportunity in recent years for political manoeuvre. De Valera, adamant for a sovereign independent Irish Republic – though possibly in 'external association' with the British Empire – and Arthur Griffith, less dogmatic on constitutional niceties, both went to London for preliminary negotiations with the British government. But the man in whose power it lay to make or break any possible settlement was the man who had made this invitation from a British government to the IRA possible in the first place: Michael Collins.

On his first visit to London after the truce he was still wearing the moustache he had cultivated for his days on the run.

On the brink of Civil War. Anti-Treaty IRA troops in the streets of Dublin, June 1922.

Chapter 11

Civil War

In London on the 6 December 1921, after months of difficult and sometimes deadlocked negotiations between an Irish delegation, headed by Michael Collins and Arthur Griffith, and the British Cabinet, an agreement was signed at Downing Street known as the Anglo-Irish Treaty.

The conclusion of that Treaty was regarded in a rather different light by both sides. The British regarded it as having solved at last the ancient problem which had bedevilled relations between the two islands for 750 years. Michael Collins, soon after signing it, is reported to have said: 'I have signed my death warrant.' This proved to be true.

The effect of the Treaty was to give to twenty-six of the thirty-two counties of Ireland the constitutional status of the Dominion of Canada at the time, with its own army and navy and total control of its own affairs at home and abroad subject to membership of the British Commonwealth and an oath of loyalty to the king: '. . . in virtue of the common citizenship of Ireland with Great Britain and her adherence to . . . the British Commonwealth of Nations.' The new state was to be called not that 'Irish Republic' which the IRA had fought for but 'the Irish Free State'.

Two aspects of these negotiations and their final outcome are often overlooked; but they do something to explain why the British government's sanguine view of the event was to prove false. Firstly, the invitation to the Irish to come to England to negotiate had defined the purpose as how the 'national aspirations of *Ireland* could best be reconciled with the interests of the British Empire. The delegates were to be representatives of Ireland: Ulster was not mentioned. Secondly, in the Treaty itself sovereign powers over the whole of Ireland were technically given to the Irish Free State. These powers were suspended, however, one month after ratification of the Treaty in six of the Ulster counties (Londonderry, Antrim, Down, Armagh, Tyrone and Fermanagh); but to be in a state of suspension they must have been in a state of theoretical existence.

It was stipulated that if at the end of that month those counties as a whole chose to opt out of the newly created Irish Free State they could do so. Everyone knew that they would; they did, and have remained outside ever since. But the Treaty had at least accepted that the Irish nationalist claim for Ireland to be one country had a seriously recognizable foundation. What was left unresolved in Irish minds, but treated by Britain as if it had been dealt with, was the question of whether the claim of the majority in the six counties to be separate from the rest of Ireland had a greater or lesser foundation. In view of the apparent certainty with which Britain had answered the question by that clause in the Treaty permitting the six counties to opt out, and in view of the continuing certainty shown by succeeding British governments to the same effect, it is worth recalling what Gladstone had said on the subject thirty years before the Treaty: 'I cannot allow it to be said that a Protestant minority in Ulster . . . is to rule the question at large for Ireland. I am aware of no constitutional doctrine tolerable on which such a conclusion could be adopted or justified.'

None of this is to suggest that settlement of the two conflicting claims one way or the other is right, only that it is not surprising in retrospect to find that the matter still gives trouble.

At the time it was clouded by other aspects of the Treaty. One of these was a clause which appointed, in the event of the six counties of Northern Ireland opting out of the Free State, a Boundary Commission to adjust the border between the two areas 'in accordance with the wishes of the inhabitants'. Many nationalists, including Michael Collins, believed that if faithfully carried out this would remove the counties of Tyrone and Fermanagh, where there was a particularly large Catholic and nationalist population, from Northern Ireland to the Free State. The remaining four counties, it was contended, would not find themselves a viable political entity, and would be forced to join the Free State. Thus the issue of 'partition' at the time could be made to look less final than it has become since.

Another aspect of the Treaty which made the failure to unite Ireland seem less urgent was the oath to the king which in the minds of many nationalist Irishmen seemed to provide a more important issue still. Clause 4 prescribed the oath to be taken by members of the Free State's Parliament, the Dail, as follows:

I do solemnly swear true faith and allegiance to the Constitution of the Irish Free State as by law established . . . and that I will be faithful to HM King George V, his heirs and successors by law, in virtue of the common citizenship of Ireland with Great Britain and her adherence to and membership of the group of nations forming the British Commonwealth of nations.

This was anathema to many republicans. Dan Breen, the man who had begun the republican violence in 1919 was to say that it made the Treaty 'the negation of everything I ever fought for . . . I wasn't going to be compelled to give allegiance to a foreign king.'

In fact, Collins, negotiating hard with Lloyd George had managed at the last moment to have the word 'allegiance' in the clause shifted as far away as possible from the word 'King'. He knew quite well what many people like Breen who had helped him to his negotiating position were going to think about it. But he was to argue that the oath could be seen as a mere symbol necessary to secure a constitutional position from which it could later be abolished. 'You'd take the oath to get rid of it,' as one of his IRA supporters put it. IRA opponents on the other hand were to argue that it was the very symbols of British rule which had helped them easily clarify what they were fighting against.

Thus, while among the ordinary population of Ireland the general reaction to the Treaty was one of relief and thankfulness that the horror of the last two and a half years had been ended, with the greater part of Ireland freer from London government than she had been for centuries, the IRA itself was split – well over half of them regarded the Treaty as a betrayal.

The fact that Collins himself had signed it of course made it easier for many of them to accept it on his terms, namely that it gave 'the freedom to win freedom'. His continued control of the still existing Irish Republican Brotherhood enabled him to disseminate this argument forcibly, although the final IRB decision was to leave the matter to individual consciences. On the other hand the opposition of Eamon de Valera to the Treaty lent its IRA opponents sober political respectability should they feel that necessary.

De Valera, the titular head of the republican 'government' which negotiated the Treaty with the British, had remained behind in Dublin, principally because he knew that some compromise on the full republican demand was inevitable and that all his political skills would be required there to make it acceptable. He had made the delegation in London his 'plenipotentiaries'; on the other hand he had instructed them not to sign a final settlement without first referring it back to Dublin. They had in fact returned to Dublin to consult with him on more than one occasion of deadlock in the negotiations, but, impressed by Lloyd George with a sense of critical urgency during the last tense night of negotiation, they had eventually signed without even resorting to the telephone – by no means such an easy means of communication in 1921 as it is today. De Valera dissociated himself from the Treaty and the split in the IRA was thus reflected among the republican politicians themselves.

But it was the split in the IRA which was important. The Dail, after a series of agonizingly emotional debates in the course of which de Valera was in tears, finally ratified the Treaty by a small majority. The country itself ratified the Treaty by a larger, though not overwhelming one, in the first Free State General Election held in June 1922. But few in the IRA had ever felt their nominal allegiance to the Dail as primarily binding, and the country had never been consulted democratically at any time as to whether or not it approved of IRA violence. Civil War between those of the old IRA who had become part of the new Free State army and those who remained aloof from it, though armed and organized and still often occupying former British barracks, broke out in June 1922. It was precipitated by a series of grim events.

Earlier, in April 1922, when tension between the pro- and anti-Treaty sections of the IRA ran high and sincere hopes on both sides that it might be resolved were beginning to evaporate, leaders of the anti-Treaty elements had occupied and set up their headquarters in the Dublin Four Courts. The most prominent of the republican leaders there who regarded the Treaty Collins had signed as a sell-out were Rory O'Connor, who had been his Director of Engineering, and Liam Mellowes, one of the few Volunteer leaders to have taken action outside Dublin in 1916. They were backed by some of the most successful leaders of flying columns in the 'war' against the British: men like Liam Lynch and Tom Barry from the south, and in Dublin, by Ernie O'Malley, who had been one of Collins's principal IRA organizers. A song was to express the feelings of their rank and file: 'Soldiers of '22', one verse of which ran:

LEFT: A prosaic end to seven and a half centuries. Michael Collins (centre), Kevin O'Higgins (ahead) and Eamon Duggan (behind) take over British administration at Dublin Castle, January 1921.

BELOW LEFT: Some of the IRA put on Free State army uniforms and take over British barracks. 10,000 rifles from the British too.

BELOW: But what about the rest of the IRA? 'The Treaty was the negation of everything I ever fought for . . .' They are reviewed by de Valera.

Take it down from the mast, Irish traitors,
The flag we Republicans claim,
It can never belong to Free Staters,
You've brought on it nothing but shame.

The enrolment in the Free State army of many Irishmen who had been officers and men of the British army confirmed republicans in their view that the new state was merely a continuation of British rule in disguise – what today might be called a neo-colonialist venture. The fact that it was headed by their old leaders, Collins and Arthur Griffith, only increased republicans' bitterness.

Collins' own feelings in this situation do not need to be imagined. In January 1922 he wrote to the Irish girl to whom he was engaged: 'I am really and truly having an awful time and am rapidly becoming quite desperate. Oh Lord, it is honestly frightful.' Such feelings were intensified by developments in what was now 'Northern Ireland'. Fears among the Protestant population there that the Boundary Commission might indeed undermine their new state had stimulated them to behave in the manner they had behaved for centuries whenever they suspected that they were going to be overwhelmed by the Catholic majority in Ireland. Serious rioting took place early in 1922. There were 138 casualties in Belfast alone in February (three-quarters of them Catholic) and 30 people were killed in a single night. Catholic refugees streamed south of the border.

The IRA, both North and South, did what they could to protect their fellow nationalists and Collins, though in honour bound by the Treaty to respect the integrity of the northern state, equally 'could not stand idly by' (a phrase that was to become famous in analogous circumstances nearly fifty years later; see page 237) and leave nationalists to be murdered. He therefore found himself in the ambiguous position of supplying arms to the anti-Treaty IRA in the North while faced by a challenge to his authority and that of the Free State, from their comrades in the Four Courts. The double crisis was brought to a head in June by revolver shots in London.

The situation in the North had by then deteriorated still further. Deaths in communal violence in the six counties in the first six months of 1922 amounted to 264 (two-thirds of them Catholics). New paramilitary police forces organized by Sir James Craig's government in the North (A and B Specials) were asserting law and order in a manner by no means meticulously consistent with the principles of law and order. Craig's security adviser in the North was the British Field Marshal, Sir Henry Wilson, a diehard Unionist in Irish affairs. On the 22 June 1922 he was shot down by two IRA men on the steps of his home in Eaton Place, London. Curiously, though the men were then acting on their own initiative, they had, before the truce, received orders from Collins himself to 'execute' Wilson. Their action now precipitated him into an even more painful phase of the crisis in which he was enmeshed, though his conscience led him to make strenuous but unavailing efforts with the British government to save them from the gallows.

That government, which for months had watched with increasing anxiety the continued passive toleration by the Free State of anti-Treaty republican headquarters in Dublin, now assumed wrongly that the orders

ABOVE LEFT: Michael Collins in Free State uniform. 'I have signed my own death warrant.'

ABOVE: De Valera reviews the electorate. Anti-Treaty meeting, Dublin 1922.

LEFT: Still trying to keep together, February 1922. Front row, fourth from the left, moving right: Arthur Griffith, Eamon de Valera, Michael Collins, Harry Boland (soon to be killed by Free State troops).

for the shooting of Wilson had come from there and insisted that Collins should take action against the Four Courts. Otherwise they would regard the Treaty as abrogated. After stalling for some days Collins, provoked on his own account by the kidnapping of one of his Generals by the republican forces, eventually gave the Four Courts twenty minutes in which to surrender and, when they refused, began to shell them from the other side of the Liffey with two field guns he had borrowed from the British. The range was ridiculously short but since the only available shells were shrapnel they took two days to have effect. Other anti-Treaty republican forces then took up their positions in buildings in O'Connell Street; guests who were breakfasting in the Hamman Hotel were told by embarrassed IRA men to get upstairs, pack their bags and leave. A week later part of O'Connell Street was once again in ruins. The Irish Civil War had begun.

After eight days fighting in Dublin during which 60 people were killed and 300 wounded the anti-Treaty republicans in O'Connell Street surrendered as those in the Four Courts had done. Cathal Brugha, a hero of 1916, had refused to do so and was mortally wounded. Rory O'Connor, Liam Mellowes and other top IRA men were prisoners in Mountjoy jail as so many IRA men had been in the time of the British. But in other parts of Ireland, particularly in the south and west, the anti-Treaty IRA were strong and they held the city of Cork.

As if relieved from the worst of his anxieties by the external breaking of the tension Collins now threw himself into the campaign against his old comrades-in-arms with the same energy he had shown against the British. He procured an extra ten thousand rifles from the British government and filled the ranks of the new Free State army both with former professionals of the British and American armies, and the old RIC, and with raw young country boys, many of whom only learned to load their rifles shortly before going into action. Sweeps were made across the countryside towards Limerick in which the one-time British field guns which had been used to shell the Four Courts were trundled down country lanes into firing positions by traction engines.

The pressure began to tell on the often scattered anti-Treaty republican forces who could no longer rely on support from the population as they had been able to do in the latter part of the fight against the British. Because communications across the south of Ireland were still being effectively harassed by republicans (soon to be known as 'irregulars') Collins sent Free State troops round by sea to take the city of Cork which they did without difficulty at the beginning of August 1922 and moved inland. Advancing apprehensively through the Cork streets they found slogans on the walls: 'Collins marches through Cork. Why not through Belfast?'

It was not only on the anti-Treaty republicans that the pressure told. A week after Cork had fallen Ireland was shattered by the news that Arthur Griffith, only fifty, exhausted by overwork, had collapsed and died of a heart attack. Collins came up from the military operations in the south to help carry his coffin at the funeral. He then returned to the Cork area to tour the newly won Free State positions there. One of his military aides, Emmet Dalton, was concerned for his safety but Collins, a Cork man himself, had replied confidently: 'Sure, they won't shoot me in my own county.'

At about 7.30 pm on the 22 August the convoy in which he was travelling, consisting of a motor cycle outrider, his own open Rolls-Royce touring car, a Crossley tender and an armoured car, ran into a set of obstacles placed across the road in a gulley called Bealnamblath between Macroom and Bandon. A party of anti-Treaty republicans had been waiting for them there all day. Firing broke out as the convoy halted. Half an hour later, and before it got dark, Collins was dead.

The death of a hero always invites legend. It is necessary to make the unbearable bearable by embroidering it in some way. As with Cuchulain, the ancient hero of Gaelic legend, so, in a more prosaic twentieth-century way it was to be with Collins. It was later said, and is still sometimes believed in Ireland even today, that he had been shot by one of his own side, either by the machine-gunner in the armoured car (who did indeed desert to the republicans later), or by one of his closest colleagues, Emmet Dalton; it was also said that the whole ambush had been engineered by de Valera, who was indeed in the vicinity at the time but had no part in republican military operations and, as a politician, was temporarily irrelevant. The truth seems to have been that as the firing died down and the ambush seemed to be over Collins stood up in the road and was hit either directly by a last lone sniper from the ridge above or by a ricochet. Emmet Dalton ran up the road and an act of contrition was whispered into the ear of the man known to be dying if not already dead from a gaping wound in the back of his head.

Devastating as the news was to many on both sides in the Civil War, particularly coming so soon after the news of Griffith's death the week before, there were also those who rejoiced when they heard it, so bitter had that civil war now become. One Dublin woman, who would have laid down her own life for Collins in the year before, looked up from her newspaper with eyes shining the next day and exclaimed: 'Isn't it great news?' Nationalist Ireland was being torn apart. But still worse was to come.

With the republicans less and less in a position to conduct military operations of any size in the field they resorted increasingly to standard 'irregular' methods: individual killings, destruction of property, blowing up of bridges, bank robberies. As for the Free State, with Collins and Griffith gone, the new leaders who took over were determined to prove their ability to hold it together at all costs. Principally these consisted of the Prime Minister William Cosgrave, who had been out in the 1916 Rising and condemned to death but reprieved, Kevin O'Higgins, a former law student and ardent Sinn Fein supporter who had been elected to the Dail in the General Election of 1918, Ernest Blythe who had been a supporter of Arthur Griffith before the 1914–18 war and Richard Mulcahy who had been Collins's old Chief of Staff and was now in charge of the Free State army. Their impeccable nationalist credentials probably helped give them the strength to do what they now did.

An Emergency Powers Bill was introduced and passed by the Dail. The decision had been taken to shoot – after a period of grace allowed for surrender – any republicans taken in arms. The first of seventy-seven executions to be carried out in the next seven months took place in November when four rank and file members of the anti-Treaty IRA caught in arms in Dublin were shot by firing squad.

RIGHT: Field Marshal Sir Henry Wilson.

BELOW: An IRA man under arrest June 1922: he had just shot and killed Field Marshal Sir Henry Wilson in Eaton Place. He was later hanged.

But it was the executions that immediately followed these which were to prove so traumatic, scarring the political life of the new free Ireland for a generation and more. On 24 November 1922, the man who had proved the most effective propagandist for the republican cause in the days of the fighting against the British and was continuing the same work now against the Free State, Erskine Childers, was shot at dawn for possession of a small revolver which Michael Collins had once given him. When the incensed anti-Treaty republican command then decreed that any member of the Dail who had voted for the Emergency Powers Act was liable to be shot on sight, and began to put their decree into practice, the Free State government had the four chief members of the republican executive who had been taken prisoner in the Four Courts five months before, including Rory O'Connor and Liam Mellowes, removed from their cells in the middle of the night and shot without trial. The decision to do this had been supported by the entire Cabinet, though O'Higgins had asked for a moment: 'Is there no other way?' recalling doubtless among other things that he had been best man at Rory O'Connor's wedding.

Such temporary squeamishness had no further place in the Free State Cabinet's thoughts. Thirty-four republicans were executed by firing squad in January 1923 alone in nine different towns of Ireland. Soon after the seventy-seventh execution in May – of William Shaughnessy at Ennis – de Valera, whose role as a republican political leader had begun to resume significance as the IRA's military effort collapsed, issued an order endorsed by the IRA to 'dump arms'. He accompanied it with a stirring message to 'soldiers of the rearguard' which told them that now 'other means must be sought to safeguard the nation's right.' He was to devote the rest of his life to that pursuit. So, after a different fashion, was a continually changing leadership of an almost mystically corporate IRA with which he was increasingly to come into conflict, but which has survived him.

Meanwhile the Free State's desperate but eventually successful struggle to survive had meant not only that a harsh bitterness now divided Irish nationalists (with 13,000 republicans in jail, many enduring long hunger strikes for their lost cause) but also that the long-term objectives for which Collins had signed the Treaty became lost to view as maintenance of the Treaty itself became the goal. This effect was reinforced by the fact that de Valera, after a year in jail himself, although elected together with other politicized republicans to mount an effective democratic opposition in the Dail, refused to take that oath of allegiance which would have enabled them to sit there. The real opposition in the country (apart from a relatively small Labour party) thus took no part in political life for the next four years. In such a situation it was too easy for the Free State simply to concentrate on consolidation of its position. In particular this meant that the issue of partition subsided by default.

It was not until 1924 that the Free State asked the British government to set up the Boundary Commission stipulated by the Treaty. This immediately produced an embarrassing problem for the British inasmuch as Sir James Craig, the Prime Minister of Northern Ireland, refused to take part in it, which, not being a signatory to the Treaty himself, he was fully entitled to do. The British had to appoint an Ulster representative of their own, a close friend of Craig's, Joseph Fisher, in addition to their official representative, an imperially-minded South African judge named Feetham. The Free State's representative was Eoin MacNeill, the Gaelic League's co-founder and nominal head of the Volunteers in 1916, who was by no means an aggressive negotiator.

A fundamental difference of view set in at once as to whether the concept of adjustment of the border 'in accordance with the wishes of the inhabitants' meant more than a mere minor adjustment. In fact there could be no doubt whatever that the inhabitants of considerable areas of Tyrone and Fermanagh, together with smaller areas of Derry, South Down and South Armagh, wished to be incorporated with their fellow nationalists in the Free State, while the inhabitants of strips of East Donegal and North Monaghan wished to be incorporated in Northern Ireland. But in an atmosphere conditioned by statements from British signatories of the Treaty to the effect that what had been intended was merely to simplify and thus consolidate the Northern government's jurisdiction over the six counties, there could also be no doubt that the two British-appointed representatives on the Commission would determine the issue in this way. After a whole year's desultory argument during which the Free State showed itself curiously inert on the subject, MacNeill resigned when by the inevitable two-thirds majority the Commission had decided that indeed only very minor adjustments would be made, actually including the transfer of some territory in Donegal from the Free State to Northern Ireland.

It is not difficult to imagine how Collins would have reacted if he had ever allowed the deliberations of the Boundary Commission to get this far. What the Free State government did was to go to London in December 1925 and agree to an amendment of the Treaty by which the Boundary Commission was abandoned altogether in return for a cancellation of certain financial obligations of the Free State to the British government under the Treaty. Cosgrave and O'Higgins, returning to Dublin, declared publicly: 'Today we have sown the seeds of peace . . .'

Ironically they had settled for a compromise on Ulster far more injurious to the cause of Irish nationalist unity than anything John Redmond and the Irish Parliamentary party had ever considered. Yet it was on the grounds that Redmond and the Parliamentary party had been too prepared to compromise over Ulster that Sinn Fein had been able to replace them in popularity with the Irish electorate. Far from 'sowing the seeds of peace' the issue remains one over which there was still to be a sort of war in Northern Ireland nearly seventy years later.

Quite apart from this legal consolidation of the partition of Ireland there had been an important psychological consolidation of it in the minds of the Protestant Unionists of the North. No one summed this up better than Kevin O'Higgins himself, explaining bitterly in the Dail what had been the effect on north-east Ulster of the Civil War and its lawlessness in the south.

We had an opportunity of building up a worthy State that would attract and, in time, absorb and assimilate those elements. . . . We preferred to burn our own houses, blow up our own bridges, rob our own banks, saddle ourselves with millions of debt for the maintenance of an army. . . . Generally we preferred to practise upon ourselves worse indignities than the British had practised on us

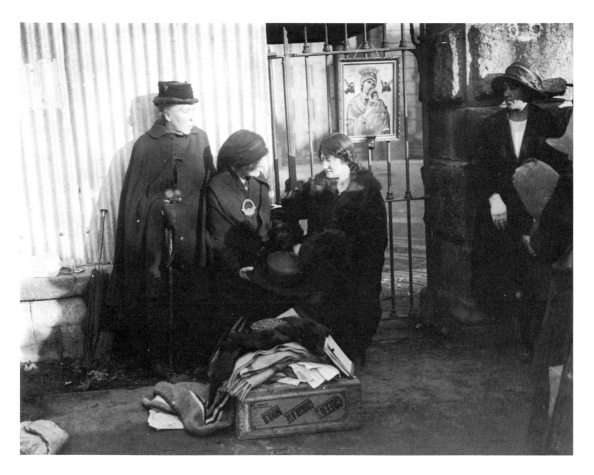

MERRY WIDOW'S SECOND HUSBAND: COURT STORY

DAILY SKETCH.

No. 4,272. Telephones {London—Holborn 6510. Manchester—City 6501. LONDON, SATURDAY, NOVEMBER 25, 1922. (Registered as a Newspaper) ONE PENNY.

ERSKINE CHILDERS EXECUTED IN DUBLIN

Mrs. Erskine Childers is an American with strong Irish sympathies. An invalid for many years, she collapsed on receiving news of her husband's execution.

Erskine Childers (left) was executed in Kilmainham Gaol, Dublin, yesterday. The Irish Master of the Rolls had refused to grant a writ of habeas corpus applied for on his behalf. Childers is here photographed with Mr. E. J. Duggan (right) when in London at the time of the Irish Treaty negotiations.—(Daily Sketch.)

Erskine Childers first became famous as author of "The Riddle of the Sands." Latterly he was De Valera's right hand.

Erskine Childers's son daily visited the courts to hear the pleas made for his father's life.

The news of the execution of Erskine Childers, after a four days' legal fight for his life, was officially announced by the Free State yesterday. Childers was arrested in Co. Wicklow and charged with "having possession of an automatic pistol without proper authority."

Erskine Childers had a distinguished war record. He served in the R.N.A.S., and was awarded the D.S.C.

Mr. Patrick Lynch, K.C. (left), appeared for Erskine Childers before the Military Court, in Dublin, by whom Childers was tried and sentenced to death. Counsel also applied to the Master of the Rolls for a writ of habeas corpus.

since Cromwell . . . and now we wonder why the Orangemen are not hopping like so many fleas across the border in their anxiety to come within our fold and jurisdiction . . .

As a statement of the Northern Protestant Unionists' case at the time it was unanswerable. Subjected as the Northern Protestants were to be from 1970–94 to lawlessness in their own midst inspired by exactly the same Republican cause, it seems more unanswerable than ever.

Chapter 12

Free State to Republic

'When all the shooting was finished, and all the dead were buried, and the politicians took over, what had you got left? A lost cause!'

The words, years later of a former member of Connolly's Irish Citizen Army and veteran of the IRA campaign of 1920–1, who, after the Treaty of 1921 and acceptance of defeat by the Republicans in the Civil War of 1922–3, continued to try to fight for what he saw as the true republican ideal.

In abstract theory his point of view is understandable. The IRA of 1920–1 had fought for an Irish Republic as a symbol of the most complete separation from Britain possible, and therefore – it almost went without saying – for a united Ireland. They had got neither. The difficulty for this 'soldier of the rearguard' and others like him who were to constitute a self-perpetuating IRA chasing a republican Holy Grail down the years, was to be that a substitute Holy Grail – not exactly instantly available but presented as being within reasonable and above all non-violent reach – was offered to the Irish people by 'the politicians'. Or by one politician in particular: Eamon de Valera. Since the majority of the Irish people had accepted the Free State in any case and were to have within it an alternative democratic way of proceeding, the IRA's principal enemy was always to be its own apparent irrelevance. Only in 1969 did an opportunity for some real new relevance appear and it eventually seized this with both hands. Between 1923 and 1969 the story of the IRA, periodically bloody, was predominantly sad and bitter.

The rebuilding of the battered Four Courts, soon a daily spectacle for Dubliners, outwardly symbolized the patient construction of the new State under new leaders – principally William Cosgrave, the President of the Executive Council, and his Minister for Home Affairs, Kevin O'Higgins. Law and order began to be painstakingly restored by a new police force, the Civic Guard. On the land, in the factories, and in the towns, normal routines of work and leisure were resumed after the peremptory and often savage dislocations of civil war. Yet the new State was founded on a terrible seam of bitterness. The execution of republicans taken in arms had continued for nearly a year after the Four Courts had surrendered; and when the bodies of those shot by firing squad in Dublin were handed back to relatives and friends, no church in Dublin would take them in; the traditional 'wakes' for the dead had to be held in a theatre. Agonizing hunger strikes of

Queen Victoria has to go, Dublin 1946.

republicans in jails left their marks on more than just the bodies of the men who undertook them. Many republicans, acknowledging in despair that their cause was indeed lost and that the Free State seemed based on unshakeable foundations, emigrated to America in the resignation that succeeds despair.

But two groups of republicans did not despair: two groups, linked by past comradeship at first, who gradually separated into enmity. One group stemmed directly from the executive of the IRA which had started the Civil War. The remnants of this group decided to re-form and continue to work for the same objective as before, a republic of the whole island totally free from Britain, using, where feasible, the same weapon as before: the gun. The other group, headed by Eamon de Valera, offered a subtler, non-violent approach.

In his last message which accompanied the order to 'dump arms' de Valera had reassured the 'soldiers of the rearguard' that in a little time the Irish people, who needed a rest, would recover and rally to the standard. Indeed the result of the General Election of May 1923 showed conclusively that there was a sizeable proportion of the Irish people on their side, for forty-four republicans had been elected, constituting about thirty per cent of the successful candidates. These, however, did not take their seats in the Dail for, as good anti-Treaty republicans they refused to take the oath of allegiance to a Free State which involved their being 'faithful to HM King George V, his heirs and successors'. But the election result was reassurance to de Valera that he had something to work on, and conversely some cause for alarm to the government – all the more so since this opposition was at first determined to remain outside the official political structure. In any case the Free State was taking no chances and had even, in the course of the election, had its troops arrest de Valera when he emerged from clandestinity to address his constituents from a platform in Ennis. Though he was in fact elected by an overwhelming majority he was imprisoned for a year, only to return to Ennis immediately on his release and continue to speak in identical terms against the Free State for its betrayal of republican ideals. He and his followers continued to refuse to take the oath in the Dail.

Meanwhile the more extreme wing of the old Civil War republican executive – the re-constituted IRA – were looking around for an effective role in the old style. The Free State's draconian anti-terrorist measures introduced by O'Higgins, which included the penalty of flogging, cramped this style severely. A further handicap was their lack of any wide support among a population too long discomfited by violence. The new IRA was temporarily reduced to destruction of such symbols of the British Imperial connection as they could find round Dublin – painted or stone crowns, lions and unicorns that were reasonably accessible – and to disruption by revolver shots of the vast armistice day crowds which as late as 1925 still packed the streets of Dublin on 11 November to wave Union Jacks and remember the southern Irish dead of the First World War – a far higher number of casualties than all those of 1916 and the 'war of independence' combined.

An IRA achievement later in the 1920s was the partial demolition of the statue of William III, victor of the Boyne, on College Green. One member of the IRA, then working on the staff of a night-club to which he brought the appropriate paraphernalia in a parcel, helped a comrade climb up in the darkness onto the base of the statue where, however, he could find nothing more substantial to which to tie the explosive than the raised fore-foot of the Orange King's horse. It was a delayed action fuse and the demolition team got well away before the explosion occurred. This failed to tumble the royal statue but succeeded, as one of the perpetrators of the deed was later to recall, in 'shaking it badly'. A more ambitious and blood-ier but equally fruitless IRA action took place late in 1926 when twelve police barracks were attacked across the country and two Civic Guards killed.

There were those within the IRA who, in view of the apparent ineffectu-alness to which it was now reduced wished to give it a new radical type of idealistic direction along the lines of James Connolly's socialism. But just as an understandably obsessional need to establish the Free State on the basis of the Treaty excluded from the minds of its politicians consideration of all but the most conservative socio-economic principles of the society they had inherited from the British, so hypnotic preoccupation with the mystical symbolism of an elusive Republic clouded the minds of most of the gun-men in the IRA, and made socio-political thinking seem a distraction from the only true objective. Socialist minded members of the IRA, among the more progressive of whom were Peadar O'Donnell and George Gilmore, continually tried, for a period of years, to lead the high command in this direction but without effect. O'Donnell recalled how on one occasion he sent a message to IRA units in a country locality to support workers involved in a dispute over wages and conditions with a local bus company – they interpreted this as an instruction to blow up one of the buses which they promptly did. O'Donnell and Gilmore were eventually to leave the IRA in despair in the 1930s because of its refusal to accept a more responsible social role, while another leftist, Frank Ryan, was to lead a group of IRA men to fight for republican Spain in an effort to assert its contemporary rele-vance. (He was taken prisoner by Franco and some time after the outbreak of the Second World War was released to spend his last years, paradoxically, in the shelter of Nazi Germany.)

But if the IRA's ineffectualness seemed unable to find resolution, this was of minor consideration to the great majority of citizens in the Free State who had little time for it. It was a different matter with de Valera and his republicans. In 1926 in fact de Valera had reorganized his supporters into a new political party. Formerly, they had called themselves by the old name of *Sinn Fein*; they now became *Fianna Fail*, (Warriors of Ireland). But at the same time they were both rendering themselves politically impotent by refusing to take the oath when they had a perfectly coherent political pro-gramme, and depriving a sizeable proportion of the citizens of the new Irish democracy of the right to try and see that programme implemented. The seriousness of their own stranglehold on themselves was emphasized by the result of the General Election of 1927 in which Fianna Fail won almost as many seats as the government party of Cosgrave and O'Higgins (forty-four against forty-seven). Indeed they might well have won more had not many Fianna Fail supporters, seeing a vote for a party that was not going into the Dail as wasted, voted for the opposition Labour Party instead.

De Valera now literally took his first steps towards entering the Free State democracy. He and his other elected supporters went to the Dail building and tried to gain admittance to the Chamber. They were asked to go through the formality of taking the oath but refused and then had the doors of the Chamber locked against them. They walked briskly out of the Dail grounds again and de Valera then addressed a large crowd in the street from the first floor of his headquarters with appropriately stirring words about refusing to take a false oath and 'prove recreant to the aspirations of the Irish people' by renouncing their principles.

A few weeks later a violent event took place which transformed the political scene in the Free State and indirectly led de Valera, by a casuistic device, to take the oath without apparently renouncing the Irish people's principles. On 10 July 1927, Kevin O'Higgins, the Minister for Home Affairs, was shot dead on the pavement outside his house while on his way to Mass. His assassins were IRA men acting not on orders of the IRA high command but on their own initiative in the hope of thus making IRA policy more aggressive.

The immediate result was a severe new Public Safety Act and the introduction of an Electoral Amendment Bill by which in future no candidate could stand at an election unless he swore beforehand to take the Dail oath if elected. In this critical moment for the new Irish democracy de Valera who had to his credit opted for democracy by dissociating himself from the IRA was forced into the Dail. Once again he and his elected supporters went to seek admittance to the Chamber so that they could take their seats. Once again he was asked by the Clerk to take the oath. But this time, while declaring firmly that he was taking no oath and removing the Bible that lay on the table alongside the book in which those taking the oath had to write their names, he nevertheless wrote his name in that book. It was judged that the necessary formality had been complied with.

So great already was the quasi-theological spell that this strangely effective man was able to cast over politics ('the constitutional Houdini of his generation' is the description applied to him by F.S.L. Lyons), that few seem to have asked at the time why, if the oath was such an easily overcome formality in 1927, it had not been so in the years before. But at least Ireland now had a properly working two-party democratic system with one party pledged to revise the Treaty in a new oath-less constitution which would one day theoretically bring about a united Ireland. The IRA might well have been thought to be more irrelevant than ever.

But curiously the IRA was, in the course of the next five years, temporarily to recover something of its lost significance and even acquire a role, though that role was in a subordinate capacity to Fianna Fail. De Valera's 'soldiers of the rearguard' might not be taking to arms literally this time but they were metaphorically on the offensive in the Dail and as such could make use of a vanguard outside it. The Cosgrave government was already beginning to experience the sort of automatic unpopularity that awaits any democratic government that is long in office and particularly one which has had to confront difficult times with strong measures. It was also about to run into a world economic depression. There was a reckless confidence about some of Fianna Fail's leaders' remarks in the Dail which struck an ambivalent note congenial enough to the republican military organization outside. 'We are a slightly constitutional party,' said Sean

Lemass, de Valera's able lieutenant on one occasion, adding, '. . . but before anything we are a Republican party.' And de Valera himself declared that he would stand by the flag of the Republic again as he had done in 1922 and made sympathetic comments about the continuity of tradition of the IRA.

To a party sailing as close to the constitutional wind as this, the illegal drilling in which the IRA increasingly indulged, even the 'executions' they periodically carried out in the name of republican 'continuity', inevitably did not seem so heinous as they did to the Cosgrave government which had built the Free State. And reciprocally the Public Safety measures which that government took in its own defence, setting up a military tribunal with powers of death, seemed almost as heinous to Fianna Fail as they did to the IRA against whom they were directed. After all Fianna Fail and the IRA did share the same republican objective, to overturn the Constitution, even though Fianna Fail proposed to do so by constitutional methods.

Thus Fianna Fail entered the General Election of February 1932 almost in tandem with the now illegal IRA. And the influence of the IRA on the streets and even in the polling booths was probably decisive in securing a narrow victory for Fianna Fail. The IRA went canvassing for Fianna Fail on doorsteps in companies so that anyone answering the door and being asked if he were going to vote for Fianna Fail would find sinister groups of men standing about watching them. Similarly the IRA organized effective plural voting in the polling booths, impersonating the dead or the sick or the merely absent, as had long been the custom in Irish elections, though possibly never so fully practised as now by Irish republicans. Some are reckoned to have voted fifty times. In the following year, 1933, such methods were hardly required, for de Valera and Fianna Fail were returned to power with an even greater number of seats and, with the support of Labour, a comfortable working majority. They were to remain in power for another sixteen years, in the course of which not only was the Constitution of the Free State constitutionally done away with, but also the whole fabric of Ireland's twenty-six-county independence from Britain was immeasurably strengthened.

So solidly in fact was de Valera's once only 'slightly constitutional' party to become a new Irish establishment that it is difficult now to remember the atmosphere of apprehension in which it first took office. Some in Fianna Fail were expecting that Cosgrave's party, *Cumann na Gaedheal*, would try and prevent them assuming their newly won power and revolvers were even issued to Fianna Fail members before entering the Dail, though according to Sean MacEntee, who was one of those to whom they were handed, no ammunition was issued with them. There is even one, doubtless apocryphal, story of an over-apprehensive Fianna Fail member of the Dail being caught in a telephone box assembling a machine gun. But any such precautions were to prove unnecessary.

It is true that the commander of the Free State troops at the Curragh Camp had earlier been approached to know what he was going to do if Fianna Fail got in. He suspected that some sort of political kite was being flown. He replied firmly that, as far as he was concerned, just as the Treaty had been accepted by a democratic vote, so he was prepared to accept de Valera as the people's choice and see what he could do with the country. He was then asked: 'What about the rest of the army?' He replied: 'I don't

PRESIDENT DeValera and his Cabinet

Seán Mac an tSaoi
Aire Airgid
Seán MacEntee, T.D.
Minister for Finance

Seán Leimeas
Aire Tionscoil 7 Tráctála
Seán F. Lemass, T.D.
Minister for Industry
and Commerce

Seosaṁ Ó Conġaile
Aire Tailte 7 Iascaiġ
Senator Joseph Connolly,
Minister for Lands and Fisheries

Séamus Ó Riain
Aire Talṁaíoċta
James Ryan, M.B., T.D.
Minister for Agriculture

Eaṁonn de Valéra, B.A., B.Sc., T.D.
Uaċtarán, 7 Aire Gnóṫaí Coigríce
President and Minister for External Affairs

Proinnsias ÓhAoḋaġáin
Aire Cosanta
Frank Aiken, T.D.
Minister for Defence

S.T. Ó Ceallaiġ
leas-Uaċtarán agus
Aire Rialtais Áitiúla
agus Sláinte Puiblí
Seán T. O'Kelly, T.D.
Vice President
and Minister for
Local Government
and
Public Health

Tomás Ó Deirg
Aire Oideaċais
Thomas Derrig, T.D.
Minister for Education

Gearóid Ó Beoláin
Aire Puist 7 Teleġrafa
Gerald Boland, T.D.
Minister for Posts and
Telegraphs

Pádraig Ruitléis
Aire Dlí 7 Cirt
Patrick J. Ruttledge, T.D.
Minister for Justice

LEFT: The losers of the
Civil War win power, 1932.
No call for revolvers.

BELOW LEFT: William
Cosgrave, guardian of the
Irish Free State 1922–32.

BELOW: General Eoin
O'Duffy, ex-IRA, ex-Free
State Police Commissioner
hoping to be an Irish
Mussolini. He and his
Blueshirts got nowhere but
Franco's Spain.

know about the rest of the army, but I'm in charge of the Curragh Camp and I have the largest body of troops there; if anybody attempts any kind of a *coup* he'll have me on his back.'

There was no coup, or any attempt at one. The change-over in which the previously defeated of the bitter Civil War assumed power from the formerly victorious took place smoothly and in exemplary democratic fashion. This was perhaps not as surprising as it seemed to some at the time. After all, for those ten years since the Civil War, Cosgrave and the Government of the Free State had been battling to assert the principle that the ballot box should prevail over the gun and they had proved themselves men of integrity. At the same time it was understandable that men who had in 1922 assumed the right to determine for themselves what was the will of the people, regardless of what the people had decided, should feel some uneasiness about the readiness of an army that had once given them short shrift to accept them as their masters.

In fact de Valera and his supporters, reassured by the correctness with which they were received in office both by the Army and the Civil Service, were immediately able, equally correctly, to set about implementing their declared programme and altering the constitutional fabric of the State which had accepted them.

De Valera declared euphorically:

It will be the dawn of a new day for Ireland. Our people in the United States, in Britain, in Australia will know a gladness they have not known since 1921. The joy born of the coming together of old friends long divided has set the youth of the country on fire . . .

How far old friends in the republican military organization, the IRA (declared illegal by the Cosgrave government), and Fianna Fail were now going to be able to come together was an interesting, though delicate question which he did not go into.

The oath was removed from the Constitution; the role of the Governor General reduced to virtual meaninglessness; the Land Annuities, the mortgage-type payments which Irish farmers had been paying into the British Exchequer under the Land Purchase Acts to make them owners of the land they farmed, were arbitrarily suspended and thus became the cause of an economic war, involving reciprocal tariff restrictions, with the British government. In short the Republican programme began to be fulfilled. Only on the issue of the six counties of Northern Ireland was there no progress. Nor was there to be for many years to come. But then, as now, this defect was so well laundered in the rhetoric that illuminates the 'injustice' of partition that, except for those with a particularly stern republican eye, it was somehow as if it were being dealt with all the time.

In these circumstances what, apart from this difference of eye on the North, was to be the role of the IRA? It had experienced one immediate benefit in the release within days, and in some cases hours, of the new Fianna Fail government coming to power, of IRA prisoners jailed by Cosgrave. Even in this matter the new government showed a certain meticulous responsibility by asking Sean MacBride, son of a rebel shot in 1916, and now on the executive of the IRA, to declare which of those men in jail who had committed crimes had done so on orders from the IRA executive and were therefore eligible for release and which had merely committed crimes on their own account and were therefore not.

A great public meeting held in Dublin under banners saying 'Republican Prisoners Free: Ireland Rejoices' suggested that there was little difference now between the two sides of the republican movement, once old comrades in arms. Indeed Sean Russell, himself just released under the amnesty, proclaimed: 'I and my comrade prisoners today celebrate the victory of the recent elections and in doing so we celebrate the downfall of the Cosgrave murder gang!' While Maud Gonne, mother of Sean MacBride and one time beloved of the poet Yeats, cried: 'Ireland has stood together in this. The IRA stood firm and they have defeated Cosgrave and the coercionists.' Both the terms 'murder gang' and 'coercion' struck popular chords in Irish history, the former being the name given to British under-cover-counter-assassins during the grim terrorism of the 1920–21 period and the latter the nineteenth-century term for the recurrent suspension of civil liberties in Ireland by the British Parliament in times of trouble. And at that year's ceremony to commemorate the dead of 1916 at Glasnevin cemetery Moss Twomey, the Chief of Staff of the IRA, read out a message from the 'Army Council' which he said was being repeated that day at all such ceremonies throughout the country. It declared that the small and at that time quite unrepresentative group of armed men who had made the 1916 rebellion had established 'the right and the authority of our nation to fight for its right to inalienable sovereign independence.'

IRA men were offered commissions in the State's army; in 1934 members of the IRA who had fought in the Civil War were awarded military pensions (an act which resolved many individual republican doubts about adherence to the Fianna Fail regime); while the year before a special auxiliary group for the police had been formed by the government, recruited from IRA men and to be known, after its first commissioner, as the Broy Harriers.

This body had come into being in order to meet an incipient threat to the new régime from a former Commissioner of the Civic Guard under Cosgrave, Eoin O'Duffy, who had earned the hatred of militant republicans by the rigour with which he had applied Cosgrave's anti-terrorist laws. Dismissed by the Fianna Fail government not long after its assumption of power, O'Duffy had taken command of a new movement designed to counter both the new open emergence of the IRA with its public recruiting campaign and tendency to violence and at the same time the 'communistic' trend of some of the elements within it. O'Duffy's movement, nominating itself the 'National Guard', took as its own ideology certain aspects of Mussolini's corporate state of the day, and, by virtue of an analogous insignia which it chose to adopt, became more popularly known as the Blueshirts. But O'Duffy who, to be fair to him, always strenuously denied that he wished to make himself a dictator, certainly had within him few of the qualities which it takes to make one, and his movement petered out, making its final appearance as an Irish legion which went to fight for General Franco in Spain. It was the IRA itself which was to prove the real difficulty for the government.

The IRA's continued open assertion of their identity in arms in public, parading and drilling in exploitation of their apparently close link with the

Fianna Fail government, was a feature which no government jealous of its authority could long tolerate. And when, in response to a request from de Valera to hand in their arms and refrain from public drilling, they refused unless de Valera promised to turn the Free State into a Republic within five years he had no alternative but to declare the IRA an illegal organization as Cosgrave had done before him and as he had with the Blueshirts. The decision, taken in June 1936, was accelerated by three vicious IRA killings of civilians which had shocked the Irish public in the course of the year.

This was the beginning of an increasingly bitter division between the republican politicians of Fianna Fail and the die-hard republican old guard of the IRA. A certain amount of sentimental ambivalence towards the IRA inevitably lingered in the less logical recesses of Fianna Fail minds for a long time, and the ghost of that ambivalence equally inevitably still walks there at times today. But when, late in 1939, a spectacular raid was carried out by the IRA on the State's principal ammunition store in Phoenix Park in Dublin and considerable quantities of arms and ammunition were removed (though almost immediately afterwards recovered), it proved a turning point in hardening the government's attitude to 'the illegal organization'. Until that raid – a fact doubtless not unconnected with it – the then adjutant-general of the IRA had been a civil servant in the Department of Defence. In the following years, as periodic IRA violence against civil peace and guardians of the state in the twenty-six counties continued, the de Valera government was to prove as 'coercionist' in its turn as Cosgrave or indeed the British had been. Four IRA men were executed in Dublin after killings in which they had been involved; one of them was an old rebel of 1916.

From these years dates the sentiment expressed in a song of the 1950s showing sympathetic understanding at least of the IRA mentality at that later time:

> This Ireland of mine has for long been half free,
> Six counties lie under John Bull's monarchy,
> And sure de Valera is greatly to blame
> For shirking his part in the Patriot Game . . .

Bitterness indeed was to become the most consistent dynamic in an IRA which, under the strain of its own ineffectualness and the pressure of the government's measures to keep it ineffectual, split into divergent tendencies. The radical leftists abandoned it in disappointment at its lack of social policies; the militants divided into those who favoured an attack on the North as a means at least of involving de Valera urgently in the problem of partition, and those who wanted to attack the English in England. It was the latter group who, under the inspiration of Sean Russell, carried out a series of bombing attacks in England in the course of 1939, placing explosive packets in letter boxes and public lavatories and killing five people with a bomb attached to a bicycle left in a crowded street in Coventry. Both Tom Barry, victor of the 1920 Kilmichael ambush, and Sean MacBride had by this time left the organization, MacBride to work in later years for peace and goodwill on the international scene and win the Nobel Peace Prize.

When war came in 1939 – traditionally Ireland's opportunity a certainly

soon to become England's difficulty – Sean Russell took the IRA into a collaboration with Germany which resulted in no real benefit to either party, and Russell himself died in a German submarine on its way to Ireland, an even more ineffectual figure at his end than Roger Casement had been nearly thirty years before.

The principal German agent to Ireland during the war was one Hermann Goertz, dropped by parachute in May 1940. His radio transmitter came down on a separate parachute but he was unable to find it. He made contact with the IRA according to plan but for a long time they were unable to provide him with an effective alternative transmitter. Those they did produce for him proved useless. Before he was arrested and interned in the following year he left them in no doubt about his view of their competence. 'You know how to die for Ireland,' he is reported to have told them, 'but to fight for it you have not the slightest idea.'

By the end of the war, in the course of which the IRA had exposed itself to a certain amount of black ridicule when its own Chief of Staff narrowly escaped execution at the hands of other members of the organization and had to take refuge in the arms of de Valera's Civic Guard, it would not have been unreasonable to think that the IRA was a force which was spent for ever.

By this time, 1945, de Valera, who had been continually in power for thirteen years, had further transformed the nature of the twenty-six-county Irish State making it a sovereign independent country in the fullest sense and a Republic in all but name. He had done this by two major contributions, one legalistic, the other psychological.

In the first place, in 1937, he had introduced a new Constitution which named the State *Eire* (or Ireland) and claimed sovereignty over the whole island inclusive of the six northern counties, where its ability to enforce that sovereignty was thus codified as being only temporarily in abeyance. Another article of the 1937 Constitution recognized what it described as 'the special position' of the Roman Catholic Church as the religion of 'the great majority of its citizens' – which was true – though it did not 'establish' it, as the Protestant Church had once been established in Ireland. This formula was in fact a compromise accepted by de Valera and his Cabinet after great pressure had been put on it by the Roman Catholic hierarchy for the Church's official establishment. De Valera, for all his personal devoutness, had been deeply opposed to it and this sometimes controversial article of the Constitution (which was to be removed in 1972) was his way of avoiding it.

In all but name the 1937 Constitution made Ireland a Republic. The only reason the word was not implanted there was that it was judged that to do so would make an eventual solution of the Northern Ireland problem harder still. This may marginally have been true. But it does not follow that the absence of the word 'Republic' made it any easier. The British Crown was now only recognized by Ireland as 'the symbol of co-operation' between Ireland and Australia, Canada, Great Britain, New Zealand and South Africa (there was no mention of 'Empire' or 'Commonwealth') so long as Ireland was 'associated' with them.

The enactment of this Constitution, which was of course an abnegation of almost all the points that Britain had insisted on as essential in the

Established. The Republic of Ireland, if not 'The Irish Republic'.
Where de Valera feared to tread. (Sean T. O'Kelly, first President,
on stand.)

Treaty of 1921, was accepted with good grace by the British government. They went further and in the following year, 1938, concluded an agreement with de Valera which not only brought to an end 'the economic war' caused by the non-payment of the Land Annuities, but also abandoned certain naval and military rights in specified ports in Ireland, which had been granted to Britain under the Treaty.

By the time Great Britain entered the Second World War most of those precautions for her own security against danger from Ireland in time of war, with which she had hedged herself round in the Treaty, and on the need for which she had based her claim to maintain authority in Ireland for centuries, had been abandoned by the scratch of a pen. The physical effect of this for Britain was soon to become significant when deprivation of the southern Irish ports and air space not only made her south-western approaches far more vulnerable, but was seriously to affect the course of the Battle of the Atlantic. The psychological effect for Eire was immense for it enabled her to maintain neutrality throughout the Second World War. Nothing could have given greater moral substance to that new status of sovereign independence now successfully manufactured by de Valera with the Constitution of 1937.

In so far as the great majority of the Irish people were glad to be out of the war and happy to have this final confirmation of a nationality, which they had never been quite as clear about as they were meant to be, neutrality was unquestionably a popular move. At the same time the term 'neutrality' as a description of the feelings of most of the people of southern Ireland towards the two sides in the war can hardly be said to be accurate. As so often in the relationship between Britain and Ireland there was an ambivalence. One republican, Kevin Boland, sums this up by saying that while there was on the part of most people no desire to see the Germans win, there was at the same time, on the part of some, always a certain pleasure when the British in particular met with some reverse. On the part of almost everyone there was an implacable determination to maintain official neutrality at all costs. When at one stage the British government were seriously considering entering Eire to regain control of the southern ports, the Irish army was put into a state of alert and troops were moved from Athlone to the border with Northern Ireland.

In spite of occasional rumours to the effect that German U-Boats were calling at Irish ports to refuel or even to land arms for the IRA there is no evidence that this happened. Only sometimes would a U-Boat surface within hailing distance of fishermen off the Irish coast to ask if they had any fish to sell. If they had they would sell it and be paid in Irish currency.

This substance given by neutrality to Ireland's twenty-six-county independence, which must be regarded very much as a personal triumph of de Valera's, was confirmed at the end of the war by a remarkable exchange of radio broadcasts between Winston Churchill and de Valera, who had incidentally shocked many people in both islands by a visit to the German Ambassador in Dublin in 1945 to offer his condolences on the death of Hitler.

Churchill had begun the exchange, alluding to the difficulties and dangers Britain had experienced during the war as a result of Eire's neutrality and deprivation of the southern ports. (He himself had fiercely opposed the

Agreement of 1938.) After deprecating de Valera's action in keeping Eire neutral '. . . so much at variance with the temper and instinct of thousands of southern Irishmen who had hastened to the battlefront to prove their ancient valour . . .' he continued:

. . . had it not been for the loyalty and friendship of Northern Ireland we should have come to – we should have been forced to come to close quarters with Mr de Valera or perish for ever from the earth. However with a restraint and poise with which I say history will find few parallels His Majesty's Government never laid a violent hand upon them though at times it would have been quite easy and quite natural. And we left Mr de Valera's government to frolic with the German and later with the Japanese representatives to their hearts' content.

Such cavalier reference to the possibility of England laying a violent hand on Ireland was bound to draw a spirited response from de Valera and it did, but in a manner so typical of him and so different from that of his adversary that it masterfully confirmed the effect of his achievement.

'I know,' began de Valera quietly, 'the kind of answer I am expected to make. I know the answer that first springs to the lips of every man of Irish blood who heard or read that speech . . . I know the reply I would have given a quarter of a century ago. But I have deliberately decided that that is not the reply I shall make tonight . . .' He then actually went on to make excuses for Churchill's remarks in the first full flush of the European victory. 'No such excuse,' he added, 'could be made for me in this quieter atmosphere.' Turning to Churchill's justification for violating Irish neutrality if needs be, he commented:

It seems strange to me that Mr Churchill does not see that this, if it be accepted, would mean that Britain's necessity would become a moral code, and that, when this necessity became sufficiently great, other people's rights were not to count. It is quite true that other great powers believe in this same code. . . . That is precisely why we have the disastrous succession of wars . . .

After which, he could not resist putting his own simplistic nationalist gloss on the complex relationship that had existed between the two peoples for the past eight hundred years. Addressing himself again to Churchill he asked:

Could he not find in his heart the generosity to acknowledge that there is a small nation that stood alone not for one year or for two, but for several hundred years against aggression: that endured spoliations, was clubbed many times into insensibility, but that each time on returning consciousness took up the fight anew; a small nation that could never be got to accept defeat and has never surrendered her soul?

It has to be admitted that if anyone had ever made that over-simplified view of the Irish nation's history *seem* true it was Eamon de Valera, and the large crowds who cheered him as he left the radio station and the ovation he received in the Dail the next afternoon testified to that fact. But what else had he done for Ireland?

Taoiseach's Broadcast
to the Nation

Reprinted from "The Irish Press," Thursday, 17th May, 1945

PRICE ONE PENNY

'I know the kind of answer I am expected to make . . .' De Valera and Churchill in radio duel, May 1945.

ABOVE: John Costello, Fine Gael (Tribe of the Gaels), first Taoiseach of the Republic of Ireland.

ABOVE RIGHT: Sean MacBride, Clann na Poblachta, ex-IRA Chief of Staff of the 1930s, now Minister for External Affairs, '. . . a new and remarkable coalition.'

RIGHT: Noel Browne, Minister of Health. A new idealism, but the Church said 'No'.

When he first came fully to power after the election of 1933 de Valera outlined the programme of his party as aiming at:

> . . . restoring the unity of Ireland and securing its independence, at placing as many families as possible upon the land so that the food we eat, the clothes we wear, the houses we live in, and the articles in common daily use in the lives of our people may all, as far as is reasonably possible be produced by Irish labour from Irish material. Ireland united, Ireland free, Ireland self-supporting and self-reliant, Ireland speaking her own tongue and through it giving to the world the ancient treasures of Christian Gaelic culture – these are the ideals.

The failure to foresee the inevitable shortfall in realization of this last ideal stemmed from that homely narrowness of outlook expressed throughout the statement, that pious dogmatism which had unfortunately blinkered so much of the noblest nationalist thinking since the days of Arthur Griffith and the early Sinn Fein. Informed with this spirit the sort of State over which de Valera presided for sixteen years, though fulfilling constitutionally some of the letter of the old Irish nationalist dream, fell short of much of the spirit. Conservative in social and economic outlook, paying limited attention to problems such as housing, slum clearance and social welfare in general, safely – some would say smugly – steeped in the orthodox moral and social teachings of the Catholic Church of that day, it offered little in the way of inspiration to the young. Emigration, so long held by nationalists to have been one of the evils of English rule and to have been caused by lack of freedom, continued. A strict literary censorship banned at different times almost all the best modern writers, including Irish ones, and some of the classics too. It was hardly the sort of State to induce Northern Protestants to join it, and it is difficult not to wonder whether, for all the pious expressions of its statesmen about the need to end partition, it minded very much whether it did include them or not.

In 1948 de Valera and Fianna Fail were finally replaced, with the swing of the democratic pendulum, by a new and remarkable coalition consisting of the inheritors of Cosgrave's party, *Fine Gael,* now under John Costello, and a new radical republican party, *Clann na Poblachta,* led by Sean MacBride. This finally completed the constitutional formality from which de Valera had held back in the belief that it would make the ending of partition more difficult: Ireland was declared a Republic – all Ireland in theory, the twenty-six counties in practice. Hopes that a fresh outlook in social affairs might result from the participation in government of new young idealists in Clann na Poblachta were dashed when Noel Browne introduced a limited National Health project known as the Mother and Child scheme. It had to be dropped as a result of pressure on the Cabinet from the Roman Catholic Church.

Civil Rights on the march – Derry 1968.

Chapter 13

Stormont

There is no question but that the government of Northern Ireland must be blamed for the manner in which they conducted the affairs of their state in the half century which followed the Anglo-Irish Treaty of 1921. They bear much of the responsibility for the outbreak of the troubles of our own time. But it is unhistorical and unfair to allot such blame and responsibility without also reiterating why the Northern Ireland government came to behave as they did.

An outsider could be forgiven for regarding the creation in 1921 of a separate Northern Ireland state as a concession to the Northern Irish Protestant's individuality and sense of freedom. But for the Northern Irish Protestant the emphasis was not like this. Men whose most potent historical memories in any case were refreshed by annual celebrations of the Battle of the Boyne and the siege of Derry saw themselves with some reason as starting from a heavily beleaguered position.

As long ago as 1911 they had accepted that they must give up their opposition to Home Rule for the greater part of Ireland. That acceptance had immeasurably strengthened their resolve to defend Ulster at all costs and under Carson and the officers of the Ulster Volunteer Force they had organized themselves very effectively to do so. A few years later they had had to agree, on Carson's recommendation, that only six of the nine Ulster counties were reasonably defensible. There had followed two years of violent terrorism and counter-terrorism in Ireland as a result of which the British government had surrendered sovereignty over twenty-six of the thirty-two counties of Ireland, including the lost three counties of Ulster.

The British invitation to representatives of the Irish 'terrorists' to negotiate had invited them to negotiate for 'Ireland'. This could certainly be read, and was so read by the Irish negotiators, as casting doubt on the continued existence of any separate six-county polity. Even the Anglo-Irish Treaty which resulted from those negotiations and which let the six counties opt out of the Free State did not necessarily ensure their independent survival. The clauses which empowered a Boundary Commission to adjust the border in accordance with the wishes of the inhabitants could be seen as threatening the new state's viability from the start. And although Sir James Craig, Northern Ireland's first Prime Minister, immediately made it clear that he would not recognize such a Boundary Commission, it remained a British government commitment for the first years of Northern Ireland's separate existence.

When Craig addressed large meetings of Orangemen early in the life of the new state he was welcomed by placards from South Tyrone (one of the areas that would have been affected by an adjustment of the border) proclaiming the old message: 'What We Have We Hold!' When Lord Derby came over to Northern Ireland to review the newly organized Royal Ulster Constabulary with their 'B Special' reserves they marched past the Union Jack that waved over the reviewing stand with sloped rifles and wearing war medals, and headed by officers still wearing khaki army uniform, with the same precision as many of them had marched not long before in the ranks of Carson's Ulster Volunteer Force. 'Ulster's Guardians of Peace', the newsreel caption called them.

From the beginning there was no doubt in any Ulster Protestant's mind about the enemy against whom the peace had to be guarded. Not only had the Irish Republican Army fought on in the south to try and replace the Free State with an all-Ireland Republic, but there had been those in the Free State who had tried also to seek a resolution of that conflict by deflecting republican energies north across the border. The very serious rioting which broke out in Belfast in the summer of 1922, resulting in 232 deaths (mostly Catholic) and thousands of Catholic refugees streaming south across the border, reflected the insecurity and unease of the Protestant-in-the-street, with the threat of the Boundary Commission still hanging over his head. The IRA has continued, in some form, with the aim of removing the border and British sovereignty, ever since. Although for decades at a time it has seemed to Britain no more than an occasional, often inexplicable irritant, to the Protestants of Northern Ireland it has seemed a permanent menace no less sinister because it was not always openly obvious. It has been the menace against which the Special Powers Act of 1922, with its severe punishments of flogging and death for the possession of firearms, was a necessary protection, and against which even the policemen on traffic duty in Belfast had to wear revolvers.

The sense of precariousness in the new northern state was reinforced by the attitude of the Catholic minority there (about one third of its population). 'At that time,' recalled Eddie McAteer, later to be a Nationalist leader in the Northern Ireland Parliament, 'we thought it was a very temporary thing and that the house of cards would crumble.' Not only did elected Catholic nationalist representatives refuse to take their seats in the new Parliament, but Catholic school managers refused to accept grants from the state and some Catholic school teachers actually refused to take their state salaries. It was not until after the collapse of the Boundary Commission in 1925 that nationalist politicians took their seats in Parliament. Even then Protestant Unionist opinion could never rid itself of the thought that the Catholic Nationalist opposition in that Parliament wanted, not just to get rid of the government, but to get rid of the state.

A new building for that Parliament was opened by the then Prince of Wales at Stormont on the outskirts of Belfast in 1932. Its front was to be dominated by a striking statue of Carson in defiant pose. Throughout that Parliament's existence – until its suspension in 1972 – Protestant Unionists were to dominate Catholic Nationalists in election after election in the

proportion of about four to one. That domination and the security it represented for the Northern Ireland Protestant was to be the most important single political factor in the life of the new state. Politically therefore it was something of a democratic freak. The economic and consequent social problems which Northern Ireland, along with the rest of the world, was to experience in the 1920s and 1930s, however urgent, were to be in the long run of secondary importance to this overriding constitutional consideration of the Protestant state's security.

Its peculiar personality in this respect was even reinforced by those economic and social problems. Though situated in an economically disadvantaged part of the United Kingdom it was always possible for its rulers to appease the discontent of its Protestant supporters by indulging them with a sense of privilege, where jobs and housing were concerned, over the Catholic minority. That some appeasement was necessary is made clear by the unemployment figures. For most of the 1920s and 1930s unemployment in Northern Ireland averaged twenty-five per cent of the insured population. However, only in 1932 during unemployed riots in Belfast, was there any momentary sign of working-class interests cutting seriously across the more fundamental barricades of the state's structure and this was to prove remarkable only as an exception. The arrival in power in the south that year of de Valera and his republican-minded Fianna Fail party soon directed the Protestant working class back to their more profound anxieties and sense of interest. The Belfast riots of 1935 in which eleven people were killed marked a return to the traditional sectarian mould.

The inflexible nature of the state's principal concern was well expressed by its Prime Minister, Sir James Craig, in 1934 when he told an approving Northern Ireland House of Commons that he prized the office of Grand Master of the Orange Institution of County Down 'far more than I do being Prime Minister . . . I have always said I am an Orangeman first and a politician and a member of this parliament afterwards . . . all I boast is that we are a Protestant parliament and a Protestant state.' The unchanging nature of that ideal is reflected in the remarkable continuity of leadership. Craig himself remained Prime Minister for twenty years until his death in 1940. He was succeeded by J.M. Andrews who had been a member of Craig's Cabinet since 1921, and Andrews in turn was succeeded by Sir Basil Brooke, later Lord Brookeborough, who had joined Craig's Cabinet as Minister of Agriculture in 1933 and himself remained Prime Minister until 1963. It was Brooke who once declared proudly in public that he did not have a single Catholic in his employ and that Catholics were 'out to destroy Ulster with all their might and power.'

The real machinery of government in Northern Ireland functioned at the level of the local authorities rather than through the Parliament at Stormont. It was at this local level that the pattern of what Catholics saw as discrimination and Protestants as the implementation of their just deserts as constitutional guardians of the state, was effected. Again it is important to recognize how generally disadvantaged was the society in which this took effect, even by comparison with the rest of the United Kingdom in the 1920s and 1930s. It was not just a question of unemployment, as the historian F.S.L. Lyons has shown in a terrifying summary. Income per head was in general less than three-fifths of what it was in Britain. Housing was seriously inadequate. Although in the mid-1920s it had been found that eighteen per cent of the population of Northern Ireland were living at a density of more than two to a room very little was done to remedy this until after the war. After eighteen years of the state's existence eighty-seven per cent of the houses in the countryside were without running water. Public health was worse than in any other comparable area of the British Isles: forty-six per cent of those who died between the ages of fifteen and twenty-five died of tuberculosis. After nearly twenty years of the state a quarter of all the children who died under the age of one died in a workhouse. Clearly in such a society such privilege as could be obtained was to be jealously prized, and resentment of it correspondingly bitter.

The existence of any discrimination at all was frequently denied by Unionist politicians. As late as 1965 Brian Faulkner, later to be regarded as something of a liberal in the context of Northern Ireland, was to deny strongly that there was any sort of discrimination against the Catholic population in Londonderry. Yet Londonderry was in fact the most flagrant single example of all and eventually to prove the explosive material which brought down the Stormont state.

The population of the city of Londonderry is roughly three-fifths Catholics and Nationalists (the two words may roughly be approximated throughout Northern Ireland, but particularly in Londonderry) and two-fifths Protestant and Unionist. This population distribution has remained more or less constant ever since the foundation of the state. For the state's first fifty years the Corporation of Londonderry was composed the other way round: three-fifths Protestant and Unionist and two-fifths Catholic and Nationalist. This effect was achieved by 'gerrymandering' or concentrating large numbers of people with majority political views in overlarge electoral districts and their opponents in smaller ones so that, in representation district by district, the minority are bound to win. Thus in Londonderry eighty-seven per cent of the large Catholic population were placed in one ward which returned eight seats, while eighty-seven per cent of the much smaller Protestant population were placed in two wards which returned twelve seats. Year after year there was a Protestant and Unionist majority on the corporation of twelve to eight.

Nor was gerrymandering the only inequitable aspect of Northern Ireland voting. The vote was confined in local elections to resident occupiers, meaning the owner or tenant of a house. Every adult did not thus have a local vote. Some, however, could have as many as six, since it was permissible to appoint additional nominees up to six for every additional £10 a year valuation of property after the first £10. This naturally gave a preferential vote to better-off sections of the community which, particularly in Londonderry, meant the Protestant Unionists. Thus not only was the Protestant vote strengthened by gerrymandering but Protestants actually had more votes per head of population than Catholics.

In practical terms all this worked to the severe disadvantage of Catholics, particularly in matters of housing. Year after year Londonderry's Protestant-dominated Corporation voted its housing powers to a sub-committee which in turn put those powers into the hands of the Protestant Mayor who, in the exercise of his preferences, was accountable to no-one but himself. Since the award of a house was also *ipso facto* the

ABOVE: 'The only people with a capability of defence for the Catholic ghettos.' IRA man and citizen, Derry.

ABOVE LEFT AND LEFT: 'The IRA back in business with a vengeance.' Provisionals in Belfast and Crossmaglen.

award of a house-vote he exercised his preference in a manner which seemed to him proper as a Protestant Mayor in a Protestant state.

Londonderry is the best known example of such social discrimination against Catholics in local government, but there were many others. As late as 1972 Dungannon's urban district, which had a population half of Catholics and half of Protestants, returned fourteen Unionists and seven Nationalists to its council. County Fermanagh, which had a Catholic population of fifty-three per cent, returned thirty-three Unionists and seventeen Nationalists to its council. The rural district of East County Down, where half the population was Catholic returned nineteen Unionists and only five Nationalists. It was not only in housing that such a state of affairs worked to the disadvantage of Catholics, but also in the allocation of jobs. In County Fermanagh, of seventy-five drivers of school buses, only seven were Catholic while in Belfast where, admittedly the Catholic population was only twenty-six per cent, ninety-seven and one-half per cent of the Corporation jobs were held by Protestants.

Proportional representation had been put into the Government of Ireland Act of 1920 by the Westminster Parliament to prevent this sort of thing happening, but was abolished by Stormont for local elections in 1922. The same Act had contained clauses forbidding discrimination on religious grounds, and, above all, asserted that notwithstanding anything in the Act, full powers of sovereignty on all matters were, in the last resort, reserved to the Westminster Parliament over Stormont. If the first had been kept in spirit, or the second implemented, earlier than 1972 (when the Stormont Parliament was to be suspended) the history of Northern Ireland would have been very different. But the attitude of Britain for the long half century after the Treaty was either one of not wanting to know what went on in Northern Ireland or of supporting and substantiating the structure within which things went on as they did.

For such an attitude Britain was amply rewarded in the Second World War when not only did the Northern Ireland Protestant most valorously express his gratitude for the privilege of having been allowed to hold what he had, but the territory of Northern Ireland itself proved essential to Britain's survival by providing a base for protection of the Atlantic convoys after the fall of France to the Germans. The emollient tone of the newsreel commentators of the day was all most British people knew of Northern Ireland: '. . . Northern Ireland is making a superb contribution to the war effort. A quarter of a million more acres are under food production . . . she's ploughing her way to victory . . .' When Sir Basil Brooke, then Minister of Commerce, visited London in 1941 to see 'what more can be done to use Northern Ireland's industrial resources and manpower in the war effort', he himself confidentially addressed cinema audiences with the words: 'As you know, we are part of the United Kingdom . . .', as if they might not have known that.

When in 1949, four years after the end of the war, the twenty-six counties of Ireland, known since 1937 as Eire, turned themselves into a Republic, claiming sovereignty over the other six, a British Labour government expressed gratitude to Northern Ireland in its turn by pledging that those six counties would remain part of the United Kingdom until the Parliament of Northern Ireland decided otherwise (a modern version of the Greek

Kalends). Neither aspect of the event attracted much attention from the British people. Again, the IRA campaign against Northern Ireland of 1956–62 in the course of which nineteen people were killed cast little shadow on Britain and when Sir Basil Brooke (by now Prime Minister, and Lord Brookeborough) appeared on the BBC's *Panorama* programme he was asked by the admirable Richard Dimbleby as the British public's enquiry agent: 'What exactly is this I-R-A?' as if the letters had been A-B-C.

But even in Northern Ireland 'the old order changeth' up to a point and Britain's view of it was also changing, at least to the extent of looking into it more closely through the television screen.

In 1963 for the first time in forty years a man not closely connected with the early days of the state became Prime Minister of Northern Ireland, Captain Terence O'Neill. A loyal Ulster Orangeman (Eton and the Guards), O'Neill was also a man of intelligence and some sensibility who saw the need to adjust Northern Ireland to the world of the 1960s, in which those of its own children who had benefited from the universal secondary education made available by the Education Act of 1947 were themselves coming to maturity. O'Neill actually did little but change the climate, bringing about the first meeting with a Prime Minister of the Dublin government (Sean Lemass by 1965) since the foundation of both states over forty years before and performing some cosmetic ceremonial rites such as visiting the girls of Catholic grammar schools. But in Northern Ireland terms such things were almost revolutionary. They proved quite enough to stir the forces of history which on all sides ran so deep and strong below the surface.

Almost at once new zest was given to the antics of a politically acute Presbyterian minister and brilliant mob orator, the Revd Ian Paisley, who specialized in regaling to spell-bound Protestant audiences how Roman Catholics consumed 'the bones, body, blood and sinews of Jesus Christ' at Mass and therefore had to be instructed not to chew 'the wafer' but 'simply let him melt away on the roof of your mouth'. When O'Neill visited a Convent school in Ballymena militant supporters of Paisley followed the Prime Minister down the ranks of nuns waving a *Protestant Telegraph* poster proclaiming 'O'Neill Arch Traitor' and 'Don't Miss This Week's Exposure of O'Neillism'. Paisley, who founded his own Protestant Unionist party in opposition to O'Neill, was, with his defiance of the Anglican establishment and the landed gentry, himself a historical throwback to Protestant dissenting radicalism of the nineteenth and even eighteenth centuries. But history was stirring from another direction too.

In 1966, at Maghera in County Londonderry, a meeting had been held at which it was decided to discuss a Civil Rights Movement for Northern Ireland analogous to that with which the second-class black citizenry of the United States had been demanding their democratic rights under the leadership of Martin Luther King. The Chief of Staff of the IRA at the time, Cathal Goulding, attended the meeting but it is indicative of the ineffectualness and low repute to which the IRA had sunk, after their rejection by the Catholic community in the failed IRA campaign of 1956–62, that he was there only as an observer and the IRA had no part in the foundation of the Northern Ireland Civil Rights Association in 1967. Eamon McCann, a young Derry republican socialist of the day (but not an IRA supporter) has

233

ABOVE: '. . . implacable determination never to become part of a united Ireland!' Northern Protestants in front of Stormont. If not the Union Jack, the flag of Ulster.

LEFT: Descendants of Carson's Volunteers. A Protestant Ulster Defence Association of 20,000 plus.

described the leadership of this movement reasonably correctly as 'middle-aged, middle-class and middle-of-the-road'.

McCann has also described, in his excellent book *War and an Irish Town*, how he and a group of young associates in Derry, who had been conducting on their own account a vigorous if unorthodox campaign against the social injustices of that city, manipulated the Civil Rights Movement into holding a Civil Rights march there on 5 October after it had been banned by William Craig, the Minister for Home Affairs, in 1968. It was broken up with gratuitous brutality by the Royal Ulster Constabulary and the history of Northern Ireland was thereafter changed irrevocably.

The Prime Minister, Captain O'Neill, announced that the Government would shortly be making certain changes such as instituting a Development Corporation for Derry and reforming local government in three years' time. But change was already ahead of him.

On 1 January 1969 a radical offshoot of the Civil Rights Movement calling itself People's Democracy set out on a march, Belfast to Derry, under slogans calling for jobs, houses and 'one man, one vote'. It was not banned but was afforded only minimal protection by the police, particularly when it arrived at Burntollet bridge seven miles from Derry on 4 January. Here the marchers were attacked on the road, from an overhanging slope which dominated it, by a Protestant mob throwing stones and wielding spiked cudgels. Television news film showed RUC in uniform among the attackers, but making little attempt to arrest them. None were in fact arrested. Instead the police arrested about eighty of the marchers whom they were supposed to be protecting. Later that evening the police moved into the Bogside in Derry where according to the British government's later Cameron report they 'were guilty of misconduct, . . . assault and battery . . . malicious damage to property . . . and the use of provocative and sectarian slogans.' The pattern had been set for the rest of the year: increasing popular Catholic impatience with resistance to reform, leading to increased popular Protestant resistance to that impatience.

The succession of events by which a movement originally intended to bring Northern Ireland out of the Stormont era into the modern world led to its return to an even older version of Irish history is soon told.

Captain O'Neill, seeking to strengthen his hand as a Protestant reformer called a General Election which had the reverse effect. In April he resigned to be replaced by an equally well-meaning but even less magnetic upper-class Orange Ulsterman, Major James Chichester Clark. Riots took place in Dungannon in April and on a horrific scale in Derry and Belfast in August in which the B Special Reserves of the RUC became barely distinguishable from the Protestant mob as, firing sub-machine guns and tear gas, they chased to their homes Catholic rioters who had been throwing stones and petrol bombs but who were otherwise unarmed. In two nights six people were killed, 300 houses burned. British troops had to be deployed in Derry on 14 August and Belfast on 16 August 1969 to preserve law and order which was suffering severely at the hands of the police.

In the fighting in Derry a republican tricolour had appeared on the top of the tallest building in the Bogside, the Rossville Street flats. People in the Republic were appalled by the spectacle of Nationalists under vicious attack in Derry. Jack Lynch, the Irish Prime Minister had given a television

1916 and All That. Patrolling the Creggan Estate, Derry.

Taking their place in line. On the blanket in the prison of history.

interview in which he said that the Irish government could no longer 'stand idly by', and some members of his government, with or without his knowledge, were involved in an attempt to get arms to the Catholics in the North for defensive purposes. But in all this so far virtually nothing had been heard of the IRA. 'IRA I Ran Away' was beginning to be chalked by Catholics on the walls of Belfast, and young Catholics looking to the IRA for defence against the Protestant mobs and the B Specials had found an organization ill-equipped on either side of the border to give them help.

In the years since the failure of the 1956–62 campaign the IRA had diverged – creditably in intent at least, it might be said – down red social revolutionary paths and away from its plain green patriotic republican tradition. Now suddenly with Nationalists on the defensive, and British troops on the streets of Derry and Belfast, it was possible to make that tradition highly relevant again. To the traditional extremist republican the fact that the troops were temporarily welcomed by many in the Catholic population as protection against the police and the Protestant mobs was of little significance beside the fact that these troops, who were after all there to establish *British* law and order, were once again, as anyone over sixty could remember, in similar positions on the streets of Ireland to those which British troops had occupied in 1920–21. In the winter of 1969 the IRA split into two groups, the Marxist-inclined 'Officials' and the traditional 'Provisionals' (named after the 'Provisional' government of Ireland announced by Pearse at the Dublin GPO in 1916) who determined to exploit the new situation to the full in pursuit of old ideals.

As in 1920–21, it was not long before searches and occasional clumsy brutality on the part of the British forces trying to preserve law and order provoked an angry reaction from the population. It was not difficult for an IRA increasingly asserting its own rigid control over the Catholic areas of Derry and Belfast to manipulate and develop this reaction for patriotic ends. Quite apart from any elements of intimidation in that control, the IRA were at first the only leadership the people had. After the events of August 1969 the Civil Rights Movement was as played out as the old Nationalist party. Young socialist radicals like Bernadette Devlin and Eamon McCann had neither the experience nor, with their primarily intellectual approach, the populist relevance necessary to provide leadership. The only people who now for a time seemed relevant, with their capability, once they began to acquire arms, of defence for the Catholic ghettos, were the IRA. This was an IRA which at least did not run away. And it could take advantage of the fact that, for many of the Catholic minority population wanting to escape discrimination in the Protestant state, there had long seemed nowhere else to go except in the direction of republicanism.

The IRA's gradual orchestration of rioting in Catholic areas, particularly in Belfast, and of the hijacking of buses, the throwing of stones, petrol bombs and even grenades at the forces of law and order made it easy for the army to become enemies. The cold-blooded killing of RUC men had started in 1970. At the end of February 1971 two unarmed RUC men were gunned down in a Belfast avenue. Police stations and off-duty RUC men and their families came under attack. Early in March three young Scots soldiers were lured from a Belfast pub and taken outside the city to be shot in the back of the head. Criticism was levelled at the Prime Minister Chichester Clark

Is it dangerous to look too closely into Irish history?

for the ineffectualness of the security forces. Protestants began to call for the B Specials to be reintroduced.

'No disrespect to the Army, but the army hasn't got a clue,' was one Protestant woman's comment. 'One of our association members has been murdered; just two weeks ago a bomb was left in my own hall and the Prime Minister says we're closing in on the terrorists. I think the terrorists are closing in on us.'

Under mounting criticism from within the Ulster Unionist Council the Old Etonian figure of Chichester Clark resigned as Prime Minister to be replaced by Brian Faulkner, an ambitious professional Unionist politician thought to be of traditionally sterner stuff. In August 1971 he said he had come to the conclusion that the ordinary course of the law could no longer deal with 'the vicious ruthlessness of the IRA'. He introduced internment without trial. There were those, and not only republicans, who demurred at this interference with the normal democratic processes of the law. 'We are,' said Faulkner, 'quite simply at war with the terrorist and in a state of war many sacrifices have to be made.'

This was a sacrifice which would make matters worse.

Nearly 300 people of republican sympathies were detained without trial, and the arrests had more than quadrupled by the end of the year. By that time, although a great proportion of those arrested had had to be released – indicating the measure's clumsy inability to get the right people – there were still more republicans interned than at any time since 1921. Relatively few were members of the Provisional IRA. The effect was to drive many internees into joining it. The ruthlessness became more vicious than ever.

Faulkner had said he had 'a war' on his hands. But this was just what the IRA wanted people to think. Internment appeared to give further plausibility to the IRA claim that they were fighting for the rights of the Irish people, as they had done in the 'Anglo-Irish War' of 1919–21. The falsity of this claim, with its dishonest alignment of two quite different sets of historical circumstances, was something which the unsubtlety of government policy did not always make it easy to expose.

This was unfortunate, for it was not only the Unionists and the British security forces who were opposed to the increasing ruthlessness of the IRA. A good part of the Catholic nationalist minority in Northern Ireland, while content to accept a certain sense of protection which the IRA could confer, were reluctant to approve the slaughter brought about by aggressive IRA violence. They looked, rather, to the democratic process to acknowledge fairly their identity and aspirations when legitimately expressed.

In fact, a new nationalist grouping, the Social Democratic and Labour Party, had recently come into being. This had been formed in 1970 by Gerry Fitt, a 'Republican Labour' member of the Westminster Parliament, assisted by John Hume, a nationalist opposition member of Stormont. And among the new party's natural supporters, some of whom had themselves been detained, internment and the treatment and conditions experienced aroused bitter resentment. A British Marine Commando officer wrote in his regimental magazine that internment had 'polarized further the Catholic and Protestant communities and reduced the ranks of the much needed Catholic moderates. In a worsening situation,' he concluded, 'it is difficult to imagine a solution.'

ABOVE: Early in 'the troubles' Gerry Fitt, SDLP leader, with deputy John Hume (right) in the barricaded home from which he was to throw out a violent republican mob in 1976.

BELOW: Belfast incident, 1972. Twenty-one years more of this to come.

OPPOSITE: Bloody Sunday, 30 January 1972. Twelve other unarmed civilians dead too.

It was still the generally held assumption that a military solution was possible, that IRA violence could be beaten technically, or at least reasonably contained at nuisance level. A historical footnote to the next twenty-four years might well want to examine why, purely technically, this did indeed so long prove impossible, for it was to be an assumption on which government policy would continue to fall back for much of that near-quarter of a century. A simple statement in which Gerry Fitt long ago expressed the SDLP viewpoint, today pierces with chastening simplicity the torpid horror of those years: 'The British government,' he said, 'must recognize that there can be no military answer to the problems here in Northern Ireland, that political action must be taken.' The years were to show only sporadic attempts to take such action, and these, until the most recent, unequal to the task which history had set.

As 1971 ended, with 174 more people killed – fifteen of them in a Belfast pub in December blown up by Unionist paramilitaries in revenge for what the IRA was doing – Faulkner concentrated on the military solution. The sort of thing this could mean was shown on the 30 January 1972, to become known as Bloody Sunday, when thirteen unarmed civilians were shot dead by British soldiers on the streets of Derry.

This last event ominously stirred historic emotions even in the Republic. A crowd of 20,000 people attacked the British Embassy in Dublin and burned it down. The Irish Foreign Minister of the day declared: 'From now on my one aim is to get the British out of Ireland.' Ireland it could seem was back in its ancient prison of history, and the IRA were there with a vengeance.

The number of deaths had been rising steadily: twenty-five in 1970, 174 in 1971. Within a few weeks of Bloody Sunday, an IRA bomb had killed five women in a military barracks at Aldershot in revenge for Derry; another had killed two people and injured 130 in a Belfast restaurant; a car bomb had killed two and injured 100 in a Belfast shopping street. On 20 March 1972, the British government of Edward Heath, against the protests of Faulkner and his Unionist administration, took control of Northern Ireland's powers of law and order, and brought Stormont itself to an end after fifty years. All its powers were replaced by direct rule from Westminster. The prison of history was at least partly changing shape.

OPPOSITE: '. . . firing bordered on the reckless . . .' Widgery report on Bloody Sunday, 30 January 1972.

Inspecting the remains of the Harrods car bomb.

Chapter 14

Dublin Is Just a Sunningdale Away

It was the British government's determination to control the deteriorating security situation under Faulkner that had brought about direct rule, but in this respect it was to have little apparent success. Leaders of the Provisional IRA, among whom at this time were allegedly Gerry Adams and Martin MacGuinness, saw the change usefully clarifying the issue as one simply with the British government. 'The war must go on,' they said.

Their campaign continued with wide use of the undiscriminating car bomb. Less than three weeks after the introduction of direct rule thirty bombs went off all over North-East Ulster in one day. May was to see more people killed than in any month since the troubles had begun. Protestant paramilitaries stepped up their reciprocal campaign with the sectarian murders of individual Catholics. Although the year also saw a British military operation, Operation Motorman – the biggest by the British army since Suez – which had been intended to 'remove the capacity of the IRA to create terror and violence', this object was not achieved. 1972 ended with the largest number of deaths recorded since 'the troubles' began: 476, a figure to remain the highest of any in the twenty-two years of 'troubles' still to come. In the political field, however, direct rule was to have a most significant effect.

In March 1972 the British Prime Minister, Edward Heath and his new Northern Ireland Secretary of State, William Whitelaw, had both made clear from the start that they saw direct rule not just as a measure for taking control of law and order in the province, but also as an opportunity to set the whole historic Northern Ireland problem to rights.

It was early days for them to be able to make clear how they thought this should be done, for they were by no means clear themselves.

No British statesman for almost fifty years had had to sit down seriously in peace-time to consider how the historical complexities of the old 'Irish question' could be accommodated to the urgency of the present. Despite the surrender of British pride involved in the Treaty settlement of 1921, an all-important part of its purpose had been to rid the British political system of the tiresome question for ever. It was reliance on the wishful thinking that this had been achieved which left the Stormont Parliament so happily to its own devices for nearly half a century, and created the situation now veering out of control.

In Whitehall, after all this time, little sense of familiarity with the

ABOVE: Incident in 'bandit country'. A 400-pound bomb triggered by radio blows up an army Saracen and kills a British soldier in South Armagh.

RIGHT: Brian Faulkner and Gerry Fitt, leaders of the power-sharing executive, at Sunningdale. It was to last six months.

NER MR G FITT

subtleties of Irish history was still to hand. In May 1969 the British Minister of Defence in Wilson's Labour government, Denis Healey, had actually been able to object to intervention in Northern Ireland on the side of the Catholics and the Civil Rights movement on the grounds that 'we know nothing at all about it'. Four months later, after such intervention had taken place without great increase in knowledge, another member of that government, Richard Crossman, noted disconsolately that with British troops tired and no longer popular '. . . the terrible thing was that the only solutions would take ten years, if they would then ever work at all'. And this was even before the rejuvenated IRA had had time to become effective.

At least the Heath government was prepared to try to grasp the nettle.

It seems probable that at this stage something not unlike the long-held orthodox Labour position prevailed in many Conservative minds, namely that in the end a united Ireland was the only feasible solution, and that this should be borne in mind in so far as it could be done without antagonizing the Unionists – evidence in itself of how unclear about the realities some minds were. Having hardly had to think about the historic emotions of the Irish question for so long, both parties had simply inherited the assumption formally expressed by statute in the Home Rule Act of 1914 and confirmed in the letter of the Treaty of 1921 to the effect that in principle a united Ireland was desirable. The Labour Party, in anticipation of their next turn in power, were then discussing options for Northern Ireland under the significant code-name 'Algeria'.

The awkwardness of present realities was soon apparent. The very extent to which the imposition of direct rule was deemed a successful move at once became part of the problem.

Unionists over a wide range of groupings were in any case unlikely to be enthusiastic about their power being taken away from them. It had made them feel safe for the past fifty years. And the welcome given to the move not only by the Catholic nationalist minority in the North, but also by the Government of the Republic, served to remind Unionists of why they had felt the need for such power in the first place. From now on and into the mid-1990s, Unionists' anxiety for their future, rooted in the history of 1912–14, 1919–22 and even further back, was to be politically as difficult a factor for British governments to handle as, in security terms, the confrontation with the IRA – though it was not always so clearly perceived. It was a difficulty which the British had fudged, successfully for themselves, with the Treaty. Now that fudge had, as fudge does, disintegrated.

For the next twenty years or so there was to be an increasing tendency for Unionist opinion to withdraw into the inner safety of traditional attitudes in the face of impending change, a tendency seen in the increasing gain of popular ground from the Official Unionist Party by more extreme Unionist groupings, principally the Democratic Unionist Party of the Reverend Ian Paisley. One of the achievements of the 1993 Downing Street Declaration was to be that it would enable Official Unionists to regain much of their original position and prestige. But in 1972, as the Heath government prepared to embark on the bold course that would reach its climax in the Sunningdale Agreement of December 1973, there was less acute awareness of Unionist difficulties ahead.

Sunningdale was, in the early 1970s, as much an attempt to 'overcome the legacy of history' and make 'a new departure', as the Downing Street Declaration which used those words in 1993. Unlike the Downing Street Declaration it was to prove painfully premature. But it was first presented cautiously enough. And because it was to be the first creative attempt to take a political initiative in Northern Ireland since 1922, and a more ambitious initiative than any, including the Anglo-Irish Agreement of 1985, to be taken before December 1993, it has a connection with our present, and the hopes and disillusion that attended it repay some scrutiny today.

After a summer which had seen the hundredth British soldier killed in eighteen months, and a day in Belfast in July to be known as Bloody Friday, when twenty-six IRA bombs killed eleven people – some of whom had to be scraped up as lumps of meat from the pavement –injuring 130 others, the British government produced in the autumn of 1972 a discussion paper. This began with an assurance to Unionists that no change could take place in the status of Northern Ireland without the consent of the majority of the people who lived there. The most recent previous statutory assurance to Unionists had been in the Ireland Act of 1949, passed when 'Eire' unilaterally declared herself a Republic. This had stated that no change could take place without the consent of the Parliament of Northern Ireland. But the Parliament of Northern Ireland was no longer there. A renewal of the pledge in relevant contemporary form was an important starting point.

But having given this pledge, the paper immediately set Unionist alarm bells ringing with its next two points. The first was an option to give the Catholic nationalist minority 'a share in the exercise of executive power'. The second reintroduced something which history had long made apparently central to the problem, and which was now respectably cloaked as 'the Irish dimension', meaning the context of the whole of Ireland and specifically Irish nationalism. This point was spelt out in the official British White Paper of March 1973 that followed, in words which, it is easy to see now, could strike an uncomfortable nerve in a conventional Unionist mind.

It was here stated to be 'clearly desirable that any new arrangements for Northern Ireland should, whilst meeting the wishes of Northern Ireland and Great Britain, be *so far as possible* [author's italics] acceptable to and accepted by the Republic of Ireland' – that Republic of which the Constitution in its Articles 2 and 3 claimed Northern Ireland as part of 'the national territory' whose 're-integration' was 'pending'.

In fact, nothing in the White Paper needed to be read as any sort of commitment to change the constitutional status quo. The initial pledge logically saw to that. Yet to a Unionist mind, conditioned by history, the tone at least conveyed that a way was being prepared for this alien Republic with its 'national' claims to begin interfering in the internal affairs of Northern Ireland.

What was envisaged under this heading was a 'Council of Ireland' to harmonize cross-border interests and concerns. Whether such harmonisation would lead to closer political ties was the sensitive question. Such a Council of Ireland had been put into the Treaty of 1921 as a sop to the Irish nationalist signatories to compensate for Northern Ireland's right to opt out of the new Free State. The abandonment of this Council in the 1920s had much contributed to the sense of safety the average Unionist felt in the security of Stormont. Now Stormont had been taken away and here was the Council of Ireland appearing again.

The average Unionist had already had to come to terms with the old order changing even before Stormont disappeared. Under the impact of the events of 1969 a set of reforms had been introduced. One man now had one vote in local elections; the Londonderry Corporation had been dissolved; the RUC had been disarmed and the B Specials disbanded. For the first time in fifty years the most conservative Unionist in Northern Ireland could hardly help looking to the future. But what now had to be contemplated in that future was not only a reinforcement of the old menace of the Catholic majority in the island, disguised as 'the Irish dimension', but also the idea of a power-sharing executive on which there were to be automatic places for Catholic nationalist politicians of that majority.

The last Stormont Prime Minister, Brian Faulkner, was Prime Minister-in-waiting for whatever new style Northern Ireland administration might next emerge. Previously 'a loyal Orange Ulsterman' of impeccable credentials, he was no Ulster Bourbon, and being a man of shrewd political intelligence and natural ambition was ready on principle to accept the lines along which the British government, in the White Paper, now prepared to give Northern Ireland a new beginning.

At a meeting of the governing body of the Ulster Unionist Council he beat off by 381 votes to 231 an attempt to reject his support for the White Paper – a comfortable enough majority in a normal democratic political context for a normal democratic party's political conference. But this was not a normal democratic political context and the Ulster Unionists had never been exactly a normal democratic political party. Here a split of the size revealed by this vote was of serious significance, a fact quickly confirmed by the immediate secession from the party of some of those who lost, led by a former minister of O'Neill's, William Craig, who formed a new party, Vanguard. Vanguard did little to conceal its links with the Loyalist paramilitary Ulster Defence Association, which liked to think of itself as facing up to the White Paper proposals much as Carson had faced up to Home Rule in 1914.

A fortnight after Faulkner had won his vote in the Ulster Unionist Council, the British government, as the next step towards implementation of the White Paper, introduced a bill to create a Northern Ireland Assembly of 78 members. The elections for it were held in June 1973 and there was a high electoral turn-out. Those Unionists who at least nominally supported the White Paper with its power-sharing and Irish dimension principles, stood as 'Official Unionists', the others just as 'Unionists'. The overall result of the Assembly election was a clear victory for Faulkner and supporters of the White Paper: 52 seats as opposed to 26 against. But it was a defeat for Faulkner as a Unionist. Of his 52 seats only 24 were Official Unionists, the rest Social Democratic and Labour nationalists and others. Among Unionists he was actually in a minority. Even some of those who technically supported him were lukewarm in their support.

The uncertainties implicit in this situation were masked for a time by formality. Three weeks later a bill to give the new Northern Ireland Assembly constitutional status received the Royal Assent as the Northern Ireland Constitution Act 1973. Its first clause re-stated the one consistent principle of every British government approach to the problem of North-East Ulster since December 1921. Northern Ireland, it said, '. . . remains part of Her Majesty's dominions and of the United Kingdom and . . . in no event will Northern Ireland or any part of it cease to be part . . . without the consent of the majority of the population of Northern Ireland . . . voting in a poll.'

This Northern Ireland Constitution Act of 1973, which remains in force today, was to figure as the statutory guarantee of that pledge in the Downing Street Declaration of 1993. It was indeed an instrument of some vision. It laid down that if a Northern Ireland executive could be found 'likely to be widely accepted throughout the community', and if there were 'a reasonable basis for the establishment of a Northern Ireland Government by consent', the Assembly should be given legislative powers by the Secretary of State, subject to the special provision that any measure which discriminated against anyone 'on the grounds of religious belief or political opinion should be void'.

It was now up to Faulkner to see if he could find an executive widely acceptable to the community. Despite his precarious position within his own party – emphasized when a lukewarm supporter in the Assembly switched to outright opposition – he pursued difficult talks with the nationalist and other minority members of the Assembly about forming a power-sharing executive, and on 21 November 1973 was able to announce success. An executive would consist of himself as leader and five other Unionists, together with five members of the Social Democratic and Labour Party, and one from the middle of the middle of the road, liberal Unionist, Alliance Party. Gerry Fitt of the SDLP was to be the Deputy Chief Executive, John Hume, Minister of Commerce and another SDLP member, Austin Currie, Minister of Housing.

The announcement was immediately greeted with a protest from Paisley's Democratic Unionist Party that this was 'the greatest betrayal since Lundy ' – the officer who had wanted to open the gates of the city of Derry to King James's troops in 1689. And when Faulkner faced the Assembly with his executive a few days later he was met with Unionist cries of 'Traitors out! Traitors out!'

Power could not in fact yet be transferred to him, for the other half of the White Paper's recommendation had first to be settled: that sensitive question of 'the Irish dimension', initially a matter for the British and Irish governments.

Talks had been taking place between the two governments for some weeks, and with the principal areas for negotiation agreed (reform of the police and the civil service, and the proposed Council of Ireland), a Conference between the two governments and the new Northern Ireland power-sharing executive was arranged for 6 December 1973 at Sunningdale in Surrey.

The 6 December 1973 was, to the day, the 52nd anniversary of the signing of the Anglo-Irish Treaty in which this modern phase of the Northern Ireland crisis had its roots. It was also the first occasion on which heads of the British and Irish governments, and a leader of Northern Ireland had met together since 1925, when the Boundary Commission to adjust the border had been abandoned. So there was some historical resonance to the occasion. The realities of the present were to have the final word.

Some of these realities were not even in Ireland. It had always been a problem for Britain that the Irish question, while central to the Irish, was, however demanding, only peripheral to British politics as a whole. That autumn a new Arab-Israeli war in the Middle East and the resulting oil crisis absorbed much of the Heath government's attention, while Heath's own battle with the miners over pay increases reached crisis point only three weeks before the meeting scheduled for Sunningdale. Heath moved Whitelaw, with his amiable conciliatory gifts, from the Northern Ireland Office to that of Employment, to help deal with the miners. He appointed in his place Francis Pym, a man largely unversed in the affairs of Ireland. The Irish Foreign Minister at Sunningdale, Garret Fitzgerald, was to describe Pym later as having been 'like a fish out of water' about the place. As things turned out this was hardly to matter.

In Northern Ireland itself many Unionist faces were turning strongly against the Conference even before it met. Although the White Paper had spoken of 'leaders of elected representatives of Northern Irish opinion' being invited, the extremists Craig and Paisley were accorded only an invitation to lunch at Sunningdale 'to give their views' but not to participate in the Conference itself – 'the same privilege as the catering staff', as Paisley put it. On the day the Conference met, there also met in Belfast a great gathering of Unionist delegates of all shades of anti-Faulkner opinion to pledge their opposition to power-sharing.

It is easy to see now that Sunningdale had no hope of success. Paradoxically it was a successful Conference. After four days the British and Irish governments, together with Faulkner's power-sharing executive, agreed the grounds on which this executive could now proceed. A major part of the work had concerned the way in which the new Council of Ireland was to function, elaborated with a detail which, given Faulkner's minority Unionist position in Belfast, now seems staggering.

There was to be a consultative Assembly for the whole island of Ireland, to consist of thirty members of the Northern Ireland Assembly and thirty members of the Dublin Dail. Above this was to be a Council of Ministers composed of seven members of the Northern Ireland executive and seven members of the Irish government. But an attempt by the SDLP members of the executive to create a joint police authority for the whole island, with equal membership for the Republic, was whittled down to no more than agreement that the two separate authorities of Northern Ireland and the Republic should co-operate through the Council of Ireland. However, the implication for a future in which an eventual united Ireland might more easily be brought about was unmistakable.

There was one important additional token of reassurance for Unionists. The Fine Gael Irish government agreed to reinforce the British pledge in the Constitution Act with one of their own, saying that there could be 'no change in the status of Northern Ireland until a majority of the people of Northern Ireland desired a change in that status'.

With this statement a significant milestone in British-Irish relations had been reached. Hitherto, the only official Irish position on this point had been the contrary one contained in Articles 2 and 3 of the Irish

Constitution where it was stated that 'the national territory' consisted of 'the whole island of Ireland', while recognizing that the Dail's laws temporarily did not apply there. It would, of course, have been more helpful to Faulkner still if the two clauses could have been removed from the Irish Constitution altogether. Both Garret Fitzgerald, the Irish Foreign Minister, and Conor Cruise O'Brien, an Irish minister also present at Sunningdale, were personally of the opinion that the clauses should go, but since a national referendum was constitutionally necessary before this could be effected, they were also of the opinion that the result of such a referendum was too doubtful to be worth risking. If the vote were to go against change it would subsequently bring any successful Sunningdale Agreement to nothing. It was not then known that it would come to nothing anyway.

For some years Fitzgerald would continue to wonder whether the risk should not have been taken and thus have made the Agreement in the end more widely acceptable to Unionists at large. However, a vote in the Dail soon afterwards suggests that the referendum would indeed have gone against change. On a motion, supported by the opposition Fianna Fail Party, to restore the traditional anti-partition rhetoric in place of the Northern Ireland majority veto conceded at Sunningdale, the Fine Gael government won by only five votes. A subsequent judgment by the High Court in Dublin was to rule that what the Irish government had agreed on this point at Sunningdale amounted in fact to no more than 'a statement of policy', and could not affect the strict constitutional position. In any event, Unionists at large, obsessed with the menace of a Council of Ireland, were in no mood to be impressed by any sort of verbal concession from the Republic.

However, in the long term, the question of the exact legal validity of the Irish government's commitment was less important than the fact that such a commitment had been made. Like so much else that got on to the record at Sunningdale, a marker of significance had been put down for the future.

Other participants too had made adjustments to traditional positions. The most startling of all of course was that made by the Unionist, Faulkner, though because he did not in fact represent the vast majority of Northern Ireland Unionists it was to be irrelevant. But, again, it was a marker for the future. A loyal Unionist *could* countenance power-sharing, however much other Unionists might disagree with him.

The SDLP, traditionally and now confidently engaged in promoting conditions for a future united Ireland through the Council of Ireland, had to compromise at least by abandoning the proposal for a joint police authority, thus also accepting that without some adjustment of traditional attitudes by all parties, there could be no constructive future.

The British government's own position at the time was the most complicated because it was still stuck with traditional attitudes that were contradictory. One was expressed in the traditional pledge that there could be no constitutional change in Northern Ireland without the approval of the majority who lived there – a pledge now reinforced by the Irish government itself. But the British were also traditionally lumbered with that conscientious feeling inherited from the Home Rule Act, and indeed the Treaty itself, that in the long run a united Ireland was desirable. This expressed itself at Sunningdale as dedication to the principle of a Council of Ireland, a dedication which at times involved British pressure on Faulkner in support of the SDLP. Symptomatic of the greenness, in more senses than one, of this approach was its failure to appreciate the strength of that majority Unionist opinion which was soon to make Sunningdale altogether redundant.

It was the Council of Ireland that was to seal the Conference's fate, with most Unionists already profoundly suspicious of Faulkner for having gone off to Sunningdale with his power-sharing executive in the first place. Within days of his return, the Protestant paramilitaries had formed an Ulster Army Council to back all Unionist politicians who would oppose a Council of Ireland.

In accordance with the Agreement the power-sharing executive formally took office on the first day of 1974. Three days later the Ulster Unionist Council voted to reject the Council of Ireland. Faulkner had to resign as Unionist Party leader, and form his own party as leader of the executive.

But these were all politicians. What did the ordinary people of Northern Ireland make of Sunningdale? It was possible to hold a sort of plebiscite almost at once.

The British Prime Minister, Edward Heath, preoccupied by his trouble with the miners, boldly called a General Election in the hope of increasing his power to deal with that problem. In Northern Ireland the election was fought almost entirely on the issue of Sunningdale. 'Dublin is just a Sunningdale away!' was the Unionist anti-Faulkner slogan. The votes were cast on February 28th. Of the twelve Westminster seats, eleven went to anti-Faulkner Unionists. The only seat won by a member of the executive was in West Belfast, won by Gerry Fitt for the SDLP. The Revd Ian Paisley immediately called for fresh elections to the Northern Ireland Assembly. A new Unionist grouping, the Ulster Workers Council, called for widespread civil disobedience unless such elections were held.

But Faulkner did still have a majority in the Assembly, if not one of Unionists, and on May 14th a motion there to reject power-sharing and the Council of Ireland was itself rejected by forty-four votes to twenty-eight. The Ulster Workers Council immediately called a province-wide strike.

The strike took some hours to get going early on the first day, but groups of so-called Tartan youths and men of the paramilitary Ulster Defence Association (the UDA) sometimes masked, wearing camouflage jackets and carrying clubs, soon saw to that. By midday, *The Times* reported from Belfast that 'intimidation was beginning to reach epic proportions'.

The need for intimidation did not indicate lack of support for the political aim of the strike, but rather mere reluctance, even in Protestant areas, by shopkeepers and wage-earners to give up their business and their wages. The election had shown clearly enough what the Unionist majority's feelings were. What the British government was about to learn was that nothing can be achieved in Northern Ireland if the Unionist majority is not prepared to support it.

By the middle of the week there were electricity black-outs of up to six hours at a time and Belfast itself was riddled with road-blocks manned by strikers. As the strike went into its second week, its grip on the facilities of ordinary life became something of a stranglehold. There was panic-buying of food; both gas and electricity supplies recurrently failed; petrol could be had only from a limited number of pumps manned by the army; the postal services fragmented. A fortnight after the start of the strike, the electricity supply for the whole of Northern Ireland was on the point of being shut down altogether.

In Britain the new Labour government of Harold Wilson which, after the discomfiture of Heath in the election, had taken office without an overall majority in the House of Commons, had inevitable problems of its own. Faulkner called for strong government action to deal with the strike, but virtually all he got from Wilson was a curious national broadcast denouncing the strikers and their supporters as people who had spent their lives sponging on the British tax-payer.

Wilson's unsure touch reflected a fundamental uncertainty about what to do. His thoughts were, as those of British Prime Ministers so often were, mainly concentrated elsewhere than on Ireland. His General Officer commanding British troops in Northern Ireland had some 17,000 men at his disposal but judged that they were not enough for the situation he faced. 'If,' the General commented, with unanswerable soldierly simplicity, 'you get a very large section of the population bent on a particular course, then it is a difficult thing to try to stop them taking that course.' That course continued.

On Monday, 27 May 1974, Faulkner handed in his resignation. The executive which he had headed could no longer conceivably be thought, as the Constitution Act had said it should be, 'likely to be widely accepted throughout the community'. Wilson's Secretary of State for Northern Ireland, Merlyn Rees, declared reasonably enough that the executive had ceased to exist. The Assembly went with it, first dissolved and then finally prorogued in 1975. The Sunningdale Agreement was no more.

Theoretically, with the return of direct rule, the British government had now to go back to the political drawing board. But for a long time it seemed as if the drawing board had gone too. The Wilson government was even to consider for a while the option of withdrawing from Northern Ireland altogether.

Britain's most imaginative effort since the Treaty of 1921 to deal with the Irish question by devolution – too imaginative and unrealistic as it had proved – was now over. There was not to be another on the same scale for nearly another twenty years. By that time a good deal more realism had entered the minds of all parties to this dangerous and degrading situation.

The rest of the news to date for 1974 was that seventy-four people had been killed in Northern Ireland by the time the Sunningdale Agreement collapsed, and that shortly before it did so Unionist paramilitaries had exploded a number of car bombs in the Republic, in Dublin and Monaghan, killing thirty-three people – the largest number of people killed in a single day in all these 'troubles'.

The Labour government of the day was at the time, and has been since, often criticised for its failure to force an end to the Ulster Workers' strike and assert the right to survival of the new political structure so painstakingly evolved. But while it is true that the decision not to act was probably determined as much by lassitude and distraction at home as by conscious determination of policy, two salient points need to be borne in mind before proceeding to condemnation. The first is that, had the military option

been decided on, and pressed to the point of success, the result would have been defeat and humiliation for most of that very majority Unionist opinion to which British government is otherwise pledged and on which it must depend for co-operation in any new attempt at political solution. This would have been the worst possible basis for a fresh start.

Secondly, it can in no way be assumed that a military operation would necessarily have been successful, even if pressed with vigour. The paramilitary leaders of the Ulster Workers (essentially the UDA) had calculated that military force might be used and had devised a tactic with which to cope with it. As one of the leaders was later to explain: 'The one thing we set out from day one was that we were not going to provoke confrontation with the security forces. The order went down to all the rank and file members of the UDA that where they were confronted they were just to walk away and leave their barricades and as soon as the army left, go back and build them up again. We deliberately set out to make sure there would be no points of provocation.'

Had this tactic been employed, the last state of humiliation for the Sunningdale Agreement could again have been worse than the first. As things were, at least this attempt at a political solution ended with a clean cut. It left the failed model of a political solution to be studied for the future by all parties, including the IRA and the Unionist paramilitaries, both of whom continued to go about their awful business, as if it were part of the natural order of things.

Chapter 15

After Sunningdale

History, although it is the story of what happened in the past, is strangely different from that story as it was being lived through. The important difference of course is that, as it was being lived through, no-one knew what was going to happen next, and history does. History thus acquires a certain arrogance by which detail in human existence, dramatically and painfully relevant at the time, gets relegated to the nondescript by the view history requires. But there are times when one is conscious of living both in ordinary life and in history as well. The period following the IRA and Loyalist paramilitary ceasefires of the second half of 1994 was such a time.

Looking back from there, the previous twenty-five years contracted easily into history, a quarter of a century in which, for all the detail of slaughter, cruelty and material destruction, the most significant thing about it was that throughout that time these things had not stopped.

Simultaneously (and this process began with the Downing Street Declaration of 15 December 1993) emphasis switched into wondering what would happen next and what history would one day make of it. In the historical package into which twenty-five years contracted only the prominent features became of interest, particularly those political features with apparent significance for the future.

In an abbreviated work of history like this, such historical imperative is accepted readily but may be prefaced by some reminders of the detail which brought it about.

First, there are the dead: 3,168 altogether, of whom 648 were British soldiers; 296 RUC officers, including women, and 2,224 civilians – men, women and children.

This last figure includes those killed 'in action' on both IRA and Loyalist paramilitary sides. If it seems unfeeling not to distinguish them from the many civilians they killed, this may be appropriate at a time when a comforting, even reconciling feature of the tragedy may be that it was awareness of its dimension that helped bring it to an end. People died, it could be said, to help make the living realize that there had been too much death.

But it would be wrong to let detail of the events of these years slip entirely into the oblivion history can conveniently offer. They all contributed to the final realization that the killing had led nowhere except to the conclusion that it had to stop. Some of the worst should be remembered.

Some of the early horrors have already been listed in the account of events to the failure of the Sunningdale Agreement. Among the worst killings of the nineteen years that followed were: 21 people killed and 182 injured in the IRA's bombing of two Birmingham pubs on 21 November 1974; the shooting of 10 Protestant workmen in a minibus in County Armagh on 5 January 1976; the killing of 12 Protestants and the injuring of 23 others in the Le Mon Hotel in County Down on 17 February 1978; the killing of 18 soldiers at Warrenpoint, County Down on 27 August 1979 and of the Queen's cousin Mountbatten with members of his family in a boat off County Sligo on the same day; the killing of 8 soldiers – 6 of them bandsmen – and civilians in parks in London on 20 July 1982; the killing of 17 people, including 11 soldiers, at a disco in County Derry on 6 December 1982; the killing of 3 civilians and 3 London policemen, with 90 other people injured by a bomb at Harrods on 17 December 1983; the killing of 5 people including one MP and the wife of the Conservative Chief Whip in the bombing of the Grand Hotel Brighton on 12 October 1984; the killing of 9 RUC officers including 2 women, at a police station in Newry on 28 February 1985; the killing of 8 IRA men and a civilian caught in the cross-fire in Loughall, County Armagh on 8 May 1987; and the killing of 11 civilians and the injuring of 63 others by a bomb at Enniskillen on 8 November 1987.

One bizarre sequence of grim events involved the killing in Gibraltar by the SAS on 6 March 1988 of 3 unarmed IRA 'active service' personnel planning to bomb a military ceremony there, followed ten days later by the killing at the subsequent IRA funerals in Belfast of 3 mourners by a Loyalist gunman, and the torture and murder three days after that of 2 British soldiers who had accidentally strayed into the funeral of those the Loyalist gunman had killed.

Later in this desultory catalogue: the killing on the 15 May 1988 in West Belfast of 3 Catholics and the injuring of 9 others in an attack with machine guns on a bar there; the killing of 8 soldiers and the injuring of 27 others in an attack on a bus in Co. Tyrone on 30 August 1988; the strapping of a Catholic workman by the IRA into a van carrying a bomb which he was forced to drive to a check point near Derry where it exploded killing him and 5 soldiers; the massacre on 17 January 1992 of 8 Protestant workmen in County Tyrone, which Gerry Adams, described curiously as being 'a horrific reminder of the failure of British policy in Ireland'; the massacre of 5 Catholics in a bookmaker's shop on 5 February 1992 by Loyalist paramilitaries; further evidence of 'the failure of British policy in Ireland' with the killing of 2 children by the IRA at Warrington in England on 20 March 1993; and, in a final frenzy of killing in the period leading to the Downing Street Declaration and the eventual ceasefires of 1994: the massacre of 10 Protestants by an IRA bomb in the Shankhill Road on 23 October 1993; the Greysteel massacre of 7 Catholics in reprisal by Loyalist paramilitaries a week later; and a final massacre of 6 Catholics in a bar in Loughin island on the 18 June 1994. The days in the 1970s when a Loyalist murderer could say, as one was reported to have done: 'I could see the IRA taking over Ulster and I thought if I killed Roman Catholics it would stop them,' seemed by then almost innocent by comparison.

Such a summary lists less than 200 deaths out of the sum total of 3,168.

Casualties of 'war' for Ireland in Hyde Park. A car-bomb
attack on the Household Cavalry, 1982.

LEFT: Gordon Wilson at the graveside of his daughter, one of eleven killed in the Enniskillen bombing 1987. '. . . no ill-will . . . no grudge . . . it's not going to bring her back.'

BELOW: The way nationalist West Belfast saw the Enniskillen bombing.

Meanwhile, what had been happening in the minds both of politicians and of ordinary people as they watched this in both parts of Ireland?

The failure of Sunningdale left attitudes in Northern Ireland frozen in a rigidity which seemingly defied further creative political initiative. It was a situation of which the IRA hoped to take political advantage. The irresolution of Wilson's Labour government seemed demonstrated to many by talks its officials held with Provisional Sinn Fein at the end of 1974, and by a temporary ceasefire and 'truce' which some of the IRA entered into for part of 1975. This eventually came to nothing but during this period, as the Northern Ireland Secretary of State of the day, Merlyn Rees, later recalled, the British government 'seriously considered', among other options, the possibility of withdrawal from Northern Ireland altogether.

Rejecting this, it considered political involvement again. But the essential political reality had not changed, indeed had become even more intractable. The great majority of Unionists refused to entertain any sort of concession either to the aspirations of the minority nationalists or to the Republic whose Constitution continued to lay claim to their state. The chance of success in these circumstances was slim and indeed soon disappeared for the foreseeable future.

Elections were held in May 1975 for a Constitutional Convention, based on the pattern of the Assembly, to consider 'what provisions for the government of Northern Ireland would be likely to command the most widespread acceptance throughout the community'. The elections certainly provided the answer to that question but it was not one that would help bring about peace. A clear majority of anti-power-sharing, anti-Irish dimension Unionists was the result: 47 anti-Sunningdale Unionists out of an Assembly of 78. The Faulkner Unionists won only 5 seats. An inevitable vote for a return to majority rule in the style of Stormont proclaimed the uselessness of the Convention for the purpose for which it had been convened, and it was dissolved in March 1976.

A new Northern Ireland Secretary, Roy Mason, was appointed the same year and the Government fell back on pursuit of the military solution. Mason's tough security policy, combined with concern for Northern Ireland's economic interests, did to some extent reduce the IRA's effectiveness for a time. He increased the strength of both the RUC and the army. The SAS were introduced to the scene on a significant scale in South Armagh. The number of deaths arising from the troubles for 1977 fell to less than half those of the year before, to 112, and for 1978 still further, to 81. And Mason showed he could be tough with the Unionists as well: he saw off the Revd Ian Paisley's attempt to emulate the Ulster workers of 1974 with a strike in May 1977 for the recall of the Assembly and the return of plain majority rule.

A distancing from the political conflicts of the province was an essential part of Mason's approach; the SDLP's democratic nationalist aspiration commanded equally little respect from him. He stood firmly by the confident statements he gave to the Press at the beginning of 1978 to the effect that 'the tide had turned', that he was 'squeezing the terrorists like rolling up a toothpaste tube . . . squeezing them out of their safe houses . . . squeezing them out of society and into prison'.

In fact there were to be 100 explosions within the province in the next

TOP: A moment in the grim sequence of events started by the Gibraltar killing of three IRA activists. Mourners at their funeral shelter from a firing Loyalist gunman.

RIGHT: The fathers of the Warrington bomb victims, Tim Parry and Jonathan Ball, meet after Tim Parry's funeral. Colin Parry (left) holds the hand of Wilf Ball.

fifty days and one of them was that which killed 12 Protestants and injured 23 others in the Le Mon Hotel. Though the total number of deaths were indeed down, the year ended with the machine-gun killing of three Grenadier Guardsmen in Crossmaglen, County Armagh, while doing their Christmas shopping. Mason himself was replaced when the Conservatives in Britain under Mrs Thatcher won the General Election of 1979.

Margaret Thatcher, who in the early days of her leadership of the party had struck Garret Fitzgerald as singularly ill-briefed on Northern Ireland, was to learn at least the facts of life there fast. Her great friend Airey Neave, whom she had ear-marked to be her Northern Ireland Secretary had been killed by an 'Irish National Liberation Army' car bomb as he drove out of the House of Commons car park two months before the election. She had been in office only three months when 18 soldiers were killed at Warrenpoint on the same day as Mountbatten was murdered off County Sligo. However disinclined, like most British Prime Ministers, to pay much attention to Ireland, Thatcher was not one to do nothing when something obviously needed to be done. If direct rule could not do better than this, then the need was to find an alternative to it by some form of political initiative.

Her Northern Ireland Secretary, Humphrey Atkins, called a constitutional conference to see what sort of progress could be made in that direction. He discovered inevitably that with both majority Unionists and democratic SDLP nationalists stuck in the positions they had assumed in the Sunningdale aftermath there was none to be made. The conference foundered.

So, what was a British Prime Minister of purpose to do instead?

The British position was, as always, a semi-contradictory one: conditioned by history to be theoretically in favour of a united Ireland, should this prove possible, it was equally conditioned by history to consider it impossible so long as the majority in Northern Ireland did not want it. The Irish Republic, the other outside party to the strange equation which required solution, was in a semi-contradictory position of its own: its Constitution indicated that the equation was both solved and not solved at the same time; the six counties were part of its territory though it could not rule them. Since this view was shared by the democratic nationalist minority in the North and since it was important that, expressing itself through the SDLP, it should not lose ground to the violent republicans of the IRA and other groups, it was to the Irish dimension that the British government now turned, and was to continue to turn for much rest of the decade. In doing so it took for granted too easily that Unionist loyalty, on the strength of so many past reassurances from British government, would remain more or less unobtrusively in place.

It was a good moment in which again to look to Dublin. Both political parties there, Fianna Fail and Fine Gael, were republican by tradition in descent from the Sinn Fein of the first Dail of 1919, but Fianna Fail, in descent from those who like the present IRA regarded the Treaty of 1921 as a betrayal, was the party whose co-operation was likely to be the most valuable and was now in power. Its leadership had just changed. The previous Taoiseach, Jack Lynch, unofficially closer to Fine Gael than much of his party in readiness to give the Unionist majority a democratic veto on

LEFT: Garret Fitzgerald comes through 'the revolving door' of Irish politics to meet Mrs Thatcher ('Northern Ireland is as much a part of the UK as my constituency').

BELOW: John Hume expounds modern Irish nationalism in Dublin, with Albert Reynolds, Fianna Fail Taoiseach, as right-hand man.

Irish unity, had recently been succeeded by Charlie Haughey, a skilled political operator with strong republican views whose father had been a leader of the IRA in the North at the time of the Civil War against the Free State. Margaret Thatcher's instinct to get somewhere near the heart of the matter by dealing with Haughey was sound inasmuch he represented the democratic republican tradition at its most politically realistic, and the Irish dimension at its most inescapable.

But while she had taken care to preface arrangements for a forthcoming summit in Dublin with reassurance to the Unionists about the constitutional future of Northern Ireland being 'a matter for the people of Northern Ireland, this government and this parliament and no-one else', when the meeting in Dublin finally took place in December 1980 a rather different sort of emphasis seemed to emerge.

It was in any case an historic encounter – the first between British and Irish Prime Ministers in Dublin since the Treaty. Judged in narrow diplomatic terms it was a personal success. In terms of political initiative for resolution of the crisis in Northern Ireland, it merely laid down guidelines for the future which, in the absence of anything else, were regarded as something of a triumph. But in the absence of anything else they were guidelines which again set alarm bells ringing in many Unionist minds. The joint communiqué spoke of 'the unique relationship between the two countries', of 'special consideration of the totality of relationships within these islands' and of 'possible new institutional structures'.

Thatcher was later to admit honestly enough that she had not involved herself sufficiently closely in the drafting of these words. But that could be another way of saying that she had not sufficiently grasped their significance. Haughey certainly took advantage of her omission to suggest that useful constitutional discussion had taken place, though this was hardly so. It was a defect of Thatcher's otherwise remarkable political self-confidence that, in Irish affairs, it led her to feel she knew all she needed to know, without looking further at the complexities. Her memoirs seem to make clear that it was only the security situation which seriously concerned her, and that her understanding of the Northern Ireland realities was otherwise minimal. The only political standpoint there to which she seems drawn with some respect is that of the old Stormont régime.

Paradoxically it was from the heart of some of the old Stormont mentality that a spirited response came to her summit meeting with Haughey. The Reverend Ian Paisley took off at once, organizing in February 1981 a military parade of some 500 men wearing combat jackets and brandishing their gun licences on a hillside near Ballymena, and a few days later signed in Belfast City Hall an 'Ulster Declaration' on the model of Carson's 1912 Covenant.

In fact, for most Unionists the words of the Thatcher-Haughey communiqué stirred a reaction rather less dramatic than that provoked by the third Home Rule Bill, but many were disturbed by the implications that a much closer relationship with the Republic was in the air, leading to direct republican involvement in the running of Northern Ireland. This was the very thing they thought they had so explicitly put an end to after Sunningdale.

It was significant that at the local government elections in May that year

Paisley's Democratic Unionists for the first time secured a slightly greater number of votes than Molyneaux's Official Unionists, though the latter won a slightly greater number of seats. The difference concerned style rather than strength of reaction. The assumption hitherto prevailing that Mrs Thatcher of all people had been unlikely to betray them had received a rude shock. Unionists might have been still more disturbed had they known that Haughey had told a journalist the day after the first Thatcher-Haughey meeting earlier in 1980 that he had the impression Thatcher had no idea what to do about Northern Ireland and no plans for it.

Haughey's own plans were clear enough. They were, he declared openly: '... to secure the final withdrawal of the British military and political presence from Ireland'. It was the same ideological goal as the IRA's, but unlike theirs to be obtained only by peaceful means when a consensus future made this possible. The British government, he stressed, should play its part in helping to bring this consensus about by encouraging support for a united Ireland. British governments were, he knew, up to a point historically pledged to do this.

His own public offers to Unionists of every sort of consideration and indeed representation for their own special interests and concerns in an eventual Northern Ireland cut no ice with them at all.

'Mr Haughey,' the Revd Ian Paisley declaimed to wild applause, 'Mr Haughey made a wonderful speech in the Dail yesterday, and he said the people of Ulster would be amazed if they knew what he was going to offer them. "Come into my parlour," said the spider to the fly. "It's the nicest little parlour that ever you did spy." I want to tell Charles Haughey that Ulster Protestants are too dead fly to go into his little parlour. We'll not be there. No surrender – that's our answer to Charles Haughey.'

And though many Unionists preferred their fears expressed in less demagogic tones, this was the standpoint which had to be accommodated if anything like a 'solution' were ever to be found. Along with the standpoint of the IRA, namely that somehow Unionist 'surrender' could be achieved once violence had got the British out, it was the apparently unalterable component in the situation. The weakness in the IRA's position was that after more than ten years of violence there was no sign whatever of their being able to get the British out, however effectively they might be able to continue to disturb the peace. The Unionists by contrast were in a position to say that what they had they would hold.

Where then was the necessary flexibility for a solution to be found? The democratic minority in the North, represented by the SDLP, had little room in which to move. Their position was clear: they were Irish nationalists who wanted a united Ireland if it could be achieved peacefully and were prepared to wait to achieve it by a combination of the democratic process and the weight of the Irish dimension. But quite apart from the fact that the majority Unionists were implacably resistant to any sort of democratic persuasion along these lines, there was at present not even any political structure in Northern Ireland within which any democratic process could take place.

It was nevertheless within the SDLP that signs of at least some passive flexibility might be discerned. Why, for instance, in spite of the failure of the nationalist ideal or even local power-sharing to materialize did there

OPPOSITE

TOP: Mothers of the hunger strikers. Falls Road, 1981.

BELOW: Gerry Adams and an IRA volley for Bobby Sands MP – first of ten hunger strikers to die for special category prison status in 1981.

seem on the part of SDLP supporters small inclination to forsake the democratic process and join in what supporters of the IRA could say with some truth was the historic republican traditional way of getting the British out of Ireland? It had got them out of most of Ireland in 1921 and, so the esoteric belief went, would have got them out of the whole of it had some republicans then 'stuck to their guns' and not 'betrayed the true cause'?

To such a question John Hume gave his own clear answer. It was from him, as early as 1980, that indications of movement from a traditionally rigid minority position were being articulated.

'What has been put forward in the name of republicanism by many people in Northern Ireland is not republicanism at all,' he said. 'It is extreme nationalism which puts forward a very narrow sectional view of Ireland, a view which takes little account of the differences that exist in this island, and of the existence of a very large tradition in the northern part of the island . . . a view which thinks that it's right not only to kill but to die to enforce this view, this sectional view of Ireland . . . I don't think that's republicanism at all . . . republicanism ought to mean the coming together of Catholic, Protestant and Dissenter, and what I would want to see on this island would be an agreed Ireland, one which all its traditions agree, an Ireland which is of course independent, and one which has a role for all sections of the Irish people to play.'

Independence was, it could seem, being placed as a somewhat secondary consideration to the importance of the quality of Ireland's social fabric.

A difference in character between the nature of the minority's nationalism in the North and that of the majority in the Republic had inevitably developed over the seven decades in which the two had been separated. In the North nationalism had become, for many in the minority, a necessary local defensive attitude within the Protestant state for a Protestant people, with, in times of real trouble, the IRA of the day regarded as some sort of defensive structure. In this sense it had a different reality from the nationalism of the South, where nationalism had become, particularly after the successful constitutional changes of de Valera and the subsequent creation of the Republic, primarily a nostalgic obligation, sacrosanct in the Constitution and much formally revered by politicians, particularly Fianna Fail, but increasingly little related to what was important in the daily lives of citizens of the Republic. For many years almost every family there had had members who in a previous generation had fought together against the British and one side or the other in the Civil War of 1922–3, but even these were beginning to die off, taking much of the whole story with them or at least consigning it to emotional historic memory, remote from the actuality of the every day life. It was towards such a less compulsive view of traditional nationalism that John Hume was keen to direct minority thinking in the special conditions of the North.

It so happened that the closer co-operation between the British and Irish governments foreshadowed by the Thatcher-Haughey summit did not immediately develop to give substance to Unionist fears provoked by the words of the communiqué.

At the beginning of 1981 a republican prisoner in the Maze, Bobby Sands, serving a sentence of fourteen years for firearm offences, started a hunger strike for the political status for prisoners which the IRA demanded

but the British refused to give. Over the next eight months he and nine other republican prisoners died on hunger strike in this cause – Sands himself after starving for sixty-six days, in the course of which he was elected at a bye-election in Fermanagh and South Tyrone as a member of the Westminster Parliament.

Hunger strikes hit a particularly acute emotional nerve in both parts of Ireland, where school children had for two generations learned of the heroic deaths of Thomas Ashe and Terence Macswiney half a century before and come to regard them as martyrs, a title which the IRA was understandably quick to apply to Sands and the others. After Sands's death his agent, Owen Carron, was elected at the subsequent bye-election with an increased majority and an increased number of votes. While a new bitterness inflamed the rioting after each hunger strike death in Northern Ireland and a certain nobility entered the perception of the IRA cause abroad (particularly in the United States) Margaret Thatcher with characteristic single-mindedness refused to make any concessions. Relations with Haughey and the Dublin government deteriorated predictably.

The impact on ordinary people in the Republic was inevitably of some emotional significance. But as the number of deaths mounted and the IRA sought to make as much effective political capital out of them as possible a curious reverse effect set in too.

There was, as one nationalist historian put it at the time, 'a certain unease among the southern citizenry at the strategy adopted by the supporters of the hunger strike: the black flags, some of the slogans, the real intimidation and even more the sense of intending anarchy which developed in certain places. There were some country towns in which H-block supporters took over the direction of traffic and other local arrangements for whole afternoons, and all this created a grave unease.'

The unease came to a head with a march on the British Embassy in Dublin. The demonstration had been largely organized from the North and proceeded to attack with remarkable violence the Irish police who were there to protect the Embassy. This, as another republican historian put it in 1983, 'turned off a great deal of such emotion as had been aroused . . . Every time the IRA attacks the institutions of our state, they lose sympathy at a tremendous rate in the Republic. The cumulative effect down the years has been to diminish very very greatly the support that was rather more widespread ten or fifteen years ago.'

'Irish people,' commented the first historian, 'didn't at all like the idea of what they regarded as imported thugs marching through Ballsbridge and confronting the Irish police in the most barbaric fashion and using weapons they had brought for the purpose. Here was a perfect example of the interests of *our* state and *our* community in the Republic of Ireland being threatened by aliens. Even if they were northern republicans their behaviour stamped them as aliens.'

Somewhere in that perceptive identification of a southern Irish nationalist personality that had developed separately over the years – a separate twenty-six county personality – there lay seeds of hope for peace in Ireland in the future.

But Mrs Thatcher was not at that moment particularly concerned with the future of Northern Ireland. She was temporarily hard pressed on the domestic front and satisfied to have demonstrated her authority in Northern Ireland over the hunger strike with characteristic bravura and to some effect. Early in the following year she would be preoccupied with the Falklands.

In the meantime the measure of her interest in finding a 'solution' for Northern Ireland can be gauged from her Foreign Minister, Geoffrey Howe's, comment that she had sent a new Secretary of State to Northern Ireland, Jim Prior, 'to get him out of her hair'.

Chapter 16

Ulster Says No!

Prior, who took up his new position in September 1981, can hardly have expected life to be much easier on the other side of the Irish Sea, and indeed within a matter of weeks violent abuse was being screamed at him by frustrated and angry Unionists at the funeral of the MP Robert Bradford murdered by the IRA. Paisley said 'the blood of the murdered' lay as much on the British government which allowed such things to happen with impunity as on the IRA. Asked by a reporter if the noisy and turbulent scenes which greeted the Secretary of State were not disgraceful for a funeral, Paisley replied that what was disgraceful was 'Mr Prior himself who has the blood on his hands.'

Prior's problem – no new one for any Northern Ireland Secretary – was how, in the face of 'successful' IRA terrorism of this sort, to introduce a creative political initiative without arousing Unionist fears of a British government sell-out. Such fears were always strengthened by failure to maintain security.

He was unlikely to get much creative political help from Downing Street. Certainly, with a forthrightness no Unionist could fault, Thatcher did her best to repair any remaining damage from the Haughey 'summit'. Probably hoping at the same time to bolster any incipient 'wetness' in Prior's approach she had made a statement in the House of Commons to the effect that Northern Ireland was a part of the United Kingdom 'as much as my constituency is'. Prior was in fact working on an idea for a new elected Assembly, with devolutionary powers which would once again be 'acceptable to both sides of the community'.

The difference this time was to be that the Assembly would develop executive powers at its own pace, a principle that came to be described as 'rolling devolution'. It would be, Prior said, a 'step by step approach', starting as a political forum and moving on from there to acquire, when the Government saw fit, administrative structure.

The White Paper introducing the idea, about which Thatcher was unenthusiastic, appeared three days after Argentina invaded the Falklands. Her attention and that of the House of Commons itself was hardly focussed on Northern Ireland for the next three months. Nevertheless the bill to set up the Assembly went through, without much interest, in July 1982 and elections for it were held in October.

Prior had expressed a conviction that the time had come when the

OPPOSITE

Aching for peace in the nationalist Falls Road. The day before the Downing Street Declaration of 15 December 1993.

273

people of Northern Ireland would really want to come together to discuss where they should go next. This turned out to be wishful thinking. The people of Northern Ireland were prepared to vote in elections for an Assembly but the Assembly proved interested only in making clear that it was not prepared to discuss any change from pre-conceived positions. It was the same story all over again: the majority of Unionists were not prepared to discuss power-sharing; the SDLP, though they had taken part in the election were, in these circumstances, not even prepared to sit down with them in the Assembly. The Irish dimension was not under consideration; in any case relations between the Thatcher and Haughey governments, strained by the hunger strikes, had worsened with unfriendly Irish neutrality over the Falklands war. The Assembly degenerated into a one-sided talking shop. Devolution rolled to a stop.

The Assembly itself was not dissolved until the middle of 1986 by which time it had long ceased to have significance. It had been displaced from any sort of political limelight in 1985 by an event which at the time appeared to unfold important possibilities for the future, the signing of the Anglo-Irish Agreement. This was in one sense an indirect product of Prior's failed venture.

At the elections for the Assembly, Provisional Sinn Fein had taken part for the first time on the curious democratic basis recently announced of 'the ballot box in one hand and an armalite in the other'. They had won ten per cent of all first preference votes and five of the seventy-eight seats. (Gerry Adams and Martin MacGuiness won two of the five.)

The SDLP were still well ahead of Sinn Fein, with just under nineteen per cent of the first preference votes and fourteen seats, but it became a reasonable concern for the Government that, in the further absence of progress towards some sort of political initiative which took the nationalist minority into account, Sinn Fein might begin to close the gap. This concern was reinforced when in the British General Election of 1983 Gerry Adams won West Belfast from the SDLP candidate, Gerry Fitt. Such results made the total republican vote in Northern Ireland, including the SDLP almost thirty per cent of the voting electorate. It was hardly surprising that in such circumstances government attention focussed on the Irish dimension and how to try to square it with overall commitment to the Union.

This was again a good moment in which to look to Dublin, although for opposite reasons from the time before. Then, the advantage of dealing with a strongly republican Fianna Fail Taoiseach like Charles Haughey had seemed to be that if mutual agreement could be reached with him, it was likely to prove of lasting value because he could carry strong republican sentiment with him. But when the initial appearance of success at the Thatcher-Haughey summit proved illusory and relations deteriorated over the hunger strikes and the Falklands, all such prospect vanished. Now at the end of 1982 what Garret Fitzgerald of Fine Gael called 'the revolving door' of Irish politics brought him rather than Haughey to power again in Dublin.

Fitzgerald had impeccable republican credentials of his own: his father had fought in the Post Office in 1916. But his position on Irish unity was far from standard rhetorical republican dogma. His view was that while he would have preferred to see a united Ireland, on the grounds that the

Gerry Adams, Sinn Fein President, twice elected to the House of Commons for West
Belfast. An old-fashioned nationalist in modern trim.

more the Protestant and Catholic traditions in Ireland were brought together the more usefully they would interact on each other for their own good, he recognised that 'in the medium term or over an unspecified period' the fears on the part of the Northern Protestants made its realization unlikely.

This fell short of the total exclusion of unity which most Unionists would themselves have preferred, but then even the British government did not subscribe to that. And if there were ever to be hope of one day coming to some accommodation with Unionists his was a more auspicious starting point than Charlie Haughey's. A commitment to amend Articles 2 and 3 of the Irish Constitution by removing the national claim to North-East Ulster was, of course, what they really wanted to hear. Privately Fitzgerald had been of the opinion even at Sunningdale that some such amendment was desirable, though only in return for a Council of Ireland or some form of joint authority in the North, both of which were anathema to them. Nevertheless, from the British point of view it could be said that, with Fitzgerald, Articles 2 and 3 might be on the table in some form, and that with him there were grounds for believing that a new political initiative was feasible. His mind permitted honest flexibility to enter conventional republican dogma.

In this spirit Fitzgerald now accepted a proposal put forward by John Hume of the SDLP that a forum should be held in the Republic at which all concerned parties, 'abandoning rhetoric' and with 'their cards on the table', should examine together the future of North-East Ulster.

This forum sat in Dublin for over a year. A creative concept, it was to reveal helpfully the extent to which democratic Irish nationalism could indeed be ready to abandon some of the rhetoric of the past. But in terms of the search for a solution to the Northern Ireland problem it was crippled from the start, for the traditional Unionists refused to take any part in it. All the forum could hope to do was to provide further limited data on which the search for a solution might proceed. But at least it was helping to start the search up again.

Sitting in Dublin it was dismissed by the majority in the North as little different from the spider and fly device discerned by Paisley in the mind of Charles Haughey. Its final report published in May 1984 could seem to some extent to justify such dismissal. It blamed Britain in an old-fashioned way for bringing partition about by 'refusing to accept the democratically expressed wishes of the Irish people' (a historical reference to the British General Election of 1918) and by creating 'an artificial political majority in the North'. However, for this one-sided approach the Unionists themselves were partly to blame for having refused to take part and being thus unable to place their view in the report. The same could be said about the report's actual proposals for a solution.

Fitzgerald was anxious to insist that these were in fact suggestions rather than proposals and they did certainly contain in the first of them an expression of what, by conventional republican standards, was his progressive view. Three options were presented: a united Ireland *by consent*; a federal state; or a 'joint authority' for Northern Ireland.

To all this Margaret Thatcher effectively voiced the authentic Unionist reply, when at the end of a summit meeting with Garret Fitzgerald in

November 1984 she rejected each option vigorously at a press conference with the words '. . . out ', '. . . out', '. . . out'.

Nevertheless, the forum had engendered a climate in which the two governments were prepared once again, for the first time since Sunningdale, to attempt some political initiative.

Negotiations were conscientiously pursued by enlightened civil servants on both sides, under the supervision on the British side of two successive Northern Ireland Secretaries who followed Prior: Douglas Hurd and Tom King.

The position of the two main parties in Northern Ireland itself remained deadlocked as before. The Unionists were unprepared to accept any initiative which involved power-sharing. The SDLP were unprepared to accept any which did not. Since the Unionists already had their prime requirement built in (commitment to the Union so long as the majority wanted it), it was in the area of the SDLP's second requirement (the Irish dimension) that there seemed room for manouevre and it was between the two governments alone that such manouevre took place.

The results of the Northern Ireland local district elections in May 1985 gave a spur to the negotiations. Sinn Fein, now contesting local elections for the first time, won nearly twelve per cent of the first preference votes; the SDLP 17.8 per cent – compared with the Assembly elections of 1982, a slight gain for Sinn Fein and a slight drop for the SDLP.

The signing of the Anglo-Irish Agreement took place at Hillsborough Castle on 15 November 1985. It maintained Thatcher's 'out . . . out . . . out . . .' response to the three forum proposals, but established instead a clear structure of involvement on the part of the Republic in the affairs of Northern Ireland. The first Article affirmed, much as the Sunningdale Agreement had done, on the part of both British and Irish governments, that there could be no change in the status of Northern Ireland without the consent of the majority of the people there; it also recognized that the present wish of the majority was for no change and said that should in future there be a clear wish for a united Ireland both British and Irish Parliaments would introduce legislation to that effect. Other articles were distinctly innovative.

A new Intergovernmental Conference was set up under the British Secretary of State and the Irish Foreign Minister to deal with Northern Ireland and relations between the two islands on a regular basis over political, security and legal matters. This Conference was to have a secretariat in place at Maryfield outside Belfast to be manned permanently by both British and Irish civil servants. Eventual devolved government was defined as a shared aim and the Irish government could use the Conference to put forward views about how the interests of the minority might be considered in bringing that about.

The Unionists were nonplussed, staggered, outraged, appalled, dismayed. The sense of betrayal by Thatcher, whom they had now come to think of as someone who would not let them down, ran right across their whole political spectrum, with the exception of the small moderate Alliance Party.

On Sunday two days later Paisley prayed to God before his congregation in church 'to deal with the Prime Minister of our country . . . Oh God, take

TOP: James Molyneaux, Official Unionist leader since 1974. 'No Surrender' velvet style.

BELOW: 'Not an Inch', again. Outside Stormont, Ulster Unionists trying to block the road to the Anglo-Irish Agreement 1985.

vengeance upon this wicked treacherous, lying woman; take vengeance upon her and grant that we shall see a demonstration of your power.'

In the House of Commons, Harold McCusker, a balanced Official Unionist of integrity, told Thatcher he had never known what desolation felt like until he read the Agreement, and that he would carry to his grave with ignominy the sense of injustice he had done his constituents by telling them to trust her.

James Molyneaux, leader of the Official Unionists, said in the House that he had never known such 'universal cold fury' adding that he had thus far managed to contain it.

All fifteen Unionist MPs in fact were to resign their seats in Parliament and fight bye-elections in protest under the slogan 'Ulster Says No!' They registered over 400,000 Unionist votes which said just that, though they were to lose one seat to the SDLP which naturally welcomed the Agreement,

The *Belfast Newsletter* wrote of the ghosts of Cromwell and Lundy walk-ing 'hand-in-hand to produce a recipe for bloodshed and conflict which has few parallels in modern history'. And bloodshed and conflict as a result of the Agreement there was to be.

The Secretary of State himself, Tom King, was attacked by Unionists when he went to Belfast City Hall in November. At the first meeting of the Anglo-Irish Conference at Stormont in December, thirty-eight RUC officers were injured in clashes with rioters there and at the site of the secretariat at Maryfield. A big protest march which arrived there early in the New Year pulled down the gates and set a police car on fire in clashes with the RUC. Much worse was to come.

A day of Unionist action was called for 3 March 1986: roads throughout the six counties were blocked or covered in nails and oil to make them impassable. There was rioting, and stoning of the RUC and even some shooting at them. There were vicious assaults by 'Loyalists' on the RUC when they halted an already banned Apprentice Boys march in Portadown at the end of that month and the RUC fired plastic bullets which killed a Protestant. There was to be trouble at Portadown with its historic memo-ries throughout the marching season.

In Belfast there were fire-bomb attacks on the homes of a number of RUC officers. 'Buy and Die' were the words then found scrawled on the houses the police abandoned. The Revd Ian Paisley, carried protesting head first by four RUC officers out of the now defunct Assembly that summer, shouted at them: 'Don't come crying to me the next time your houses are attacked; you'll reap what you sow.' David McKittrick of the *Independent* wrote two months later:

Northern Ireland is at the moment a tense and dangerous place. [British] Government ministers venture out of their heavily fortified bases only furtively and under heavy escort. Unionist politicians refuse all contact with them; some Unionist MPs now appear regularly at menacing midnight shows of strength with masked men carrying cudgels . . .

Though all Unionists were adamantly opposed to the Agreement, and Molyneaux and Paisley had at one time announced a joint plan for civil

The Reverend Ian Paisley, with Peter Robinson beside him, reads
the open letter given to both Prime Ministers at the Anglo-Irish
Conference in Dublin Castle.

disobedience involving withdrawal of rates and the disruption of local authorities, the existence of the two separate Unionist parties continued to mark a division between moderation and extremism in Unionism which was capable of assuming real political significance. An organization calling itself Ulster Resistance received at least tempered support from Paisley and his younger and sharper, though less charismatic Deputy, Peter Robinson.

The character of the Official Unionist protest under Molyneaux was appropriately expressed at the beginning of 1987 by presentation of a petition to the Queen calling for a referendum on the Agreement. It collected 400,000 signatures. An estimated 200,000 people of one party or the other had attended a protest at Belfast City Hall on the first anniversary of the Agreement, the previous November. Gangs of looters had come to endorse that protest by breaking into shops in the city centre, from one of which – a sports outfitter – they threw golf balls at the RUC who eventually fired back with plastic bullets.

The most effective radical resentment was polarized in Protestant paramilitary organisations like the Ulster Defence Association and its offshoots. Over the coming years there was to be a corresponding increase in their ruthless and sectarian terrorism to match that of the IRA to which they were opposed.

Over the coming years there was also to be a strange political vacuum in Northern Ireland, strange because though intense political feeling was at work at various levels, no internal democratic structure was available in which that feeling could express itself other than local district councils. Strange too because at the same time a political structure, though not a democratic one, *was* available: that Intergovernmental Conference established by the Agreement at which representatives of the two governments met regularly, and at which issues could be discussed and outside party talks arranged or monitored. The political scene in Northern Ireland became for a few years a sort of shadowland of talks.

Perhaps contacts is a more accurate word with which to describe the all-important activity spasmodically occurring once the Unionists had faced up to the fact that the Agreement was firmly in place and no mere protest was going to shift it. What could shift it was some form of eventual co-operation with the British government (and by definition therefore now with the Irish government too) in order to supersede it with something else. This meant a return to negotiating mood, a mood to which the Official Unionists under Molyneaux were more inclined than the Democratic Unionists of Paisley and Robinson. And to this purpose initial contacts were made with the Government while Tom King was still Northern Ireland Secretary in 1988. Subsequent talks took place under Peter Brooke who replaced King in 1989.

Indicative of changing moods in the political atmosphere generally was a statement that Brooke made in November of that year to the effect that Sinn Fein itself might be brought into talks were it to renounce its support of IRA violence. Brooke was also the first Northern Ireland Secretary to say openly that though the IRA could be contained by military means it could not be totally defeated and that therefore 'a flexible and imaginative' approach might be pursued if the IRA itself would give up violence. It is easy now with the hindsight of history to see that the foundations of what four years later was to be the Downing Street Declaration were being set in place. But history is not always noticeable as such at the time. The political picture then looked opaque.

A separate set of contacts had started in 1988 between John Hume of the SDLP and Gerry Adams of Sinn Fein, who had again won West Belfast in the General Election of the year before – though in the Sinn Fein tradition of seventy years before he had again not taken his seat. Hume's aim was to persuade Adams that the nationalist goal they both shared was more likely to be attained peacefully through the democratic process than by IRA violence. This was a view which Adams, a highly intelligent republican extremist, must occasionally have considered for himself after eighteen years in which the goal of driving the 'Brits out' by violence continued to seem more distant than ever. However, while on the one hand he may at times have reasoned that Michael Collins had managed to drive them out of a much greater part of Ireland after only three years, he had modelled himself not on Collins, who had accepted British control of the North, but on those anti-Free State republicans who had continued to fight unsuccessfully until striving for success rather than success itself became the test of republican patriotism. However, personal considerations to the effect that his astute political skills might be deployed more satisfactorily to himself in the wider range of democratic politics may already have been troubling him. In fact Hume and Adams made little progress together at this stage. It would certainly have occurred to Adams that were he to change his views in favour of peace he would have a problem persuading his former comrades, and the relatives of those whose funerals he had assiduously attended, to change their views too.

The feature of this whole period in which talks were held and contacts pursued in the half-light of politics, was that all parties – with the exception of the Democratic Unionists – were having to consider adjustments to previous positions and eventual compromise if there were to be any worthwhile progress for themselves in the future at all.

It was the British government which could be said to have the greatest responsibility for finding an alternative to the deadlock in which, for all their good intentions, the Anglo-Irish Agreement had landed them. It was the British government whose sovereignty in Northern Ireland was, from any angle, central to the situation there. And it was degrading to any self-respecting democratic sovereignty to be responsible for the sort of things that were going on there and be unable to do anything more to stop them. The number of deaths from 'the troubles', though now considerably lower than in the early days, remained more or less constant at a steady average of nearly two a week for every year between 1988 and 1993. It actually rose each year between 1988 and 1992 when, though the total number was slightly down (to 85), the number of civilians killed was the highest since 1976. Most were killed by so-called 'Loyalist' paramilitaries.

The Irish government's position was in some ways the least compulsive. Though they had conceded by the first article of the Agreement that, for all the claim in their Constitution, there could be no question of it being realized until the majority there accepted it, they had already conceded this eleven years before at Sunningdale, and in any case had hardly seemed anxious to press the claim except rhetorically for over half a century before that. Whatever the Constitution might say, the reality was that after seventy years of separation something very like a separate 26-county nationalism had been emerging in the Republic. This emphasized an emotional need sympathetically to look after the interests of the nationalists in the North rather than any obligation once again to go through the motions of the old rhetorical posture. History had indeed shown the aspiration for a united Ireland, ever since the failure of the United Irishmen in 1798, to have been largely a matter of words.

Nationalism for the minority in the North had been subject to its own shift of emphasis. Irish nationalism for most of the minority had become a necessary part of identity with which to assert the right to fair treatment from a majority long not prepared to give it. The linking of the need to remove British rule with this important defensive attitude could be seen as something like an historical irrelevance when viewed from a Republic which had rid itself of British rule so long ago. Now, through the Intergovernmental Conference and the secretariat at Maryfield, the Irish government could look after that minority's interests in a manner regularly institutionalized. And though there was a degree to which traditional rhetoric might still drive the Republic to want to extend its say, this could hardly seem an urgent priority since it would have to be negotiated against Unionist demands that it should be reduced.

One line of argument open to the Irish government to pursue to help salve its rhetorical conscience lay in the area of the Government of Ireland Act of 1920, still applicable to Northern Ireland. A clause in this asserted the Westminster Parliament's authority over any devolved government in Northern Ireland. But any change here was also likely to be unacceptable to Unionists unless virtually meaningless. And it could hardly be more than that, since British sovereign power in Northern Ireland, which the Irish government temporarily recognized as effective, could only derive from the Westminster Parliament.

The major concession the Irish were likely to be pressed to make was for an amendment to Articles 2 and 3 of their Constitution. These, by reason of the historic allegiances which had divided the two main parties in the twenty-six counties for decades, carried simpler domestic political under-tones than suggested by the high patriotic sentiments they enshrined. Many in republican political life, not least Garret Fitzgerald of Fine Gael when Taoiseach, had been prepared to consider putting the amendment to a referendum.

It was the Unionist position which was on paper the most secure of all. The British and Irish governments had pledged themselves that there could be no change in the constitutional status of Northern Ireland without the consent of the majority there. This was embedded in the Anglo-Irish Agreement and also by statute in the Northern Ireland Constitution Act, which not only set out the principle, but laid down that the majority's opinion should be determined by 'a poll'. In these circumstances it might have been expected that the Unionists would be ready to compromise on other matters. But this would be to ignore the real presence of their historic fears as a minority in the island of Ireland.

They were a minority which in the past a British government, for all its present promises, had tried to separate from the Union and put into a united Ireland and, but for Ulster intransigence in the early part of the century, would have succeeded in doing so. They were unlikely in any case for many generations to forget this or forgo the fears those historic memories kept alive. Had they been inclined to do so the IRA had been there for many years of recent memory to remind them of the fate that might await them to which they were determined never to succumb. Where anything to do with the Irish dimension was concerned, they were always going to be abnormally sensitive. It had already been manifested twice in the past two decades – at Sunningdale and at Hillsborough – that no 'solution', and certainly no 'solution' with devolved government, had a chance of success unless it took into account such abnormal sensitivity. This was a realistic fact of life which those looking for a solution would always have to live with. Although the talks Brooke held with Unionists did not technically come to any successful conclusion, points did emerge to indicate some likelihood of later progress. Were the Anglo-Irish Agreement to be superseded, it was clear that Molyneaux's Unionists at any rate had small fear of some cross-border harmonization on practical matters such as tourism, communications, and fisheries, and, what was far more important, would, in return for abandonment of the Agreement, no longer maintain their old Sunningdale intransigence about power-sharing in an eventual Assembly.

This latter point was of course of great importance particularly to the SDLP and John Hume, whose own perception of what it meant to be a national Irishman – and he was proud to be one – had clearly been affected by his experience of adumbrated nationalism within the European Community, in the Parliament of which he was one of Northern Ireland's members.

Whichever way Hume was beginning to see the correct emphasis in Irish nationalism – and he had already made clear long ago that he saw classic extreme republican dogma as irrelevant to modern times – clearly no development was going to be possible at all without an atmosphere of peace in which to proceed. This meant, in short, persuading those in Sinn Fein with influence on the IRA of the day to persuade the IRA that it was in the best interests of the Irish nation to cease the violence which in nearly a quarter of a century had failed to bring nationalist victory and to try something else instead.

In the early 1990s, Hume again engaged in talks with Gerry Adams of Sinn Fein to find principles they could both accept, as nationalists, on which to base an approach to the Irish government, in the first place, and thus to the British government, to encourage them both to find a framework for a new and better future.

On 15 December 1993 the Downing Street Declaration, the product ultimately of some years of talks and contacts at many different levels (some not without political risks), but owing its instigation as much to the Hume-Adams talks as to any of them, was signed by John Major, Prime Minister again after being returned to power in 1992, and Albert Reynolds for the Irish Republic, Taoiseach of a Fianna Fail dominated coalition.

In one way this last political fact was the most important thing about the Declaration. For the first time the Irish party with the strongest national and republican tradition had put its name to a solemn document guaranteeing Northern Ireland's statutory constitutional status, and stating that 'it

would be wrong to attempt to impose a united Ireland in the absence of the freely given consent of a majority of the people of Northern Ireland'.

One of the most important bases of agreement in the Hume-Adams talks had been to the effect that the decision on a united Ireland should be the product of Irish 'self-determination'. But how was Irish self-determination itself to be determined? There could have been no possible chance of any Unionist ever accepting such a decision based on the vote of the Irish people voting as a whole. And indeed the exclusive 'statutory' basis for Northern Ireland's position accepted by the Irish in this document ruled that out. So what was here again spelt out very clearly and agreed by the leader of the most traditional republican party in the Dail was that while it was 'for the people of Ireland alone to exercise their right of self-determination', any agreement over a united Ireland should be 'between the two parts respectively ', and that 'self-determination of the people of Ireland as a whole' meant that the result was 'subject to the agreement and consent of a majority of the people of Northern Ireland'. The document was a brilliant piece of verbal drafting on which clever civil officials of both governments had been working for months.

It recognized, as both Sunningdale and the Anglo-Irish Agreement had failed to do, that whereas the recipe for a successful formula required the most delicate balance between Unionist fears, Northern Irish minority anxiety for their identity, and Irish nationalist tradition as a whole, the one element without whose co-operation in any future democratic structure for Northern Ireland there could be no hope of success was the Unionist. The Taoiseach here 'in recognition of the fears of the Unionist community' said he would 'examine with his colleagues any elements in . . . the Irish state that can be represented . . . as a real and substantial threat to their way of life an ethos . . .' This was, of course, likely to be interpreted by most Unionists as just another version of Haughey's spider and fly devices. But more to the point, it seemed, was the approach to Articles 2 and 3 of the Irish Constitution. Acknowledging that these were 'deeply resented by Northern Unionists' the Taoiseach confirmed that 'in the event of an over-all settlement the Irish Government will . . . put forward and support proposals for change in the Irish Constitution which would fully reflect the principle of consent in Northern Ireland.'

By and large it was unusual for such a portentous public document to carry such genuine conviction of sincerity and hope in its often dignified phrases. Some of the two major participants' real personal commitment seemed evident in the language. It had, and this was perhaps its most impressive and encouraging general aspect, an awareness of the great range of Irish history in its subtext. It saw its purpose, laying the foundation of some future framework, as being '. . . to remove the causes of conflict, to overcome the legacy of history, and to heal the divisions which have resulted, recognizing that the absence of a lasting and satisfactory settlement of relationships between the people of both islands has contributed to continuing tragedy and suffering'.

What will history eventually have to say about it?

Viewed from five years before the end of the century it is possible already to make some judgements. That it provided a more hopeful start to a new era than Sunningdale or the Anglo-Irish Agreement, the two most

How the Loyalists of the Shankill Road received the
IRA ceasefire of 31 August 1994.

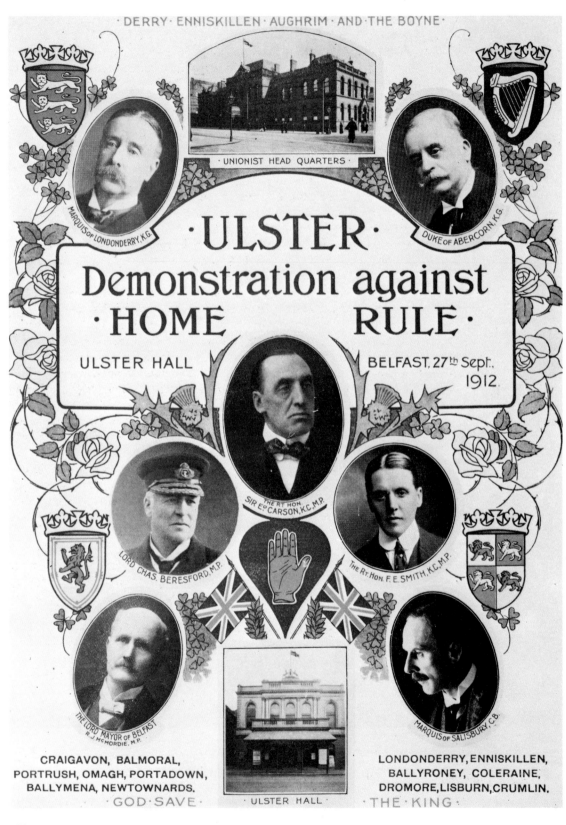

DERRY · ENNISKILLEN · AUGHRIM · AND · THE · BOYNE ·

· UNIONIST HEAD QUARTERS ·

MARQUIS of LONDONDERRY, K.G.

DUKE of ABERCORN, K.G.

· ULSTER ·
Demonstration against
· HOME   RULE ·

ULSTER HALL

BELFAST, 27th Sept.,
1912.

THE RT. HON.
SIR Ed CARSON, K.C., M.P.

LORD CHAS. BERESFORD, M.P.

The RT. HON. F. E. SMITH, K.C., M.P.

THE LORD MAYOR OF BELFAST
R. J. McMORDIE, M.P.

MARQUIS of SALISBURY, C.B.

CRAIGAVON, BALMORAL,
PORTRUSH, OMAGH, PORTADOWN,
BALLYMENA, NEWTOWNARDS.

· ULSTER HALL ·

LONDONDERRY, ENNISKILLEN,
BALLYRONEY, COLERAINE,
DROMORE, LISBURN, CRUMLIN.

· GOD · SAVE ·   THE · KING ·

ambitious political initiatives of the previous quarter of a century, is unquestionable. It recognized, as they did not, that in trying to square the circle of Unionist and Irish nationalist tradition it is today the Unionist tradition that can always dominate the attempt's success or failure. Though the Democratic Unionist Party's routine dismissal of the Declaration ran true to form, this can be partly explained by the need to attract maximum attention to yourself if you are the weaker of two similar parties about to enter major negotiations with others. The guarded but sympathetic reception accorded the Declaration by the Official Unionists is one important measure of its achievement. More important was the IRA ceasefire that came into force at the end of August 1994, to be followed two months later by the ceasefire of Protestant paramilitaries.

The solemnity of these two decisions, more unlikely to be rescinded every day they last because those formerly giving passive support to terrorism now rejoice every day in peace, itself breaks the pattern of the last quarter century. At the very least the pattern events take in future will have a different character, or scale, or both.

By no means all prognoses are optimistic. One distinguished observer and former participant in Irish government affairs has already forecast a reversion to violence on a prodigious scale. This will happen, he says, when the IRA comes to terms with the fact that, at least for the foreseeable future, it is as unlikely to get the British out of Ireland through the democratic process as it was over the past twenty-five years through violence. The heightened civil war in Northern Ireland to which that doomsday observer sees renewed violence escalating will, he predicts, lead to a sudden British withdrawal on the analogy of Palestine and India, to be followed by limited intervention by the Irish army, an IRA military coup in Dublin and total war in Ireland.

The many inevitable disruptions which were foreseen by others in the early stages of the long peace process – walk-outs, furore over leaked documents, arguments in public that should be taking place around a table behind closed doors over the Irish dimension, the 'decommissioning' of arms, the release of prisoners – are all part of a political future in which uncertainty will long be the only constant.

There is though one thing of which we can be sure. The Downing Street Declaration ended by saying that it hoped it had laid 'the foundations for a more peaceful and harmonious future devoid of the violence and bitter divisions which have scarred the past generation'.

It is not only the past generation that will say 'Amen' to that.

The rest will one day be history.

LEFT: Ulster Unionists refuse the Third Home Rule Bill (1912–14).

Selected Further Reading

NB All the books listed below contain their own, often very extensive bibliographies

General
J. Bardon *A History of Ulster* (Belfast 1992)

J.C. Beckett *A Short History of Ireland* (1977; paperback)

J.C. Beckett *The Making of Modern Ireland* (1969; paperback)

D.G. Boyce *Nationalism in Ireland* (London 1982)

L.M. Cullen *An Economic History of Ireland since 1660* (London 1976)

R.F. Foster *Modern Ireland 1600–1972* (London 1988)

R. Kee *The Green Flag* (1976; 3 vols. paperback)

F.S.L. Lyons *Ireland Since The Famine* (1973; paperback)

O. Macdonagh *Ireland: The Union and Its Aftermath* (1977; paperback)

N.S. Mansergh *The Irish Question* (1975; paperback)

T.W. Moody and F.X. Martin *The Course of Irish History* (1966; paperback)

M. and C.C. O'Brien *A Concise History of Ireland* (1972; paperback)

Cormac Ó Grada *Ireland: A New Economic History 1780–1939* (Dublin 1994)

G.D. Zimmermann *Songs of Irish Rebellion* (Dublin 1967)

The Gill History of Ireland (Dublin) consists of 11 useful detailed paperback volumes ranging from *Ireland Before The Vikings* (vol. 1) (Dublin 1972) to *Ireland In The Twentieth Century* (vol. 11) (Dublin 1975)

Specific Subjects
CHAPTER 2

M. and L. de Paor *Early Christian Ireland* (London 1978)

T.W. Moody, F.X. Martin and F.J. Byrne (Editors) *A New History of Ireland Vol. III: Early Modern Ireland 1534–1691* (Oxford 1978)

CHAPTER 3

T.W. Moody, F.X. Martin and F.J. Byrne *A New History of Ireland Vol. III* (Oxford 1978)

A.T.Q. Stewart *The Narrow Ground: Aspects of Ulster* (London 1977)

CHAPTER 4

J. C. Beckett *The Making of Modern Ireland* (1969; paperback)

M. Elliott *Wolfe Tone* (Yale 1989)

M. Elliott *Partners in Revolution* (Yale 1982)

W.E.H. Lecky *Ireland In The Eighteenth Century* (5 vols. Chicago 1972)

O. Macdonagh *The Hereditary Bondsman* (New York 1989)

O. Macdonagh *The Emancipist* (London 1989)

T. Pakenham *The Year of Liberty* (1972; paperback)

M. Wall *The Penal Laws* (Dublin 1961)

CHAPTER 5

R. Davis *The Young Ireland Movement* (Dublin 1988)

R.F. Foster *Modern Ireland* (London 1988)

C. Kinealy *This Great Calamity* (Dublin 1994)

D. Williams and K. Edwards (Editors) *The Great Famine* (Dublin 1956; now paperback)

C. Woodham-Smith *The Great Hunger* (1970; paperback)

CHAPTER 6
L. O'Broin *Fenian Fever* (London 1971)
D. Ryan *The Fenian Chief: James Stephens* (Dublin 1967)
R.V. Comerford *The Fenians in Context* (Dublin 1985)

CHAPTER 7
P. Bew *Land and The National Question* (Dublin 1980)
R. Foster *Charles Stewart Parnell* (1979; paperback)
R. Kee, *The Laurel and the Ivy* (1994; paperback)
F.S.L. Lyons *Charles Stewart Parnell* (1978; paperback)
C.C. O'Brien *Parnell and His Party* (Oxford 1957)
C. Townshend *Political Violence in Ireland* (1988; paperback)

CHAPTER 8
P. Bew *Ideology and the Irish Question* (Oxford 1994)
R. Blake *The Unknown Prime Minister* (London 1955)
A.T.Q. Stewart *The Ulster Crisis* (London 1967)

CHAPTER 9
R.D. Edwards *Patrick Pearse* (London 1977)
L. O'Brion *Dublin Castle and the 1916 Rising* (1966; paperback)
M. Wall (Editor) *The Making of 1916* (Dublin 1969)

CHAPTER 10
T.P. Coogan *Michael Collins* (London 1990)
T.P. Coogan *De Valera* (London 1993)
D. Macardle *The Irish Republic* (London 1951)
C. Townshend *The British Campaign in Ireland 1919–21* (Oxford 1978)

CHAPTER 11
F. Pakenham *Peace by Ordeal* (1972; paperback)
Calton Younger *Ireland's Civil War* (1970; paperback)

CHAPTER 12
J. Bowyer Bell *The Secret Army* (London 1970)

J. Lee (Editor) *Ireland 1945–1970* (Dublin 1979)
F.S.L. Lyons *Ireland Since The Famine* (1973; paperback)
K. Nowlan and D. Williams *Ireland In The War Years and After* (Dublin 1969)

CHAPTER 13
P. Bew and G. Gillespie *Northern Ireland: A Chronology 1968–1993* (Dublin 1993)
P. Bishop and E. Mallie *The Provisional IRA* (London 1987)
P. Buckland *The Factory of Grievances* (Dublin 1979)
J. Darby *Conflict in Northern Ireland* (Dublin 1976)
D. Hamil *Pig In The Middle* (London 1985)
R. Hull *The Irish Triangle* (1977; Princeton paperback)
E. McCann *War and an Irish Town* (1974; paperback)
C.C. O'Brien *States of Ireland* (London 1972)
E. Phoenix *Northern Nationalism 1890–1940* (Belfast 1994)
R. Rose *Governing Without Consensus* (London 1971)
A.T.Q. Stewart *The Narrow Ground: Aspects of Ulster* (London 1977)

CHAPTERS 14–16
P. Arthur and K. Jeffrey *Northern Ireland Since 1968* (Oxford 1988)
J. Bardon A *History of Ulster* (Belfast 1992)
P. Bew and G. Gillespie *Northern Ireland: A Chronology 1968–1993* (Dublin 1993)
P. Bew, P. Gibbon and H. Patterson *Northern Ireland 1921–1994* (London 1995)
K. Boyle and T. Hadden *Northern Ireland: The Choice* (London 1994)
G. Fitzgerald *All In A Life* (London 1991)
D. McKittrick *Despatches from Belfast* (Belfast 1989)
D. McKittrick *Endgame* (Belfast 1994)

Acknowledgments

Pictures were supplied or reproduced by kind permission of the following:

Black and white illustrations:

BBC Hulton Picture Library 19 above, 73 above, 84 below right, 89 below, 105 above, 118, 121 above, 127 below, 167 below, 170 above, 173 above, 176 above, 181 below, 183 below, 184 above, 186 above, below left and right, 190, 194 above and below left, 196 above left, above right and below, 199 above and below, 200 above left, above right and below, 203 above and below, 212 below left, 216 above left and right

British Library 18 above and below, 31 above and below, 62 above left, 72 below, 76, 81 above, 84 left, 105 below left and below right, 114, 125 above and below, 127 above, 130, 164 above right

British Museum 45 below

Cambridge University 25 below

Camera Press 230 below, 234 below, 236 above, 238

Cork Examiner 212 below right

Leo Daly/Source 28 below

Colman Doyle/Source 224, 230 above left and right, 233 above and below, 234 above

G.A. Duncan 206, 218, 222 above left, above right and below, 227 below left and below right

Mary Evans 102

Fotomas Index 19 below, 45 above

Hulton Deutsch 240 above, 246 above and below, 265 above, 272, 285 above

Independent Newspapers, Dublin 184 below

Irish Tourist Board, Dublin 25 above, 26 right

Keystone Press Agency 17 bottom right

Library of Congress 109 below, 116

Linen Hall Library, Belfast 288

Donald McCullin, 14

Magnum 240 below, 241, 242, 255 above left and right, 269 above

Mansell Collection 47 above and below, 81 below, 84 above right, 89 above, 93 above and below, 98 above right, 99

Joyce Marlow 130 below left and below right

George Mott 70 above, below left and below right

Museum of the City of New York 108 below

National Gallery of Ireland 38, 67 above left and below, 68 above

National Library of Ireland 57 below, 58, 62 above right and below, 67 above right, 68 below, 72 above, 73 below, 108 above, 139, 143 above and below, 154 above left, above right and below, 158 below, 162 above left, above centre, above right and below, 164 below left, 167 above, 170 below, 176 below right, 181 above left and above right, 183 above, 212 above

National Museum of Ireland 26 left, 28 above, 109 above, below left and below right, 148 below, 164 above left and below right, 173 below, 174, 176 below left, 204

National Parks and Monuments, Dublin 22

National Portrait Gallery 17 top left, top right, centre left and centre right, 98 above left

Pacemaker Press 227 above left and above right

Popperfoto 17 bottom left, 194 below right, 216 below, 260, 263 above

Press Association Photos 20

Private Collection 221 above

Report/Derek Speirs 236 below

Syndication International 258, 261 above and below

Topham 244, 255 below, 263 below, 265 below, 269 below, 275, 278 above and below, 280, 283 below, 287

Trinity College, Dublin 36

Ulster Museum 52, 136, 144 above and below, 148 above

University College (Dept. of Folklore), Dublin 57 above

Colour illustrations:

Between pages 32 and 33:
(in order of sequence)
Above Rex Features (photo Bojesen); *Below* Rex Features (photo Frilet)
Above Kelly Daly; *Below* Brian Seed
Full page Trinity College, Dublin
Above left and below left National Library of Ireland; *Above right and below right* Trinity College, Dublin

Between pages 64 and 65:
Above Ulster Museum, Belfast; *Below* Robert Ashby/Source
Above The Parker Gallery, London; *Below* Robert Ashby/Source
Full page Kelly Daly
Above National Gallery of Ireland; *Below* National Library of Ireland

Between pages 128 and 129:
Above Sheffield City Art Gallery; *Below* City of New York Museum
Full page British Library
Above The Mansell Collection; *Below* National Library of Ireland
Above, below left and right Ulster Museum, Belfast

Between pages 160 and 161:
Full page E.T. Archive Ltd
Above Kelly Daly; *Below* Crawford Art Gallery, Cork
Above Sligo County Museum; *Below* Municipal Art Gallery, Dublin
Above Kelly Daly; *Below* Robert Ashby/Source

Picture research by Anne-Marie Ehrlich and Linda Silverman

Index

Page numbers in *italic* indicate illustrations

Murphy, Walter J., 145

National Guard (O'Duffy's movement), 214–15
National Volunteers, 151
nationalism, Irish
    Catholic emphasis in, 53, 66, 75
    Protestant origin, 66
    and Gaelic culture, 141–2
    and Northern Ireland question, 268, 282–4
    see also Home Rule; Irish Republican Brotherhood;
        Irish Volunteers
Neave, Airey, 16, *20*, 264
New Ross: Wexford rebels defeated at, 65
Newgrange (prehistoric site), 23–4, *25*
Normans, *28*, 29–30
Norsemen (Vikings), 27, *28*
Northern Ireland
    outbreak of troubles (1960s), 15
    workers' strike (1974), 138, 253–4, *254*
    civil rights and disobedience in, 153–4, 232, 235,
        237, *255*
    administered as separate state, 225–6
    Assembly (Stormont parliament), 226, 228, 243,
        249–51, 273–4
    Catholic minority in, 226–9, 237, 239
    conditions and character, 228–9
    voting system, 229, 241
    IRA campaign of violence in, 239, 243, 245, *246*,
        259, 264
    casualties, 243, 245, 254, 257, 259, 262, 264, 282
    direct rule from London (1972), 243
    loyalist paramilitary actions in, 243, 281–2
    pledges of consent given to, 250–1, 283, 286
    local elections, 267, 277
    British sovereign power in, 283
    future prospects, 289
    see also Home Rule; Protestants; Ulster
Northern Ireland Civil Rights Association, 232
Northern Ireland Constitution Act (1973), 249–51,
    254, 283

O'Brien (executed Fenian), 115
O'Brien, Conor Cruise, 252
O'Brien, William Smith, 104–6, *105*
O'Connell, Daniel, *72–3*
    and Catholic Emancipation, 66, 71, 75
    achievements, 69, 74–5
    seeks repeal of Act of Union, 71
    wins Clare by-election (1828), 71
    'Monster Meetings', *72*, 74–5
    death, 74
    on Irish famine, 80
    see also Catholic Association
O'Connor, Rory, 193, 197, 201

O'Donnell, Hugh Roe, Lord of Tyrconnell, 35–7, 39
O'Donnell, Peadar, 209
O'Donnell, Rory, 1st Earl of Tyrconnell (son of Hugh
    Roe), 39–40
O'Duffy, Eoin, *212*, 214
'Official' IRA, 237
    see also Irish Republican Army
Official Unionist Party (Northern Ireland), 247, 249,
    262, 267, 281, 289
    see also Ulster Unionists
O'Hanrahan, Michael, 172
O'Higgins, Kevin, *194*, 198, 202, *203*, 207, 210
O'Kelly, Sean T., *218*
Old English, the, 30–5, 44
O'Mahony, John, 107, *108*, 111
O'Malley, Ernie, 193
O'Neill, Hugh, 2nd Earl of Tyrone, *34*, 35–7, 39–40
O'Neill, Owen Roe, 43–4
O'Neill, Captain Terence, 227, 232, 235
O'Rahilly, Michael, 160, *167*, 168
Orange Society (Order), 48, 61, 137–8, 228
O'Shea, Katharine, 128–9, *130*, 132–5
O'Shea, Captain William, 128, *130*, 133–4
Oulart Hill: Wexford rebels victory at, 64

Paget, Sir Arthur, 149
Paisley, Revd Ian, *227*
    oratory, 232
    extremism, 247
    protests against Northern Ireland executive, 250
    and Sunningdale Agreement, 251
    and 1974 General Election, 253
    Mason opposes, 262
    signs 'Ulster Declaration', 266
    mocks Haughey, 267, 276
    blames British government for IRA terrorism, 273
    prays against Thatcher, 277–9
    resists Anglo-Irish Agreement, 279, *280*, 281
    RUC remove from Assembly, 279
Pale, the, 30
paramilitaries (loyalist), *see* loyalist (Unionist)
    paramilitaries
Parliament Act (1911), 145
parliament, Irish, 58–9, *59*, 65, 74, 142
    see also Dail Eireann; Home Rule
parliament, Northern Ireland (Stormont) *see*
    Northern Ireland: Assembly
Parnell, Charles Stewart, *118*, *121*
    on 'Manchester murders', 117
    career and dominance, 119, 122–3
    and Land League, 120, 123
    imprisoned in Kilmainham Jail, 126–9
    nationalist aims, 126, 131–2, 247
    and Katharine O'Shea, 128–9, 132–5